T0190516

Praise for Daniel L. Everett's

DON'T SLEEP, THERE ARE SNAKES

"A story of language and faith along the sweeping banks of the Maici River. . . . Verdict: read."   —*Time*

"Destined to become a classic of popular ethnography."
                                          —*The Independent* (London)

"A genuine and engrossing book that is both sharp and intuitive; it closes around you and reaches inside you, controlling your every thought and movement as you read it. . . . Impossible to forget."
                                          —*Sacramento Book Review*

"Three stars. . . . [A] spiritual adventure story."   —*People*

"A fascinating look into the lives of the Pirahã, an Amazonian community of hunter-gatherers."   —*Minneapolis Star Tribune*

"*Don't Sleep, There Are Snakes* makes the rain forest sound like a magic mushroom."   —*Harper's Magazine*

"A riveting account of a Christian missionary 'converted' to the viewpoint of the Amazonian Indians he had intended to evangelize."
                                          —*The Huntsville Times*

"Vivid. . . . The book is fascinating. . . . May serve to bring the furor of linguistics and language research to readers who otherwise never catch sight of it."   —*Science* magazine

Daniel L. Everett

DON'T SLEEP, THERE ARE SNAKES

Daniel L. Everett is the Chair of Languages, Literatures, and Cultures at Illinois State University. He is pictured here with Kaabohoá.

DON'T SLEEP, THERE ARE SNAKES

Life and Language in the Amazonian Jungle

Daniel L. Everett

VINTAGE DEPARTURES
VINTAGE BOOKS
A DIVISION OF RANDOM HOUSE, INC.
NEW YORK

FIRST VINTAGE DEPARTURES EDITION, NOVEMBER 2009

The Library of Congress has cataloged the Pantheon
edition as follows:
Everett, Daniel Leonard.
Don't sleep, there are snakes : life and language in the
Amazonian jungle / Daniel L. Everett.
p. cm.
Includes bibliographical references.
1. Pirahã Indians—Amazon River Region—Social life
and customs. 2. Pirahã dialect—Social aspects—Amazon
River Region. 3. Jungles—Amazon River Region.
4. Amazon River Region—Social life and customs.
I. Title.
F2520.1.M9E94 2008
305.898'9—dc22 2008016306

Vintage ISBN: 978-0-307-38612-0

Author photograph © Martin Schoeller
Designed by Anthea Lingeman

www.vintagebooks.com

Printed in the United States of America

This book is about past events. But life is about the present and the future. And so I dedicate this book to my wife, Linda Ann Everett, the constant encourager. Romance is a good thing.

I thus learnt my first great lesson in the inquiry into these obscure fields of knowledge, never to accept the disbelief of great men or their accusations of imposture or of imbecility, as of any weight when opposed to the repeated observation of facts by other men, admittedly sane and honest. The whole history of science shows us that whenever the educated and scientific men of any age have denied the facts of other investigators on a priori grounds of absurdity or impossibility, the deniers have always been wrong.

—ALFRED WALLACE (1823–1913)

The notion that the essence of what it means to be human is most clearly revealed in those features of human culture that are universal rather than in those that are distinctive to this people or that is a prejudice that we are not obliged to share. . . . It may be in the cultural particularities of people—in their oddities—that some of the most instructive revelations of what it is to be generically human are to be found.

—CLIFFORD GEERTZ (1926–2006)

Contents

Part Three: CONCLUSION

Some Notes on the Pirahã Language as Used in This Book

Although Pirahã has one of the smallest set of speech sounds (phonemes) known, it can still be very difficult to pronounce without a little help. Here is a rudimentary guide to pronunciation, using the writing system that my missionary predecessors to the Pirahãs, Arlo Heinrichs and Steve Sheldon, and I developed for the language.

b Pronounced at the beginning of a word like the *m* in *mama*. Between the vowels *i* and *o* it is pronounced as a trill, with the lips vibrating (as in some American children's imitation of a car motor running). Elsewhere it is pronounced like the *b* of *baby*.

g Pronounced at the beginning of a word like the *n* of *no*. Between the vowels *o* and *i*, as in the word *xibogi* (milk), it can be pronounced as either *g* or an *l*-like sound found in no other language of the world, where one makes an *l* but then lets the tongue continue out between the lips to touch the bottom of the tongue on the lower lip. Elsewhere, it is pronounced like the *g* in *god*.

p Pronounced like the *p* sound in English words like *pot*.

t Pronounced like the English *t* sound in *tar*.

k Pronounced like the English *k* sound in *skirt*.

x This is a glottal stop. It is pronounced like the medial sound in the English negative interjection *uh-uh:* "Do you have any sugar?" "Uh-uh" (the sound where the "-" is). This is not a full consonant in English and is not represented in the English alphabet. In the International Phonetic Alphabet its symbol is ʔ.

s Pronounced like the English *s* sound in *sound*, except before the letter *i*, where it is pronounced like the English *sh* sound in *sugar*.

h Pronounced like the American English sound at the beginning of the word *here*.

i Usually pronounced like the English *i* vowel in *hit*, though occasionally like the English *e* vowel in *bed*. On some occasions it is pronounced like the *ea* sequence in *bead*.

a Pronounced like the British English *a* vowel in *father*.

o Usually pronounced like the English *o* vowel in *who*, though occasionally the vowel *o* in *abode*.

The acute accent (´) indicates a high tone and is written over a vowel when a high pitch is needed. When there is no symbol above a vowel it has a low pitch. Think of the English words *PERmit* (a license or form of permission) versus *perMIT* (to allow). The capitalized syllables normally have high pitch in English. In Pirahã, every vowel always has a pitch associated with it, depending on the function or location in the sentence of the word it occurs in.

I have tried in most places to translate Pirahã into idiomatic English. This has the consequence of presenting the language differently from the way the people actually speak. For example, many of the translations, unlike the original Pirahã sentences, include recursion. Anyone with a keener interest in the grammar can examine the Pirahã stories that are included in the book or my many linguistic writings about the Pirahãs, such as my chapter in the *Handbook of Amazonian Languages*, volume 1 (edited by Desmond Derbyshire and Geoffrey Pullum, published by Mouton). The stories in the book will be sufficient for most readers, since they provide literal translations (though these translations are likely to be more difficult for non-Pirahã speakers to follow).

Preface

Science is not just about research teams in lab coats working under the direction of an eminent scientist. It can be pursued by lone individuals slogging it out in hard times and hard places—feeling lost and over their heads, yet challenged to bring new knowledge out of their difficulties.

This book is about scientific work of the latter type and about intellectual growth in the crucible of an Amazonian culture, living among the Pirahã (pee-da-HAN) Indians of Brazil. It is about them and the lessons they taught me, both scientific and personal, and how these new ideas changed my life profoundly and led me to live differently.

These are *my* lessons. Someone else would no doubt have learned other lessons. Future researchers will have their own stories to tell. In the end, we just do the best we can to talk straight and clear.

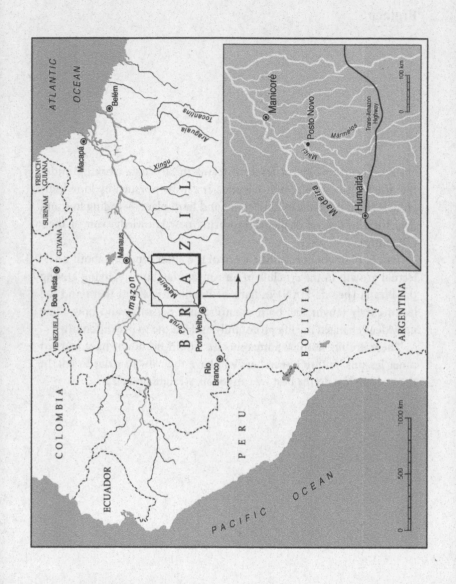

Prologue

"Look! There he is, Xigagaí, the spirit."
"Yes, I can see him. He is threatening us."
"Everybody, come see Xigagaí. Quickly! He is on the beach!"

I roused from my deep sleep, not sure if I was dreaming or hearing this conversation. It was 6:30 on a Saturday morning in August, the dry season of 1980. The sun was shining, but not yet too hot. A breeze was blowing up from the Maici River in front of my modest hut in a clearing on the bank. I opened my eyes and saw the palm thatch above me, its original yellow graying from years of dust and soot. My dwelling was flanked by two smaller Pirahã huts of similar construction, where lived Xahoábisi, Kóhoibiíihíai, and their families.

Mornings among the Pirahãs, so many mornings, I picked up the faint smell of smoke drifting from their cook fires, and the warmth of the Brazilian sun on my face, its rays softened by my mosquito net. Children were usually laughing, chasing one another, or noisily crying to nurse, the sounds reverberating through the village. Dogs were barking. Often when I first opened my eyes, groggily coming out of a dream, a Pirahã child or sometimes even an adult would be staring at me from between the *paxiuba* palm slats that served as siding for my large hut. This morning was different.

I was now completely conscious, awakened by the noise and shouts of Pirahãs. I sat up and looked around. A crowd was gathering about twenty feet from my bed on the high bank of the Maici, and all were energetically gesticulating and yelling. Everyone was focused on the beach just across the river from my house. I got out of bed to get a better look—and because there was no way to sleep through the noise.

I picked my gym shorts off the floor and checked to make sure that there were no tarantulas, scorpions, centipedes, or other undesirables in them. Pulling them on, I slipped into my flip-flops and headed out the door. The Pirahãs were loosely bunched on the riverbank just to the right of my house. Their excitement was growing. I could see mothers running down the path, their infants trying to hold breasts in their mouths.

The women wore the same sleeveless, collarless, midlength dresses they worked and slept in, stained a dark brown from dirt and smoke. The men wore gym shorts or loincloths. None of the men were carrying their bows and arrows. That was a relief. Prepubescent children were naked, their skin leathery from exposure to the elements. The babies' bottoms were calloused from scooting across the ground, a mode of locomotion that for some reason they prefer to crawling. Everyone was streaked from ashes and dust accumulated by sleeping and sitting on the ground near the fire.

It was still around seventy-two degrees, though humid, far below the hundred-degree-plus heat of midday. I was rubbing the sleep from my eyes. I turned to Kóhoi, my principal language teacher, and asked, "What's up?" He was standing to my right, his strong, brown, lean body tensed from what he was looking at.

"Don't you see him over there?" he asked impatiently. "Xigagaí, one of the beings that lives above the clouds, is standing on the beach yelling at us, telling us he will kill us if we go to the jungle."

"Where?" I asked. "I don't see him."

"Right there!" Kóhoi snapped, looking intently toward the middle of the apparently empty beach.

"In the jungle behind the beach?"

"No! There on the beach. Look!" he replied with exasperation.

In the jungle with the Pirahãs I regularly failed to see wildlife they saw. My inexperienced eyes just weren't able to see as theirs did.

But this was different. Even I could tell that there was nothing on that white, sandy beach no more than one hundred yards away. And yet as certain as I was about this, the Pirahãs were equally certain that there *was* something there. Maybe there had been something there that I just missed seeing, but they insisted that what they were seeing, Xigagaí, was still there.

Everyone continued to look toward the beach. I heard Kristene, my six-year-old daughter, at my side.

"What are they looking at, Daddy?"

"I don't know. I can't see anything."

Kris stood on her toes and peered across the river. Then at me. Then at the Pirahãs. She was as puzzled as I was.

Kristene and I left the Pirahãs and walked back into our house. What had I just witnessed? Over the more than two decades since that summer morning, I have tried to come to grips with the significance of how two cultures, my European-based culture and the Pirahãs' culture, could see reality so differently. I could never have proved to the Pirahãs that the beach was empty. Nor could they have convinced me that there was anything, much less a spirit, on it.

As a scientist, objectivity is one of my most deeply held values. If we could just try harder, I once thought, surely we could each see the world as others see it and learn to respect one another's views more readily. But as I learned from the Pirahãs, our expectations, our culture, and our experiences can render even perceptions of the environment nearly incommensurable cross-culturally.

The Pirahãs say different things when they leave my hut at night on their way to bed. Sometimes they just say, "I'm going." But frequently they use an expression that, though surprising at first, has come to be one of my favorite ways of saying good night; "Don't sleep, there are snakes." The Pirahãs say this for two reasons. First, they believe that by sleeping less they can "harden themselves," a value they all share. Second, they know that danger is all around them in the jungle and that sleeping soundly can leave one defenseless from attack by any of the numerous predators around the village. The Pirahãs laugh and talk a good part of the night. They don't sleep much at one time. Rarely have I heard the village completely quiet at night or noticed someone sleeping for several hours straight. I have learned so much from the Pirahãs over the years. But this is perhaps my favorite lesson. Sure, life is hard and there is plenty of danger. And it might make us lose some sleep from time to time. But enjoy it. Life goes on.

I went to the Pirahãs when I was twenty-six years old. Now I am old enough to receive senior discounts. I gave them my youth. I have contracted malaria many times. I remember several occasions on which the Pirahãs or others threatened my life. I have carried more heavy boxes, bags, and barrels on my back through the jungle than I care to remember. But my grandchildren all know the Pirahãs. My children are who they are in part because of the Pirahãs. And I can look at some of those old men (old like me) who once threatened to kill me and recognize some of the dearest friends I have ever had—men who would now risk their lives for me.

This book is about the lessons I have learned over three decades of studying and living with the Pirahãs, a time in which I have tried my best to comprehend how they see, understand, and talk about the world and to transmit these lessons to my scientific colleagues. This journey has taken me to many places of astounding beauty and into many situations I would rather not have entered. But I am so glad that I made the journey—it has given me precious and valuable insights into the nature of life, language, and thought that could not have been learned any other way.

The Pirahãs have shown me that there is dignity and deep satisfaction in facing life and death without the comfort of heaven or the fear of hell and in sailing toward the great abyss with a smile. I have learned these things from the Pirahãs, and I will be grateful to them as long as I live.

Part One LIFE

1 Discovering the World of the Pirahãs

I t was a bright Brazilian morning on December 10, 1977, and we were waiting to take off in a six-passenger plane provided by my missionary agency, the Summer Institute of Linguistics (SIL). The pilot, Dwayne Neal, put the aircraft through its preflight inspection. He walked around the plane and checked to see how well the load was balanced. He checked for external signs of damage. He drew a small vial from the fuel tank to check for water in the fuel. He tested the action of the propeller. This is a routine that has become as normal to me now as brushing my teeth before going to work, but then it was my first time.

As we prepared to take off, I thought hard about the Pirahãs, the tribe of Amazonian Indians I was going to live with. What was I going to do? How should I act? I wondered how the people would react to seeing me for the first time and how I would react to them. I was going to meet people different from me in many respects—some that I could anticipate, others that I could not. Well, I was flying there to do more than just meet them, actually. I was going to the Pirahãs as a missionary. My income and expenses were to be paid by evangelical churches in the United States so that I could "change the Pirahãs' hearts" and persuade them to worship the god I believed in, to accept the morality and the culture that goes along with believing in the Christian god. Even though I didn't even know the Pirahãs, I thought I could and should change them. This is the nexus of most missionary work.

Dwayne sat down in the pilot's seat, and we all bowed our heads while he prayed for a safe flight. Then he shouted, *"Livre!"* ("Stand clear" in Portuguese) out the open pilot's window and started the engine. As the engine warmed he spoke with Porto Velho's air-traffic control and we began to taxi. Porto Velho, the capital of the Brazilian state of Rondônia, was to become my base of operations for all future

Pirahã trips. At the end of the dirt airstrip, we turned around and Dwayne revved the engine. We sped off, the rust-red earth of the *cascalho* (gravel) airstrip becoming blurry and then falling away quickly beneath us.

I watched the jungle eventually consume the cleared land around the city. The open spaces around Porto Velho became smaller as the trees became more numerous. We flew across the mighty Madeira (Wood) River and the transformation was complete—a sea of green, broccoli-like trees arched to the edge of vision in all directions. I thought about animals that might be down there right now, just below us. I wondered if we crashed and I survived whether I would be eaten by jaguars—there were plenty of stories about crash victims killed not by the crash but by animals.

I was going to visit one of the least studied people in the world, speakers of one of the world's more unusual languages—at least judging by the trail of disappointed linguists, anthropologists, and missionaries they had left in their wake. Pirahã is not known to be related to any other living human language. I didn't know much about it except how it sounded on tapes and that previous linguists and missionaries who had studied the language and the people had decided to work elsewhere. It sounded like nothing I had ever heard before. The language, it seemed, was intractable.

The small air vent above my head in the Cessna began to blow out colder air as we gained altitude. I tried to get more comfortable. I leaned back and thought more about what I was about to do and how different this trip was for me than for the others in the plane. The pilot was doing his day job and would be back home in time for supper. His father had come along as a tourist. Don Patton, the missionary mechanic accompanying me, was getting a minivacation from the hard work of maintaining the missionary compound. But I was flying to my life's work. I was to meet for the first time the people I planned to share the rest of my existence with, the people whom I hoped to take to heaven with me. I would have to learn to speak their language fluently.

As the plane began to be buffeted by the midmorning updrafts—typical of the Amazon in the rainy season—my reverie was rudely halted by a more pressing concern. I was airsick. For the next 105 minutes, as we flew above the forest on breezes, I was nauseated. Just as I had willed my stomach to remain quiet, Dwayne reached back with a tuna sandwich, loaded with onions. "You guys hungry?" he asked helpfully. "No thanks," I replied, tasting the bile in my mouth.

Then we circled the airstrip near the Pirahã village of Posto Novo so that the pilot could get a better look. This maneuver increased the centrifugal force on my stomach, and I was already using every bit of restraint I could draw on to keep from heaving. For a couple of dark moments before we landed, I thought that it would be much better to crash and explode than for this nausea to continue. I admit that this was a rather shortsighted thought, but there it was.

The airstrip had been cleared from the jungle two years before by Steve Sheldon, Don Patton, and a team of teenagers from American churches. To build a jungle airstrip like this, you must first fell more than a thousand trees. Then their stumps need to be pulled up, because otherwise the wood will rot in the ground, the earth over the stump will collapse, and some plane will lose its landing gear and perhaps all its passengers. After pulling these thousand or so stumps, some several feet in diameter, you need to fill in the holes left by the extraction. Then you need to make sure the airstrip is as level as it can be without the use of heavy equipment. If you are successful, you conclude this process with a strip thirty feet wide and six hundred to seven hundred yards long. These were roughly the dimensions of the Pirahã strip we were about to land on.

The day we flew in, the grass on the strip was waist high. We had no way of knowing whether there were logs, dogs, pots, or other things in the grass that could damage the aircraft—and us—on landing. Dwayne "buzzed" the strip once and hoped that the Pirahãs would understand, as Steve had tried to explain to them, that they should run out and check the airstrip for dangerous detritus (once a Pirahã house had been built in the middle of the strip and had to be torn down before we could land). Several Pirahãs did then go out and we saw them running off the strip with a small log—small, but enough to flip the plane end-over-end if we had hit it on landing. All turned out well, though, as Dwayne brought us in for a safe, smooth landing.

Finally, when the plane came to a stop, the windless jungle heat and humidity hit me full force. As I exited, squinting and woozy, the Pirahãs surrounded me, chattering loudly, smiling, and pointing with recognition at Dwayne and Don. Don tried to tell the Pirahãs in Portuguese that I wanted to learn their language. In spite of knowing almost no Portuguese, a couple of the men got the idea that I was there to replace Steve Sheldon. Sheldon had also helped them understand my coming by explaining to them in Pirahã, on his last visit, that a short red-headed guy was coming to live with them. He said that I wanted to learn to speak like they did.

As we walked down the path from the airstrip to the village, I was surprised to encounter swamp water up to my knees. Carrying supplies through warm, murky water, not knowing what might bite my feet and legs, was my first experience with the Maici's flood stage at the end of the rainy season.

The most striking thing I remember about seeing the Pirahãs for the first time was how happy everyone seemed. Smiles decorated every face. Not one person looked sullen or withdrawn, as many do in cross-cultural encounters. People were pointing to things and talking enthusiastically, trying to help me see what they thought I might find interesting—birds flying overhead, hunting paths, huts in the village, puppies. Some men had on caps with the slogans and names of Brazilian politicians, bright shirts and gym shorts received from river traders. The women all wore the same type of dress, with short sleeves, hemmed just above the knee. These dresses had started out with different brightly colored patterns, but the colors were now obscured by a general brown stain from the dirt floors of their huts. Children younger than ten years of age or so ran naked. Everyone was laughing. Most touched me gently as they came up to me, as though I were a new pet. I could not have imagined a warmer welcome. People were telling me their names, though I did not remember most of them.

The first man whose name I did remember was Kóxoí (KO-oE). I saw him crouching in a bright clearing off the path to the right. He was tending something by the side of a fire in the sun. Kóxoí had on ragged gym shorts and wasn't wearing a shirt or shoes. He was thin and not particularly muscular. His skin was dark brown and lined like fine leather. His feet were wide, thickly calloused, and powerful-looking. He glanced up at me and called me over to where he was, on a patch of sandy ground, baking hot, where he was singeing the hair off a large rat-like animal. Kóxoí's face was kind, with a broad smile that took over his eyes and mouth, welcoming and comforting me on this day of new experiences in a new place. He talked to me pleasantly, though I didn't understand a single word. In my still nauseous state, the pungent smell of the animal almost gave me dry heaves. The tongue of the creature was hanging across its teeth, tip in the dirt, with blood dripping down it.

I touched myself on the chest and said, "Daniel." He recognized this as a name and immediately responded by touching his chest and saying his name. Then I pointed at the rodent on the fire.

"*Káixihí*" (KYE-i-HEE), he responded to the object of my pointing.

I repeated it back to him immediately (while thinking, Holy twenty-pound rat burger!). Sheldon had told me that the language was tonal, like Chinese, Vietnamese, and hundreds of other languages. This meant that in addition to paying attention to the consonants and vowels, I would need to listen carefully to the pitch on each vowel. I had managed to pronounce my first Pirahã word.

Next, I bent over and picked up a stick. I pointed to it and said, "Stick."

Kóxoí smiled and said, "*Xií*" (ií).

I repeated, "*Xií*." Then I let it drop and said, "I drop the *xií*."

Kóxoí looked and thought, then quickly said, "*Xií xi bigí káobií*" (ií ih bigí KAo BIí). (As I later learned, this literally means "Stick it ground falls," with the words in that order.)

I repeated this. I pulled out a notepad and pen I had put in my back pocket in Porto Velho just for this reason and wrote these things down, using the International Phonetic Alphabet. I translated the last phrase as "stick falls to the ground" or "you drop the stick." I then picked up another stick and dropped both sticks at once.

He said, "*Xií hoíhio xi bigí káobií*." "Two sticks fall to the ground," or so I thought at the time. I learned later that this means "A slightly larger quantity (*hoíhio*) of sticks falls to the ground."

I then picked up a leaf and went through this entire process again. I moved on to other verbs, such as *jump, sit, hit,* and so forth, with Kóxoí serving as my willing and ever more enthusiastic teacher.

I had listened to tapes of the language given to me by Steve Sheldon, and I had seen some short word lists that he had compiled. So I was not completely unfamiliar with the language, even though Sheldon had advised me to ignore his work, since he was unsure of its quality, and though hearing the language was very different indeed from seeing it written.

To test my ability to hear the tones of the language, I asked for some words that I knew to be distinguished mainly by tone. I asked for the word for *knife*.

"*Kaháíxíoi*" (ka-HAI-I-oi), he said.

And then the word for *arrow shaft*.

"*Kahaixíoi*" (ka-hai-I-oi), he answered as I pointed at the shaft of the arrow at the side of his hut.

The field linguistics classes I had taken with SIL before coming to Brazil were very good, and I had found a talent for linguistics that I did not realize I had. Within an hour of working with Kóxoí and others (as interested Pirahãs surrounded us), I had confirmed earlier findings by Sheldon and his predecessor, Arlo Heinrichs, that there were only eleven or so phonemes in Pirahã, that the basic organization of their sentences was SOV (subject, object, verb)—the most common ordering among the world's languages—and that their verbs were very complicated (now I know that each Pirahã verb form has at least 65,000 possible forms). I grew less worried about the situation. I could do this!

In addition to learning the language, I wanted to learn about the culture of the people. I looked first at the spatial layout of the houses. The village arrangement seemed to make little sense at first. There were huts clustered in different places along the path from the airstrip to Steve Sheldon's old home, now mine. Eventually, though, I realized that all the huts were on the side of the path closer to the river. And they all had views of the river from bend to bend. They were built close to the riverbank, none more than twenty paces from it, and parallel to it lengthwise. Jungle and undergrowth surrounded every home. There was a total of about ten huts. Brothers lived near brothers in this community (in other villages, I later learned, sisters lived near sisters, and in some villages there didn't seem to be any obvious kinship pattern of settlement).

After unloading our supplies, Don and I began to clean a small space in Sheldon's storeroom for our small pile of supplies (cooking oil, dried soup, canned corned beef, instant coffee, some salted crackers, a loaf of bread, some rice and beans). We walked with Dwayne and his father back to the plane after they had taken pictures and looked around. Don and I waved as they took off. The Pirahãs screamed with delight when the plane lifted up, all shouting, "*Gahióo xibipíío xisitoáopí*" (The airplane just left vertically)!

It was about two in the afternoon. And I felt for the first time the surge of energy and sense of adventure that comes naturally on the Maici with the Pirahãs. Don went to put Steve's imported Sears & Roebuck fishing boat (a wide, stable, aluminum boat with a cargo capacity of nearly one ton) into the river and test the outboard engine. I sat down in the middle of a group of Pirahã men in the front room of Sheldon's house, which was built like a Pirahã house, though larger. It was raised on stilts and had only half walls—no doors, no privacy, except in the bedroom for the children and in the storeroom. I got out my pad and pencil to continue language learning. Each man looked fit, lean, and hard—just muscle, bone, and gristle. They were all smiling broadly, and it seemed almost as if they were trying to outdo one another in their expressions of happiness around me. I repeated my name, Daniel, several times. One of the men, Kaaboogí, stood up after huddling with the others and addressed me in very rudimentary Portuguese: "*Pirahã chamar você Xoogiái*" (The Pirahãs will call you OO-gi-Ai). I had received my Pirahã name.

I knew that the Pirahãs would name me, because Don had told me that they name all foreigners, since they don't like to say foreign names. I later learned that the names are based on a similarity that the Pirahãs perceive between the foreigner and some Pirahã. Among the men there that day was a young man named Xoogiái, and I had to admit that I could see some resemblance. Xoogiái would be my name for the next ten years, until the very same Kaaboogí, now called Xahóápati, told me that my name was now too old and that my new name was Xaíbigaí. (About six years after that my name was changed again to what it is today, Paóxaisi—the name of a very old man.) As I learned, the Pirahãs change names from time to time, usually when individual Pirahãs trade names with spirits they encounter in the jungle.

I learned the names of the other men there—Kaapási, Xahoábisi, Xoogiái, Baitigií, Xaíkáibaí, Xaaxái. The women stood outside the house looking in, refusing to speak, but giggling if I spoke to them directly. I was writing down phrases like *I drop the pencil, I write on paper, I stand up, My name is Xoogiái*, and so on.

Then Don got the boat motor started and all the men ran out immediately to ride with him as he did a few circles in the river in front of the house. Looking around at the village, I suddenly found myself alone, and I noticed that there was no central village clearing, just two or three huts together, nearly hidden by the jungle, connected to other houses in the village by narrow paths. I could smell smoke from the fires burning in each hut. Dogs were barking. Babies were crying. It was very hot at this time of the afternoon. And very humid.

Now that I was working among the Pirahãs, I was determined to record language data as quickly and carefully as I was able. But each time I asked an individual Pirahã if I could "mark paper" (study—*kapiiga kaga-kai*) with them, although they would happily study with me, they would also tell me about another Pirahã I should work with, saying, "*Kóhoibiíihíai hi obáaxáí. Kapiiga kaagakaáíbaaí.*" I began to understand. There was some guy named Kóhoibiíihíai who would teach me to speak Pirahã. I asked my missionary colleague if he knew someone by this name.

"Yes, the Brazilians call him Bernardo."

"Why Bernardo?" I asked.

"The Brazilians give all the Pirahãs Portuguese names because they can't pronounce the Pirahã names." He went on, "This is the same reason, I suppose, that the Pirahãs give all outsiders Pirahã names."

So I waited all day for Bernardo/Kóhoibiíihíai to return from hunting. As the sun began to set, the Pirahãs started talking loudly and pointing to the farthest bend downriver. In the fading twilight, I could just make out the silhouette of a canoe and paddler coming toward the village, hugging the bank to avoid the strong current of the main stream of the Maici. Pirahãs from the village were yelling to the man in the canoe, and he was replying. People were laughing and excited, though I had no idea why. As the man tied his canoe at the bank, I could see the reason for the excitement: a pile of fish, two dead monkeys, and a large curassow on the floor of the canoe.

I walked down the muddy bank to the canoe and spoke to the arriving hunter, practicing a phrase I had learned that afternoon: "*Tii kasaagá Xoogiái*" (My name is Xoogiái). Kóhoi (Pirahãs shorten their names much as we do in English) looked up at me, his arms crossed over his chest, and grunted without emotion. Kóhoi's features were more African than the Asiatic features of so many Pirahãs, such as Kaaboogí, who looked Cambodian to me. Kóhoi had kinky hair, light black skin, and chin stubble. He was reclining in the canoe, yet the tautness of his muscles made it clear that he was ready to move quickly as he eyed me subtly. He appeared stronger than other Pirahãs, though he was no taller or heavier than any other man in the village, so far as I could tell. The squareness of his jaw and the firmness of his eye contact gave him a look of confidence and control. As other Pirahãs came running to get food, he handed out parts of animals with instructions as to who should receive what part. He had on orange pants but no shoes and no shirt.

On my second day I began to work with Kóhoi in the mornings at a table in the front room of the Sheldons' large jungle house. I spent the afternoons walking about the village, querying various Pirahãs about their language. I continued to follow the standard linguistic monolingual method for gathering data when no language is spoken in common: pointing, asking for words in the native language, and then writing down whatever response the native speaker gives, hoping it is the right one. Then practicing that immediately with other native speakers.

One of the things about Pirahã that immediately fascinated me was the lack of what linguists call "phatic" communication— communication that primarily functions to maintain social and interpersonal channels, to recognize or stroke, as some refer to it, one's interlocutor. Expressions like *hello, goodbye, how are you?, I'm sorry, you're welcome,* and *thank you* don't express or elicit new information about the world so much as they maintain goodwill and mutual respect. The Pirahã culture does not require this kind of communication. Pirahã sentences are either requests for information (questions), assertions of new information (declarations), or commands, by and large. There are no words for *thanks, I'm sorry,* and so on. I have become used to this over the years and forget most of the time how surprising this can be to outsiders. Anytime someone visits the Pirahãs with me, they ask how to say these things. And they stare suspiciously at me when I say that the Pirahãs have no such forms of communication.

When a Pirahã arrives in the village, he or she might say, "I have arrived." But by and large, no one says anything. If you give someone something, they might occasionally say, "That's right," or "It is OK," but they use these to mean something more like "Transaction acknowledged," rather than "Thank you." The expression of gratitude can come later, with a reciprocal gift, or some unexpected act of kindness, such as helping you carry something. The same goes when someone has done something offensive or hurtful. They have no words for *I'm sorry*. They can say, "I was bad," or some such, but do so rarely. The way to express penitence is not by words but by actions. Even in Western societies, there is considerable variation in how much we use phatic communication. Brazilians used to tell me when I was learning Portuguese, "Americans say 'thank you' way too much."

On my second afternoon in the Pirahã village, after a long day of language learning, I got myself a hot cup of strong black instant coffee and sat down at the edge of a steep bank to gaze at the Maici. Several Pirahã men had gone fishing with Don in the boat, so the village was quieter. It was about 5:45, the most beautiful time of day, when the sun glows orange and the river's reflective darkness stands out against the rusty color of the sky and the luxuriant spinach green of the jungle. As I sat idly watching and sipping my coffee, I was startled by the sight of two small gray porpoises jumping in sync out of the river. I had no idea that there were freshwater porpoises. Almost immediately, from around the bend came two Pirahã canoes, their riders paddling for all they were worth, in pursuit of the porpoises, trying to touch them with their paddles. It was a game of tag, porpoise tag.

Apparently the porpoises also enjoyed this because they continually came up just out of reach of the men in the canoes. This went on for half an hour, until darkness brought an end to the chase. The Pirahãs in the canoes and on the banks (for by now a crowd had gathered) were laughing hysterically. As they stopped chasing the porpoises, the porpoises disappeared. (In all my years watching this contest between mammals, no porpoise has ever been "tagged.")

I thought about where I was, the privilege of being in this marvelous world of the Pirahãs and nature. In just these first two days I had already experienced a myriad of new things, such as hearing the screechy metallic sound of toucans and the raspy cry of macaws. I smelled scents from trees and plants I had never seen before.

On the following days among the Pirahãs I watched their daily routines, in between sessions working on the language. Pirahãs start their days early, usually about five o'clock, though for a people who sleep very little during the night, it isn't clear if it's better to say that they start their day or simply never end it. In any case, I was usually awakened by various women of the village talking in their huts. They would begin speaking loudly to no one in particular about the day's events. One woman would announce that so-and-so was going hunting or fishing, then say what kind of meat she wanted. Other women would echo her from other huts or shout out their own culinary preferences.

Once the day has begun, fishing is the most common activity for men. Most of them leave before light, to favorite fishing spots hours downriver or upriver. If a fishing trip is expected to last overnight, the men take their families with them. But normally men go fishing alone or with one or two friends. If a pond has formed from receding river water, several men will be found in that single location, because it will be full of fish that cannot escape. Fishing is mainly by bow and arrow, but line and hook are also used if they can get some through trading. The men usually paddle off into the morning darkness, laughing loudly and challenging one another to canoe races. At least one man remains in the village to watch over things.

After the men have gone, the women and children leave to forage or pull manioc—also called cassava, the tuber of life—out of their jungle gardens. This takes hours and is hard work, requiring a good deal of endurance, but women (like their men) head into the jungle joking and laughing. Women are usually back by early afternoon. If the men are not yet back, they gather firewood in preparation for cooking the fish they expect their husbands to catch.

This initial visit to the Pirahãs came to an end after just a few days. In December of 1977 the Brazilian government ordered all missionaries to leave Indian reservations. We had to pack up. But I hadn't come to stay long in any case, just to get a feel for what the Pirahãs and their language were like. In those first ten days, I had learned a bit about the Pirahã language.

Leaving the village under these forced circumstances made me wonder whether I'd ever be able to return. The Summer Institute of Linguistics was concerned too and wanted to find a way around the government's prohibition against missionaries. So SIL asked me to apply to the graduate linguistics program at the State University of Campinas (UNICAMP), in the state of São Paulo, Brazil. It was hoped that UNICAMP would be able to secure government authorization for me to visit the Pirahãs for a prolonged period, in spite of the general ban against missionaries. But although I went there primarily to secure authorization to reenter the Pirahãs' village, UNICAMP turned out to offer me the greatest academic and intellectual environment I have ever experienced.

My work at UNICAMP paid off as SIL hoped it would. The president of the Brazilian National Indian Foundation (FUNAI), General Ismarth de Araujo Oliveira, authorized me to return to the Pirahãs, with my family, for a six-month stay to gather data for my UNICAMP M.A. thesis. My wife, Keren; our oldest daughter, Shannon, then seven; our daughter Kris, four; our son Caleb, one; and I left São Paulo by bus for Porto Velho in December, for our first family visit to the Pirahãs. It took us three days to reach Porto Velho, where a group of SIL missionaries were stationed and would help us travel to the Pirahãs' village. We spent a week there, preparing for the village and readying ourselves mentally for the upcoming adventure.

It is not easy for a Western family to prepare to live in an Amazonian village. Planning for our trip began weeks before we traveled. We purchased our supplies in PV, as missionaries call Porto Velho. There, Keren and I had to anticipate, buy for, and prepare for up to six months of family isolation in the jungle. Everything from laundry soap to birthday and Christmas presents had to be planned for months in advance of their actual usage. For most of our time with the Pirahãs, from 1977 through 2006, we were almost wholly responsible for all the medical needs of both our family and the Pirahãs, so we spent hundreds of dollars on medicine, from aspirin to snake antivenom, before each trip. Malaria treatments of all sorts—Daraprim, chloroquine, and quinine—topped our list.

We needed to take schoolbooks and school supplies so our children could study in the village. Each time we returned from the village to the SIL center in Porto Velho they would be tested by the SIL school, which was itself accredited by the state of California. The books (including an encyclopedia set and a dictionary) and other school materials added to the large inventory of goods for running our household—hundreds of liters of gasoline, kerosene, and propane, a propane-fueled refrigerator, dozens and dozens of cans of meat, dried milk, flour, rice, beans, toilet paper, trade items for the Pirahãs, and on and on.

After our buying and other preparations, I decided to fly in a week before my family, along with SIL missionary Dick Need, to prepare the house for the children's arrival. Dick and I labored from 6 a.m. to 6 p.m. every day, subsisting almost entirely on Brazil nuts (we could have gotten fish from the Pirahãs, but since I wasn't familiar enough with the culture yet to know whether the Pirahãs would consider our requests an imposition, we decided to get by on Brazil nuts, which the Pirahãs offered to us freely). We lacked food because our tools weighed too much for us to bring any food on the plane. We repaired the roof and floor of Sheldon's house and built a new kitchen counter. We also spent several days with machetes, assisted by a couple of Pirahãs, cutting the airstrip grass for the Cessna's arrival. I knew that for my children, at least, the first impression of the house would be crucial to their desire to stay. I was asking so much of them, to leave their friends and city life to spend the next several months in the jungle, with a people they didn't know, hearing a language none of us spoke.

The day my family was to arrive I woke up before dawn. At first light I paced the airstrip, checking for holes. There were always new sinkholes opening up. I also searched carefully for any large pieces of wood, such as firewood, the Pirahãs might have left on the strip. I was excited. This was really the beginning of our mission to the Pirahãs, for without my family, I knew that I could never stick it out. I needed their support. This was their mission too. They were stepping into a world without Western entertainment, without electricity, without doctors, dentists, or telephones—they were traveling back in time in many ways. This is a lot to ask of children, but I was confident that Shannon, Kristene, and

Caleb would handle it well. I knew that Keren, the most experienced of all of us in this kind of life, would do very well and that the children would draw confidence and strength from her experiences. After all, Keren had been raised among the Sateré-Mawé Indians and had lived in the Amazon since she was eight years old. She loved it. And nothing about the missionary life was too hard for her. In many ways I too drew strength from her confidence. She was the most committed missionary I had ever known.

When the plane was about five minutes away, the Pirahãs started shouting and running to the airstrip. I heard it a couple of minutes later and ran excitedly to welcome my family to the jungle. My children and Keren were waving enthusiastically as they landed. After the plane finishing taxiing and the pilot had opened his hatch, I approached the plane and shook his hand vigorously. Keren then stepped off, ecstatic, smiling, and immediately trying to talk to the Pirahãs. Shannon, with her dog, Glasses, Kris, and Caleb exited the passenger doors. The kids looked uncertain, but were glad to see me. And they smiled broadly at the Pirahãs. As the pilot prepared to return to Porto Velho, Dick said as he was boarding, "I'm going to think of you, Dan, while I'm eating a juicy steak tonight in Porto Velho."

We carried all our supplies to the house with the Pirahãs' help and then rested for a few minutes. Keren and the children inspected this home I had brought them to. It was still in need of serious organizing. But within a couple of days, we would get into a routine of work and family life.

After unpacking our supplies, we set up house. Keren had made mosquito nets and hanging cloth organizers for our dishes, clothes, and other belongings. The children began home-schooling, Keren managed the home, and I threw myself into full-time linguistics. We attempted to carry on an American Christian family culture in the middle of an Amazonian village. There were lessons for all of us.

None of us, not even Keren, had anticipated all that this new life would entail. One of our first nights as a family in the village, we were having dinner by gas lamp. In the living room I saw Glasses, Shannon's puppy, chasing something that was hopping in the dark, though I couldn't make it out. Whatever it was, it was hopping toward me. I stopped eating and watched. Suddenly, the dark thing hopped on my lap. I focused the beam of my flashlight at it. It was a gray-and-black tarantula, at least eight inches in diameter. But I was prepared. I worried about snakes and bugs, so I kept a hardwood club with me at all times. Without moving my hands toward the tarantula, I stood quickly and thrust my pelvis to throw the spider to the floor. My family had just seen what was on my lap and they stared wide-eyed at me and the hairy hopper. I grabbed my club and smashed it. The Pirahãs in the front room were watching. When I killed the spider they asked what it was.

"*Xóooí*" (Tarantula), I replied.

"We don't kill those," they said. "They eat cockroaches and do no harm."

We adapted to these situations after a while. And at that time, we felt that God was taking care of us and that these experiences gave us good stories to tell.

Though I was a missionary, my first assignments from SIL were linguistic. I needed to figure out how the grammar of the language worked and write up my conclusions before SIL would allow me to begin Bible translation.

I soon discovered that linguistic field research engages the entire person, not just his intellect. It requires of the researcher no less than that he insert himself into the foreign culture, in sensitive, often unpleasant surroundings, with a great likelihood of becoming alienated from the field situation by general inability to cope. The fieldworker's body, mind, emotions, and especially his sense of self are all deeply strained by long periods in a new culture, with the strain directly proportionate to the difference between the new culture and his own culture.

Consider the fieldworker's dilemma: you are in a place where all you ever knew is hidden and muffled, where sights, sounds, and feelings all challenge your accustomed conception of life on earth. It is something like episodes of *The Twilight Zone,* where you fail to understand what is happening to you, because it is so unexpected and outside your frame of reference.

I approached field research with confidence. My linguistics training had prepared me well for the basic field tasks of collecting data, storing it properly, and analyzing it. I was out of bed by 5:30 each morning.

After hauling up at least fifty-five gallons of water in five-gallon containers for drinking and dish washing, I would prepare breakfast for the family. By eight o'clock I was usually at my desk, beginning my "informant" work. I followed several different field guides and set measurable language-learning tasks for myself. My first couple of days back in the village, I made crude but useful drawings of the locations of all the huts in the village, with a list of the occupants of each. I wanted to learn how they spent their days, what was important to them, how children's activities differed from adults' activities, what they talked about, why they passed their time the way they did, and much more. And I was determined to learn to speak their language.

I tried to memorize at least ten new words or phrases per day and to study different "semantic fields" (groupings of related items such as body parts, health terms, bird names, etc.) and syntactic constructions (looking for active versus passive, past versus present, statements versus questions, and so on). I entered all new words on three-by-five-inch index cards. In addition to transcribing each new word phonetically on a card, I also recorded the contexts in which I had heard the word and a guess as to its most likely meaning. Then I punched a hole in the upper left corner of the card. I put ten to twenty cards on a ring (taken from a three-ring binder, so it would open and close) and put the ring through a belt loop on my pants. I would frequently test myself on the pronunciation and understanding of the words on my cards by working them into conversations with Pirahãs. I refused to let the Pirahãs' constant laughter at my misapplication and mispronunciation of their language slow me down. I knew that my first linguistic goal was to figure out which sounds of those I was hearing in Pirahã speech were actually meaningful and perceptible to the Pirahãs. These are what linguists call the phonemes of a language, and they would be the basis for devising a writing system.

My first big breakthrough in understanding how the Pirahãs see themselves in relation to others came during a trek into the jungle with some Pirahã men. I pointed at the branch of a tree. "What's that called?" I asked.

"*Xii xáowí*," they replied.

I pointed again to the branch, the straight portion of the branch this time, and I repeated, "*Xii xáowí.*"

"No." They laughed in unison. "*This* is the *xií xáowí*," pointing toward the juncture of the branch with the tree trunk and also to a smaller branch's juncture with the larger branch. "*That*" (what I had pointed at, the straight portion of the branch) "is *xii kositii.*"

I knew that *xii* meant "wood." I was pretty sure that *xáowí* meant "crooked" and that *kositii* meant "straight." But I still needed to test these guesses.

On the jungle path walking back toward home at the end of the day, I noticed that one long stretch of the path was straight. I knew that *xagí* meant "path," so I tried "*Xagí kositii*," pointing toward the path.

"*Xaió!*" came the immediate response (Right!). "*Xagí kositii xaagá*" (The path is straight).

When the path veered sharply to the right I tried "*Xagí xáowí.*"

"*Xaió!*" they all responded, grinning. "*Soxóá xapaitíisi xobáaxáí*" (You already see the Pirahã language well). Then they added "*Xagí xaagaía píaii*," which I later realized meant "Path is crooked also."

This was wonderful. In a few short steps I had learned the words for *crooked* and *straight*. I had already learned the words for most body parts by this time. As we walked along, I remembered the words that had been given to me by the Pirahãs in their language for *Pirahã people* (*Híaitíihí*), *Pirahã language* (*xapaitíisí*), *foreigner* (*xaoói*), and *foreign language* (*xapai gáisi*). *Pirahã language* was clearly a combination of *xapai* (head) and *tii* (straight), plus the suffix *-si*, which indicates that the word it is attached to is a name or a proper noun: "straight head." *Pirahã people* was *hi* (he), *ai* (is), and *tii* (straight), plus *-hi*, another marker similar to *-si*: "he is straight." *Foreigner* meant "fork," as in "fork in the tree branch." And *foreign language* meant "crooked head."

I was making progress! But I was still only scratching the surface.

What makes the Pirahã language so difficult to learn and to analyze are things that do not appear in the first few days of work, however cheerful one's immediate successes make one. The most difficult aspect of learning Pirahã is not the language itself, but the fact that the situation in which the learning takes place is "monolingual." In a monolingual field situation, very rare among the languages of the world, the researcher shares no language in common with the native speakers. This was my beginning point among the Pirahãs, since they don't speak Portuguese, English, or any language other than Pirahã, except for a few limited phrases. So to learn their language, I must learn their language. Catch-22. I can't ask for translations into any other language or ask a Pirahã to explain something to me in any language but Pirahã. There are methods for working in this way. Not surprisingly, I helped develop some of those methods as a result of my ordeal. But the methods for monolingual field research were mostly around long before I came on the scene.

Nevertheless, it is hard. Here is a typical exchange, after I had been there long enough to learn the Pirahã expression for *How do you say* ———— *in Pirahã?*:

"How do you say that?" (I point to a man coming upriver in his canoe.)

"*Xigihí hi piiboóxio xaaboópai*" (The man upriver comes).

"Is this right: '*Xigihí hi piiboóxio xaaboópai*'?"

"*Xaió. Xigihí piiboó xaaboópaitahásibiga*" (Right. The man upriver comes.)

"What is the difference between '*Xigihí hi piiboóxio xaaboópai*' and '*Xigihí piiboó xaaboópaitáhásibiga*'?"

"No difference. They are the same."

Clearly, from the perspective of a linguist, there *must* be a difference between the two sentences. But until I learned Pirahã on my own, I had no way of knowing that the difference was that the first sentence means "The man returns upriver" and the second means "I am an eyewitness to the fact that the man returns upriver." This makes learning the language very rough going indeed.

Another thing that makes the language hard to learn is something already mentioned—Pirahã is tonal. For every vowel, you must learn whether the pitch on the vowel is high or low. Many of the languages in the world are like this, although this number includes almost no European languages. English is not tonal in this sense. I had already decided to write vowels that had a high pitch with an acute accent (´) over the vowel and vowels with a low tone with no mark over the vowel. This can be illustrated by the simple pair of words meaning *I* and *excrement*:

Tií (I) has a low tone on the first *i* and a high tone on the final *i*. Impressionistically, this would be "tiI."

Tíi (excrement) has a high tone on the first *i* and a low tone on the second *i*—"tIi."

The language is hard to learn too because there are only three vowels (*i, a, o*) and eight consonants (*p, t, h, s, b, g,* the glottal stop, and *k*). This small number of sounds means that the words of Pirahã have to be much longer than in a language with more speech sounds. To have short words each word needs enough sound differences to tell it apart from most other short words. But if your language has only a few sound differences, like Pirahã, then you need more space in each word, that is, longer words, to be able to tell the words apart. The effect for me at first was that most Pirahã words sounded the same.

Finally, the Pirahã language is notoriously difficult because it lacks things that many other languages have, especially in the way that it puts sentences together. For example, the language has no comparatives, so I couldn't find expressions like *this is big/that is bigger*. I couldn't find color words—no simple words for red, green, blue, and so on, only descriptive phrases, like *that is like blood* for red or *that is not ripe yet* for green. And I couldn't find stories about the past. When you can't find something, but you expect it to be there, you can waste months looking for something that doesn't exist. Many of the things I had been taught to look for in field linguistics I could not find at all. This not only made things hard, but it also was at times downright discouraging. Still, I was optimistic that with enough time and effort, I would figure out this language.

But the future is not ours and our plans are only our wishes. It was folly to believe that I could just ignore where I was and focus strictly on linguistics. We were in the Amazon.

2 The Amazon

Once you have made your peace with the Amazon, a Pirahã village is a relaxing place. The first step toward this peace is for you to learn to ignore, even enjoy, the heat. That is not as hard as it might sound. The human body, when clothed properly, can handle the 90 to 110°F temperatures well, especially since the jungle provides plenty of shade and, in the case of the Pirahãs, the Maici River, which is always cool, wet, and relaxing. The humidity is harder to accept, though. Perspiration—that otherwise effective tool for lowering body temperature via evaporation in temperate climates—produces little more than athlete's foot and crotch rot in the Amazon, unless your skin, like the Pirahãs', is weather-beaten and usually dry because you rarely perspire.

Apart from such minor bodily discomforts, the Amazon region is not merely a place; it is an awe-inspiring force. The Amazonian rain forest covers nearly three million square miles: 2 percent of the total surface of the earth and 40 percent of the South American landmass. This forest is nearly the size of the continental United States. Fly from Porto Velho near the Bolivian border to the city of Belém at the mouth of the Amazon, a four-hour jet flight, and on a clear day you will see the jungle stretch out to the horizon in every direction: a green carpet, as far as the eye can see, with blue streaks of water from north to south, flowing toward the "moving sea," as the Tupi Indians called the Amazon.

The Amazon flows over four thousand miles from Peru to the Atlantic. The river is over two hundred miles wide at its mouth, with a delta, the island of Marajó, which is larger than Switzerland. There is enough dark and unknown land in Amazonia to consume a million imaginations. In fact it almost has—there is a nearly endless list of books about it, on its ecology, its histories, its peoples, and its politics. It has aroused the wanderlust and the imagination of Europeans and their descendants since the Spaniards and Portuguese first beheld it at the beginning of the sixteenth century. Two of my favorite American writers, Mark Twain and William James, felt its pull.

Mark Twain left Ohio in 1857 hoping to depart from New Orleans for the Amazon River, apparently to try to get rich in the coca trade. One wonders what books or stories we have missed because he changed his plans and decided to train as a riverboat pilot on the Mississippi. Might we have had a *Life on the Amazon,* as opposed to *Life on the Mississippi*?

William James actually made it to the Amazon and was able to explore a significant portion of the main river and its tributaries. While on a trip with the Harvard biologist Louis Agassiz in 1865 to collect zoological specimens, James traveled for some eight months through Brazil and along the Amazon and its tributaries. After his Amazonian experience, James abandoned his goal of becoming a naturalist—one might say that there is no place to go but down for a naturalist after the Amazon. (More than one-third of all species known on earth live in the Amazon.) He decided instead to focus on philosophy and psychology, eventually becoming the main force in the founding and development of the philosophical school known as American pragmatism.

The vast bulk of the Amazon rain forest, river basin, and river lie in Brazil. Brazil is the world's fifth-largest country in landmass, larger than the forty-eight contiguous United States. Its population of nearly 190 million people is diverse, containing large groups of Portuguese, Germans, Italians, other Europeans, and Asians, including the largest population of Japanese outside of Japan. To the majority of Brazil's urban-dwelling inhabitants, the Amazon sounds as distant and fantastic as it does to Europeans or North Americans. Though they pride themselves on the beauty of the Amazon and its attraction for the rest of the world, the majority of Brazilians have never seen anything that one could call jungle. The Amazon is two thousand miles from the major population areas of southeastern Brazil, where over 60 percent of Brazilians live. But this doesn't prevent Brazilians from being somewhat umbrageous and defensive when anyone suggests that the governance of the Amazon (such as its preservation) follow rules or regulations of foreign provenance. As they say throughout Brazil, "A

Amazônia é nossa"—"The Amazon is ours!" Some Brazilians' concern about foreign intervention in the Amazon can almost border on paranoia, as when some of my Brazilian colleagues insist to me that U.S. schoolchildren learn in their official textbooks that the Amazon belongs to the United States.

As the curators of the world's largest natural history preserve, Brazilians are by and large in favor of conserving the diversity of minerals, water, flora, and fauna in the Amazon. But they don't want to be preached at by the United States or Europe—who themselves destroyed much greater forest areas than have yet been destroyed in the Amazon. Local conflicts concerning preservation of the Amazon among Brazilians are well known and generally draw significant press coverage. (One well-known case is that of Chico Mendes. Mendes was murdered for organizing rubber tappers to use the Amazon's commercial resources in an ecologically friendly way that was ultimately at odds with their employers' view of how they should work.) But such stories can be misleading. In reality, these conflicts are less significant than the widespread agreement among Brazilians that the Amazon should be preserved.

Perhaps the best evidence for Brazilian interest in conservation is the Brazilian agency IBAMA, the Instituto Brasileiro do Meio Ambiente e dos Recursos Naturais Renováveis (Brazilian Institute for the Environment and Renewable Natural Resources). IBAMA is ubiquitous in the Amazon, well equipped, with a professional staff and a genuine and keen concern for the preservation of the Amazon's natural beauty and resources.

The Amazon River system has two types of land and two types of rivers, broadly speaking: white (or muddy) rivers or dark-water rivers. Both types in the Amazon are "old" rivers; that is, they meander along with slow-flowing currents, because their headwaters are only slightly more elevated than their mouths. Unlike dark-water rivers, muddy-water rivers, such as the Amazon and the Madeira (the Mississippi and the Mekong are others), are rich in flora and fauna and have higher concentrations of nutrients for fish and other forms of river life. They are also rich in insect life though insects are found on all rivers.

During my first days among the Pirahãs I discovered the curse of lit-

tle flies with V-shaped wings that land on your exposed skin during the day. These flies, *mutucas,* suck your blood and leave you with intense itching at the point of their bite, along with respectable welts if your skin is very sensitive, as mine is. You must not hate the *mutucas,* though, nor even the various types of horseflies that bite and welt the tender skin of your inner thigh, your outer ear, your cheeks, and your ass. You must not hate them even when you notice their deviousness—always flying to shaded parts of the body—exactly those parts you are not paying any attention to. Why not hate them? Because the frustration will kill you faster than the bug bites. I will admit that I have often wished that these insects had better-developed nervous systems so that I could torture them. But the feeling passes—most of the time.

There are insects at night too. If you spend a night unprotected by a mosquito net on the banks of one of these rivers, as I have on the Madeira, it will be one of the longest and most miserable nights of your life, as black clouds of mosquitoes swarm around you, flying up your nostrils, into your ears, biting you through your clothes, your hammock, and even your heavy jeans, in every imaginable spot. And, heaven forbid, if you have to relieve yourself during the night, they will swarm around any exposed flesh.

The river system traditionally dominated by the Pirahãs and the closely related tribe known as the Muras (who no longer speak their original language) is the Madeira River. The Madeira possesses the fifth-largest water flow in the world. It is the second-longest tributary in the world (after the Missouri). The Madeira River basin is three times the size of France. Among the hundreds of tributaries of the Madeira is the dark-water river, the Rio dos Marmelos, about eight hundred yards across at its mouth, averaging a width of perhaps four hundred yards and a depth of fifteen yards in August. The major tributary of the Marmelos is the Maici, the home of the Pirahãs. No one else lives on the Maici. At its mouth the Maici is more than two hundred yards wide. For most of its length it averages perhaps thirty yards in width. It varies in depth from six inches in some places just before the onslaught of the rainy season to perhaps eighty feet by the end of the rainy season.

The Maici is a dark-water river, a tea-colored flow carrying fish and leaves at a speed of twelve knots to the Marmelos. In the rainy season it is murky. In the dry season the color lightens and it becomes very clear and shallow, and its sandy bed is easily visible. Einstein proposed that the distance between two points following the course of an old river is roughly the distance of a straight line between those points times pi. The Maici conforms to this prediction. From the air it looks like an enormous snake slithering through the forest. Traveling it by boat after the rainy season, some of the curves are so tight that the wake generated by the boat travels between the flooded trees from one side of the loop to the other so quickly that the craft runs into its own wake as it comes around the corner. The Maici is startlingly beautiful. When floating on it, there are times I think it must be like Eden: gentle breezes, clear water, white sand, emerald trees, flaming macaws, awe-inspiring harpy eagles, monkey calls, toucan cries, and the occasional roar of jaguars.

The Pirahãs are settled along the Maici from its mouth to the point where the Transamazon Highway crosses it, roughly fifty miles. By motorboat, the distance is about 150 miles. The Pirahã village I have worked in the most, Forquilha Grande, is located on the Maici River near the Transamazon Highway. The Maici River intersects the Transamazon roughly fifty-six miles east of the town of Humaitá (Oomy-TA), Amazonas. The initial serious purpose to which I put my first handheld GPS was to record the coordinates of the village where I lived. They are: S 7° 21.642′ by W 62° 16.313′.

There are two major views on how the Amazon was originally settled, represented by the work of archaeologists such as Betty Meggers and Anna Roosevelt. Some people, such as Meggers, believe that the agricultural potential of Amazonia's soil, at least for prehistoric technology, was too low to sustain large civilizations and that, consequently, the Amazon has always been the home of small bands of hunter-gatherers. Consistent with this view is the idea of some linguists, especially the late Joseph Greenberg of Stanford University, that there were three waves of migration to the Americas across the land bridge of Beringia, which today lies beneath the waters of the Bering Strait. The first group to cross, some 11,000 years ago, were "pushed" southward by the second group to migrate, who were in their turn largely forced to the south by the final group to cross the land bridge— the Inuit, or Eskimos. The first group across Beringia settled South America and, aside from notable exceptions like the Incas, were mainly hunter-gatherers.

According to Greenberg, evidence for this migration can be found in the relationships among the languages of the Americas, both living and extinct. He claims, for example, that the languages of Mexico southward, by and large, are more closely related linguistically than those of central and northern North America. In Greenberg's view, Pirahã would have to be more closely related to other South American languages than to any language anywhere else. However, the Pirahã language is not demonstrably related to any living language. Greenberg's claims that it is related to languages belonging to the family that he calls Macro-Chibcha are nearly impossible to evaluate, and the evidence that I have been able to uncover over the years suggests that Pirahã and the now extinct related dialect, Mura, form a single language isolate, unrelated to any other known language. However, it is impossible to prove that Pirahã was not related to any other Amazonian languages in the distant past. Historical linguistics methods, used for classifying and reconstructing the history of languages, simply do not allow us to look back far enough to say certainly that two languages never developed from a common source language.

An alternative to Meggers's and Greenberg's views has been developed by Roosevelt and her colleagues, including my own former Ph.D. student Michael Heckenberger of the University of Florida. According to Roosevelt, the Amazon was and is capable of sustaining large settlements and civilizations, including, if Roosevelt is correct, the Marajoara civilization of the island of Marajó. According to Roosevelt, *Homo sapiens* has been in South America much longer than the Greenberg-Meggers set of ideas would allow.

The existence of language isolates like Pirahã and Mura (known by early explorers, when the Mura language was still spoken, simply as Mura-Pirahã, two very similar dialects of a single language) might be understood as supporting Roosevelt's ideas, because large amounts of time are required to sufficiently "erase" the similarity between languages to produce a language isolate. On the other hand, if the Pirahãs had been separated from other languages and peoples very early on in the peopling of the Americas, this could explain their linguistic and cultural uniqueness by either the Meggers or Roosevelt theories. The likelihood is that we will never know where the Pirahãs or their language came from—not unless a cache of early documents is discovered that record extinct but related languages. In that case, we could use the standard methodology of comparative and historical linguistics to recreate something of the Pirahãs' past.

Some evidence already exists that the Pirahãs are not originally from the part of the jungle where they currently reside, from the lack of native vocabulary for some species of monkeys found around the Maici. The Brazilian monkey *paguacu* (a name from the Tupi-Guarani linguistic family) is referred to by the Pirahãs by the same name, for example. That makes *paguacu* a loan word, one borrowed from Portuguese or one of the two Tupi-Guarani groups, the Parintintin and the Tenharim, that the Pirahãs have had long contact with. Since there is no evidence that the Pirahãs have ever given up one of their own words in order to borrow a word from another language, this suggests that the language had no word for this species of monkey because it wasn't found in their homeland, wherever that might have been.

Since Pirahã is not related to any other known living language, I came to realize that we had not been assigned to work merely with a difficult language, but with a unique language.

We adjusted as a family to life in the Amazon, completely on our own, with no one but ourselves to turn to for help. We became closer than we had ever been, taking great satisfaction and enjoyment in family companionship. We thought that we were in control of our lives as we had never been before. But the Amazon was about to remind us who was boss.

3 The Cost of Discipleship

We went as disciples of Christ to the Pirahãs. And the Bible
warns disciples that service is fraught with dangers. So we
began to discover. One late afternoon Keren began to
complain that the Pirahãs were making her tense. She was frying the
meat from an anteater that Kóhoi had killed. She was surrounded as
usual by about a dozen Pirahãs, curious about our cooking and eating
habits (and hungry for some anteater steak). She asked me to walk with
her on our airstrip. The airstrip was like our personal park. It didn't just
serve as a landing site for the plane, it gave us a place to walk, to jog, and
to escape the village once in a while.

"I can't take this anymore," Keren reported in a shaky voice.

"What's bothering you?" I asked. It was common for me to complain
about how difficult the constant scrutiny of the Pirahãs was. But Keren
rarely noticed it. And when she did notice that she was surrounded by
staring, curious Pirahãs, she didn't seem to mind at all; she'd just ami-
cably talk to them.

I told her I would finish cooking dinner and that she should try to
get some rest. As we walked back on the path to our hut, she mentioned
that her back was aching and that she was starting to get a headache. We
didn't understand the significance of these symptoms at the time,
though, and chalked them up to tension.

That night, Keren's head was aching even more. Her spine was hurting so that she frequently arched her back. Then she began to feel hot
and feverish. I got out our medical manual and started to read about
her symptoms. As I was reading, our older daughter, Shannon, began to
complain that her head was hurting too. I felt her forehead with the
back of my hand. She radiated heat.

We had medicine enough for any common Amazonian health problem, I thought. I was sure that all I needed to do was to read about the different sets of symptoms in my missionary medical book and the diagnosis would be easy. As I looked through the symptoms, I concluded that Keren and Shannon had typhoid fever. I believed this because I had contracted typhoid during our jungle training in Mexico and their symptoms were like mine had been.

I began antibiotic treatment for typhoid fever. Neither one improved at all. They were both getting very ill very quickly, and Keren's decline in health was dangerously fast. She stopped eating. She did not want to drink anything, though occasionally she would take some water. I tried to record her temperature with a thermometer, but the mercury rose to the end and never fell, no matter how many times I took it. Shannon's fever hovered between 103 and 104 degrees.

The hot tropical sun was not helping. While I cared (ineptly) for Keren and Shannon, I also had to cook and clean for Caleb (then only two) and Kris, four years old. I was unable to sleep. Keren and Shannon had diarrhea, so I had to help them on and off the chamber pot at night, empty and clean the pot, and help them back to bed.

At the head of our bed we had given ourselves a small bit of privacy by putting up a wall of *paxiuba* palm slats. The Pirahãs crowded close and peered in through the slats. They knew something was wrong. I later learned that everyone in the village except me and my family knew that Keren and Shannon had malaria.

The lack of privacy, my concern about my wife's and daughter's health, and my exhaustion from work and lack of sleep all aggravated my natural tendency to worry, so that by the end of five days, I was desperate for help. Keren was nearly comatose. She and Shannon were moaning in pain, and Keren was starting to have spells of delirium, sitting up and shouting at people who were not there, saying things that made no sense, slapping me, Kris, and Caleb if we passed too closely to her when she was sitting during one of her hallucinations.

The fourth night of her illness, during a thunderstorm so loud that I could hear almost nothing except wind and thunder and rain, Keren sat up and told me that Caleb had fallen out of his hammock in the next room.

I replied confidently, "No, he's OK. I've been awake and listening this whole time. I didn't hear him fall."

Keren became agitated and said, "Go help Caleb! He's on the dirty floor with the cockroaches."

To humor her I got up and went into the kids' room, next to our half-walled bedroom. Their room had three-foot-high board walls, with the four-foot space above them closed by plastic screen. Caleb and Kristene shared a mosquito net. Caleb slept in a hammock and Kristene in a single bed beneath him. We also had put a chemical camping toilet in this room, with privacy given by curtains hung around the toilet. We kept a kerosene lamp in the room as well. Each evening after bathing in the river and eating dinner, we would retreat to the relative comfort and privacy of the kids' room and I would read out loud to the family— from books like the *Chronicles of Narnia*, *To Kill a Mockingbird*, and *The Lord of the Rings*.

I walked into the room with my flashlight. Caleb was on the floor, cockroaches nearby. He was trying to get back to sleep but looked bewildered and uncomfortable. I picked him up and hugged him and put him back in his hammock. Keren's motherly sensitivity had overcome her malaria to alert her to the fact that her son needed help.

The next morning I knew that I had to do something. Shannon and Keren were too ill for me just to sit by and watch. But I didn't know how to get back to Porto Velho on my own. The mission plane had flown us in, so I had not traveled the river before. Without the plane we were lost. And at this time the Brazilian government would not allow foreigners to have two-way radios, so we had no contact with the outside world. I did not have a boat capable of traveling dependably, nor did I even have enough gasoline to make a river trip.

However, there was a Catholic lay missionary, Vicenzo, visiting the Pirahãs, and he had a small aluminum canoe with a new 6.5-horsepower Johnson outboard and nearly fifty liters of gasoline. I asked him the enormous favor of loaning me his boat for an indefinite period of time. If he did this, he would himself be stranded among the Pirahãs. He immediately agreed, though he assured me, wrongly it turned out, that whatever Keren and Shannon had, they must have brought it with them because there were no diseases among the Pirahãs. (Only two weeks after I left the Pirahãs Vicenzo nearly died of malaria contracted among the Pirahãs.) I asked him then if he could tell me how to get to the nearest settlement with a doctor and a hospital.

Vicenzo told me I would need to get to either Humaitá or Manicoré (ma-ni-ko-REH), two small towns along the Madeira River. He recommended Humaitá because there was a road from there to Porto Velho, the capital of the state of Rondônia and, unbeknownst to him, the location of my mission's headquarters. To get to Humaitá, he said, I would need to travel down the Maici and Marmelos rivers for about twelve hours to a place called Santa Luzia, which he pronounced "SANta loo-CHEE-a." From there I could get men to help me carry my family across a jungle path connecting the Marmelos and Madeira rivers. On the Madeira I would go to a settlement called the Auxiliadora (named for "Our Lady the Helper"), a small town founded about twenty years previously by Salesian priests. From there we could catch a large boat to Humaitá, a place I had never heard of until this conversation. It now seemed like Mecca.

I went home and began packing for the trip, though I had no idea what that would entail or what we would need. Vicenzo wasn't sure how long the boat trip from the Auxiliadora to Humaitá would take, since he had never made that trip. I didn't know if we'd need to take our own food. But there was barely enough room in his canoe for the five of us plus the gasoline, so I would be able to take very little in any event.

By now it was too late to leave. We'd have to get an early start the next day. It was too dangerous to risk getting stranded on the river after dark. I packed some canned meat and canned peaches, spoons, and a couple of enamel-coated tin plates. I gathered a machete, matches and candles, two changes of clothes for everyone, and a container for water. I set these things aside and prayed. Then I went to bed. The next morning, as soon as the sun came up, I brought Vicenzo's canoe over to the bank in front of my house and began to load it. The sun was already bright at seven and the sky was cobalt blue. A morning breeze cooled me as I worked.

After the supplies were in, I carried Shannon down and laid her in the canoe. It tipped a bit with her weight. Pirahãs lined the banks of the river, watching. I next walked Caleb and Kristene down and told them to stand by the canoe. Then I went to the house and picked up Keren, thinking how much lighter she seemed (she had weighed ninety-eight pounds before getting ill and had lost, I calculated, perhaps ten pounds in the past five days). She was only semiconscious when I started from the house. As we got to the riverbank and I began my careful descent, Keren awakened and started yelling and struggling.

"What are you doing?! Are you running away? Don't you believe in God? Don't you have any faith? We have to stay here and reach these people for Jesus!"

This made it very hard for me to continue with plans to depart. I was already tired, uncertain, and insecure. Now if something went wrong, if someone got hurt or worse, I would be morally wrong as well. But I knew that I had no choice. Keren, and maybe Shannon, would die if I did not press on and get us out of there. And, nontrivially, I simply was at the end of my endurance. I was too tired to keep up with the demands of a sick family in the village.

For many reasons, it had been hard for me to make the decision to leave. There were the uncertainty and danger of the journey, and the complications and stress of handling everyone on my own, as I was already exhausted. I was sure that the other missionaries at home base would share Keren's view that I was a faithless coward. (As it turned out, they were not condemning but were very understanding and helpful.) I also knew that in just over a week a supply flight was scheduled to arrive in the village. This plane could take the family out to Porto Velho. But if I waited, I thought the chances were strong that Keren would die. The risks of leaving earlier were less than the risk of waiting for the flight. But really I simply did not want to wait, with each additional lost night's sleep wearing me down until I was useless to myself and my family. I had to do something.

As I came up the bank to get Keren, Xabagi, an old Pirahã man, approached to ask me if I could bring back matches, blankets, and other goods when I returned from the city. I responded angrily, "Keren is sick. Shannon is sick. I am not going to buy anything" (if I had known how to say *goddammit* in Pirahã, I would have). "I'm going to the city to take them to get water [medicine] to make them well again."

I was angry, and I am sure that it showed. Here I was, my entire family in danger, and all the Pirahãs could think of was themselves? I pull-started the small Johnson engine and it came to life. The canoe tipped from side to side, a danger before we were even under way, since we had only about three inches of freeboard, and the water was deep, over fifty feet in most places this time of year. If I tipped us over from my lack of experience, there would be a disaster. I had no life vests but I did have two small children and two very sick passengers who could not swim to shore. I could not have saved them all in the powerful current of the Maici. But I had no choice.

OK, God. Now I am in one of those missionary stories that used to inspire me so much. Keep us safe, God, I thought.

We pulled away from the bank. The Pirahãs were shouting, "Don't forget the matches! Don't forget the blankets! Bring back manioc meal. And canned meat!" And the list went on. Above the whine of the two-cycle motor, I could hear the cawing of a pair of red macaws flying overheard, indifferent to me as they flew to their nest. The sun was shining brightly. It was already in the upper seventies and it wasn't yet 8 a.m.

But the canoe's nine miles per hour speed gave us a breeze. Keren's and Shannon's faces were bright in the sunlight. We'd been going for an hour or so when Kristene said she was hungry. I slowed down and opened a can of peaches. I told Kristene to wash her hands over the side in the river, then just pull peaches out of the can with her hands. Caleb did the same. Kristene turned to Keren and asked, "Mommy, you want some peaches?" Keren surprised me by sitting up and slapping Kristene on the face. She told her to shut up. Then Keren collapsed. Kristene didn't cry. She gave me a pained and puzzled expression. I said, "Mommy's sick, sweetie. She doesn't know what she's doing." Kristene knew this already. So did Caleb. Shannon didn't want anything. So we finished the peaches and I let Kristene and Caleb drink the syrup from the can.

The jungle passed us on both sides, an impassive green. No other boats were on the river. The water was high so I had to be careful to stay on the main channel and not follow false channels into swamps. Fortunately, the main current was usually easy to spot. But not always. When the water suddenly spread out before me into what looked like a swamp instead of a river, or into several apparent channels at once, I became disoriented.

After another hour or so, Keren sat up and asked for water. I tried to pour her some, but she jerked the canteen out of my hand and took the cup. Then she held the cup away from her and began to empty the canteen into her lap. I tried to get it back from her by saying, "Honey, let me do this for you. You're just spilling the water."

She looked at me angrily and replied, "This trip would be a lot more fun if you weren't along." She then put the canteen in her mouth and had a drink. I gave Shannon some too and we continued on.

Several hours later I saw a house in a clearing on the bank to my left. I pulled over. Could we already be at the path to the Madeira? My Portuguese was still rudimentary, but I went up the bank and clapped in front of the house until a woman came to the window opening. I asked her if this was Santa "Loo-CHEE-a."

The woman said, "I never heard of that place."

"Is there anyone else who could help me?" I nearly pleaded.

It was about two in the afternoon and we had less than a quarter of a tank of gasoline left, enough for one or two more hours. If I didn't find Santa Luzia soon, I would have to paddle. We might have to spend the night sleeping in the canoe.

She pointed upriver and said, "Up there at Pau Queimado they may know where the place you're looking for is."

"But I just came from upriver and I didn't see any settlement."

She clarified, "It's in the first inlet off the river on your left."

I thanked her and ran back to the boat. It was hot and I was red with sunburn. So was everyone in my family. As I was getting back in the canoe, I took another look at this woman's house, seeing for the first time how her family lived. The house was whitewashed—that could not have been easy or cheap for a family living at subsistence level. Why did they want to do that? To reflect the heat? No, they wanted their house to be attractive, even though it was in the jungle, where new people rarely came. There were *jambu* trees, producing red, succulent, sweet, applelike fruits. There were papaya plants. A field of manioc, sugarcane, sweet potatoes, and *cará* was close by, visible down the path from the house. The area around the house was clear and clean, some parts with green, machete-trimmed grass, other parts sandy soil. The house was made of boards hand-hewn, no doubt, by her husband. Near my canoe, I saw a string of live yellow-spotted Amazon River turtles tied to a stick at the house's dock in shallow water. These turtles are a favorite item of food and trade for Amazonian *caboclos* (as Portuguese-

speaking residents of the Brazilian interior are known). I thought as I untied the canoe and pointed it upriver that it must be hard to make a living catching turtles.

Life for these people is not easy. Yet they live as though it were, greeting people with grace, good humor, and helpfulness. I had so much more than they, and yet as I looked at my behavior more closely I realized that I was more tense, less welcoming, less hospitable than these people. And I was a missionary. I had a lot to learn.

But I would have to learn it later. Right then I had to get help. I started the motor. Another thought prayer: "God, I have come to the Amazon for You. I came with my family to serve You and to help people. Why are You letting me get lost? I am almost out of gasoline, God. What good will it do if my wife dies because I am out of gas and lost? C'mon, God. Help me."

I looked again at the beauty around me. From the river I could see Ipê trees, towering more than forty yards above the river, at least a yard in diameter, their bright yellow and purple flowers highlighted against the surrounding green. Brazilians of the region call the Ipê the *passar bem* (get well) tree. I half hoped that the sight of them would bring good luck. The sun was bright, the breeze cool. The forest was green, and today it seemed welcoming. The terrain here just up from the mouth of the Marmelos River was hilly, with steep banks on all sides and numerous inlets, which my novice eyes had a hard time distinguishing at times from the main river.

Farther in the distance, I could even see mighty Brazil nut trees towering over the forest. I looked at it all in a new way. Is nature beautiful if your family dies in it without help? I determined that the beauty in nature is really the beauty of our perception of it. No, it wouldn't be beautiful without humans to declare it so. But, my God, it was beautiful. Whatever the source, the breeze-blown ripples on the water, the swaying branches of the trees, the pale blue sky, the health and strength in my arms, the clearness of my eyes, the determination in my heart—these were beautiful things and I felt one with nature in the ubiquitous struggle for life.

I eventually saw the inlet to Pau Queimado and directed my shiny canoe into it. After a minute or so, as the steep banks of this miniature fjord surrounded us, I saw a clearing, a field of manioc, and a thatch-roofed hut. The bank was at about a 60 percent incline, more than forty yards up. It was a rich brown color, with some grass near the top. Brazilians along the rivers keep clean homes and village areas and are impressively industrious, valuing cleanliness and order around their houses. I sprinted up the steps the owners had carved in the bank, each step framed by wood about three inches thick. I reached the top panting and looked around. There were several people sitting on the floor of the hut, apparently having a meal.

"Do you know how to get to Santa Loo-CHEE-a?" I blurted out, not bothering with the normal caboclo niceties of introduction, calm small talk, and way-smoothing for any request.

A mother was nursing a baby boy in the corner. A man sat stirring a gruel of fish and farinha (manioc meal) in a hollowed gourd. Hammocks were neatly wrapped around crossbeams in the low roof. In spite of its height above the river, the hut was raised on eighteen-inch stilts, with a board floor, board walls, and board shutters. Caboclos close up their homes tight at night, in spite of the heat, out of fear of animals, spirits, and thieves.

"*Não existe por aqui nenhum lugar por esse nome*" (There is no place around here by that name), a man replied, as they all stared at me, this red-skinned, wild-eyed foreigner.

"But Vicenzo, the guy who works with Padre José—you know Padre José?—said there was a path at Santa Loo-CHEE-a from the Marmelos to the Madeira," I attempted to clarify.

A woman in the background suggested, "He must mean Santa Loo-ZIa. There is a path there."

"Oh, sure, that's it," the others replied in unison.

Some hope! They told me it was about thirty minutes downriver, just past the little house with the turtles. They said that a finger of land parallel to the river obscured the settlement's location to people going downriver but that I would see it if I kept looking leftward. I yelled back *"Muito obrigado!"* (Much obliged) as I ran back down the steps. Kristene and Caleb were still sitting quietly in the canoe, talking to each other. Shannon complained that she was burning up. Keren said she was going to jump in the river to relieve her fever. I started off at full speed, the 6.5-horsepower engine leaving a pathetically feeble wake behind us.

In thirty minutes I looked to the port side and thought I could see an inlet. I almost passed it but then there it was, a clearing at the top of another steep bank, this one more like sixty yards high, with the same carved steps. I stopped and moored the canoe at the bottom of the steps. I picked up Kristene in one arm and Caleb in the other. I told Shannon and Keren I'd be right back for them. I ran to the top, heart pounding, and looked for an adult.

The small settlement was also very clean and orderly, with broad paths and well-swept clearings around the brightly painted houses. A church building sat in the middle of the small cluster of six houses along the shore of the Marmelos. Hand-hewn benches of thick board were built under a couple of the trees. The Marmelos was more than three hundred yards across here, bluish black from this angle. There was a light breeze, and with the shade the benches would have made for a comfortable place to rest, but there was no time.

I saw some women talking under a shade tree about fifty yards away and walked briskly toward them. They were already looking in my direction and were no doubt discussing the arrival of these gringos from upriver—a location we could have only flown into, since to get to the Pirahãs by boat, it is necessary to pass in front of Santa Luzia.

Again, I wasted no time with pleasantries, asking my question immediately as I got into hearing distance.

"*É aqui que tem um varador para o Rio Madeira?*" (Is it here that there is a path to the Madeira River?)

"*Sim tem um caminho logo ali*" (Yes, there is a path right over there), a woman responded.

I told her that I had two very ill people in the canoe and asked if I could get some help to carry them to the Madeira. She sent a little girl to tell her father. I ran down and carried Shannon up in my arms. When I got to the top of the bank again I saw the most beautiful sight. Men coming in a line down the path, men with strong backs and arms, men coming to help me, a hopelessly inept gringo who had never done a thing for them in his life. But clearly a man with a family in need. I learned then that caboclos will always come to the aid of someone in need, even to their own hurt.

Before I could say anything, though, we all heard a loud splash and a woman yelled, "*O meu Deus! Ela pulou na agua!*" (Oh my God! She jumped in the river!)

Keren was in the river, trying to pull herself back into the canoe. I ran down to her.

She said, "The water is so cool. I was too hot."

I picked her up in my arms and ran up the bank for the third time. Keren had sounded coherent just then. Maybe she was thinking clearly now, I thought as I sat her down under the shade tree with Shannon, Kris, and Caleb.

As she sat on the log underneath this beautiful mango tree, Keren said in Portuguese to the people standing around, "I remember this place. There are elephants over there and lions over that way. My daddy used to bring me here when I was a little girl."

All the Brazilians looked at her, then at me. They realized she was delusional. No one said anything except "*Pobrezinha*" (Poor little thing).

Men went into the forest and came back in a few minutes with two six-inch-thick logs, each about eight feet long. From each one of these they suspended a hammock. We put Keren in one and Shannon in the other. Four men took off with them, two to a hammock, down the path.

I strapped on all our baggage and asked another man to take care of Vicenzo's boat (someone at Santa Luzia used his boat without mixing oil in the gas and ruined his motor before I returned). I asked them to tell Padre José that Vicenzo wanted a boat sent to bring him out of the village. My bags weighed about fifty pounds. I then picked up Caleb and told Kristene to follow. We set off down the path after the men.

Kristene slowed us down a bit as she picked jungle flowers along the path, skipping and singing to herself "Jesus Loves Me." Her hair was still partially in the little buns that Keren had put it into days before. She wore shorts, a small T-shirt, and tennis shoes. She smelled the flowers and smiled with delight at their fragrance. Even though my arms were burning with exhaustion at the weight of carrying Caleb and the bags, I could not help smiling. I always called Kris the sunshine of my life and that day her sunshine kept me from despair. Caleb was asking where the men were taking his mother and sister. Caleb was and is a sensitive person, and his mother has always been the most important person in his life.

After forty-five minutes walking down the cool, leaf-canopied jungle path to the Madeira, we came to a clearing. I could see dozens of painted wooden houses on stilts, a large church, which the locals referred to as "the cathedral," small stores, and broad dirt avenues laid out parallel to one another. This was the Auxiliadora, a small town, not merely a village just beginning. The men asked me where to put Keren and Shannon. This little settlement was obviously too small to have rooms to rent. I told the men to set them down in the shade and I went to inquire. I located the very modest home of Maici River trader Godofredo Monteiro and his wife, Cesária. I knew that they lived here because on a trip up the Maici just after we arrived they had asked us to visit them at their home in the Auxiliadora. Their house reflected their prosperity. It had the common board walls and floor typical of caboclo homes, but it also had very clean wooden steps and a partially thatched, partially aluminum roof. It was painted white with green trim; the phrase *Casa Monteiro* (Monteiro House) was painted in green block letters on the front. There was an outhouse in the backyard, visible from the front, which indicated an above-average concern with that aspect of hygiene, since most in the area used the jungle as their bathroom.

Godo and Cesária welcomed us to their small home, so I had the men carry Keren and Shannon there. Since it was evening and we were clearly very tired, Cesária asked if she could help me hang my family's hammocks.

"Hammocks?" I asked, confused. I guess I had thought we would sleep in beds or on the floor.

"We only sleep in hammocks here, Mr. Daniel, even the priest. People here don't use beds," Cesária answered. She went on to explain to me how everyone, even people traveling in boats on the rivers, slept in hammocks.

"We have no hammocks." I was growing more depressed with the situation and my lack of planning. The hammocks that Shannon and Keren had been carried in belonged to people, I didn't even know who, from Santa Luzia.

Cesária left immediately and came back in about half an hour with five hammocks borrowed from neighbors. She started dinner and told me she'd watch Keren while I took the children to bathe in the Madeira. Now, the Madeira is not like the small, clear Maici. It is a muddy behemoth, rivaling the Mississippi, perhaps more than a mile across at the Auxiliadora at high water. The riverbank was some three hundred yards from Godofredo's house and the bank was roughly sixty yards high, the highest of any settlement I had seen. I waded in to knee depth and washed off. I didn't care that there were alligators (black caimans) in it and that you could not see them in the river's muddy water. I didn't care that there were candirus, tiny fish that would swim up any bodily orifice. I didn't even care that there were piranhas, anacondas, stingrays, electric eels, and other denizens of the murky Madeira, because I was dirty. But in recognition of the potential danger, I washed Caleb and Kristene by pouring water over them and soaping them up and then dipping them quickly in and out of the river. We were somewhat clean at the end of this, but got muddy and sweaty as we walked back up the steep bank and then to the house. It was nearly dark. Unlike the Maici, the banks of the Madeira swarm with mosquitoes. They were buzzing throughout Godo's home. We had no bug repellent, no long pants, nothing to protect us. Cesária borrowed a room-size mosquito net for us, though, and put it up in her living room, so we could sit inside this netting (which made the room much hotter because it cut out all breezes) and avoid the mosquitoes. But I couldn't avail myself of this protection, because Godo wanted to talk. We sat on his steps and talked, I trying to appear unconcerned and at ease. I was slapping at biting mosquitoes without stop, my skin welting up under every bite.

"The mosquitoes are really horrible here," I complained.

"Really? There are hardly any out tonight" came Godo's reply, tinged with a bit of defensiveness about his town. But I noticed that he held his T-shirt in his hands to slap regularly at his back, front, and sides.

We settled down for a dinner of beans heavily flavored with onions, salt, oil, and cilantro, accompanied by rice and some fish. I had very little money to pay for this food. We were living on the charity of the poor.

Men inquired and reported to me that the next boat to Humaitá would pass by in two or three days. This was a letdown. We would be stranded in this place. But at least Keren and Shannon could rest and we had help washing clothes and getting food. And we had hope that we would make it to a doctor.

"How will I know when the boat is coming?" I asked.

"*A gente vai escutar de longe, seu Daniel*" (We will hear it from afar, Mr. Daniel) was the enigmatic reply.

How could they hear it from enough distance for me to get my family and things together in time to reach the riverbank and flag it down? I again wondered whether I had made the right decision to leave rather than wait for the plane.

Keren called me to her hammock and said that she wanted to go back to the village and wait for the plane. She seemed so much stronger and clearheaded that I considered returning after another night's sleep. In any case, before the next morning when I might have returned to the Maici, Godofredo woke me up. It was about 2 a.m.

"*O recreio já vem, seu Daniel*" (The recreation boat—a name that still causes me to scratch my head—is coming).

I started to get the family up and pack, but Godofredo said, "Relax. It won't be here for a while. We can have some coffee first."

We had coffee, I growing more anxious at the thought that the boat was going to pass by and we'd be stranded here for at least another week. As we finished our coffee, though, I heard voices outside his house. Men were coming, unbidden, to help me carry my family to the boat. After conversing for about fifteen minutes, the men slung hammocks on poles and I gathered our belongings together. Keren and Shannon were put back in the hammocks. Cesária picked up Caleb, I got Kris in my arms, someone else took our bags, and we began walking in a procession illuminated by kerosene lamp and flashlight through clouds of mosquitoes in the humid blackness toward the port. There were no lights anywhere. But as we neared the bank, off in the distance like a spaceship, the boat's searchlight intermittently roamed the bank and river, looking for floating logs that could damage its wooden hull, checking the distance of the boat from the banks, searching for rock shoals that could sink it. We began the precarious descent in the dark, down the steep bank, straining our eyes to see by the light of a flashlight. Suddenly I heard someone fall and tumble down a few steps. It was the man who had been holding the back end of Keren's hammock pole. But even before he hit the ground, another man had taken his place and Keren didn't seem to have noticed.

We blinked our flashlights at the boat to signal it that we wanted a ride. As it approached out of the blackness of the starless, moonless night, more than twenty feet high and seventy feet long, its enormous searchlight came to rest on us down at the river's edge. It looked us over, puny little earthlings on this Martian shore.

The men unloaded Shannon and Keren onto the lowest deck of the three-deck boat. I put everything else on board, including Kristene and Caleb, and the boat pulled out. Suddenly the friends from the Auxiliadora were gone, swallowed up in the Amazonian night. Would I ever see them again? What would happen now? I hung all five hammocks that we had been loaned by folks at the Auxiliadora in a near frenzy, worried that Kristene and Caleb might fall into the river, that Keren or Shannon would be stepped on as they lay unprotected on the deck, and that someone might try to steal our few belongings. After hanging our hammocks, I moved everyone and our baggage to the second deck. Then I gathered all our bags underneath my own hammock, settled my family in, and tried to get some sleep. I put everyone close to me so that I could hear and feel if anyone awoke or needed me.

The top deck of our boat was a bar area. Underneath the bottom deck there was storage. The boat was dirty, with thick brown paint covering the floors, whitewashed rails about one yard high around the sides, and blue paint on the hull. It was painted white everywhere else. I had known about these boats from reading, but this was the first time I had seen one up close. There were perhaps one hundred passengers on the vessel.

Throughout the Amazon River system, whether in Brazil, Peru, Colombia, or any other Amazonian country, a passenger boat is built pretty much the same. One begins with a massive frame for the hull, built from three- or four-inch-thick planks of a water-resistant, sturdy wood, such as *itauba*. The frame for a smallish boat will be about ten yards long and three yards wide. The rest of the heavy wooden structure of the hull is fashioned from two- to three-inch-thick boards, with spaces between them filled tightly with rope or other fiber and caulk, then covered with putty and paint. The rope and fibers are driven in with a caulking mallet and a caulking iron (like a chisel). The hull (*batelão* in Portuguese) has to be able to withstand blows from floating logs, some longer than the boat itself, in the rainy seasons, and survive grounding on the sand or rocks in the dry season.

The lower deck of the boat is used for storage at the prow and for the motor and drive shaft at the stern. Over this is another deck and over that, more often than not, a final deck. Each deck's ceiling is about five feet, ten inches high. These passenger decks often have no walls, at least in bigger commercial passenger boats, because of the heat—only short railings like picket fences and support posts. The ceilings usually have one-by-three-inch boards placed just for hanging hammocks. In case of rain, a plastic tarp can be lowered at the sides. The boats leak but they are by and large reliable and practical vessels. And since their design, motors, and operation are standard throughout the Amazon system, parts and labor are abundantly available—so long as you stick with this standard. Deviating from the norms of construction and operation or using engines that are uncommon is asking for trouble, because a breakdown or need for technical assistance can go unanswered. You can be inconvenienced and stranded if the parts and labor you need fall outside normal expectations.

Once these boats are constructed, they go to those who have commissioned them, usually relatively well-off traders. They are used as passenger boats or as trade vessels. Those owned by traders are used to purchase jungle products from Indians and jungle-dwelling Brazilians, who receive in exchange manufactured goods, such as matches, powdered milk, canned meats, tool files, machetes, hoes, shovels, needles, thread, rolled tobacco, liquor, fish hooks, ammunition, guns, and canoes. Many traders possess fleets of such craft. The most common home ports for these fleets of trade boats are Porto Velho, Manaus, Santarém, Parintins, and Belém—the major cities of the Amazon system. The boats transport a never-ending supply of *kopaiba*, Brazil nuts, hardwoods, latex, and other jungle products. The crews of these boats purchase the raw jungle products from Indians like the Pirahãs, the Tenharim, the Apurinãs, Nadëb, and dozens of others, as well as from caboclos.

The crews are usually caboclos as well. A typical crew consists of two to four men who operate the motor, steer the boat, repair the hull, and so on. During the hours of operation, the crew can relax. So long as the motor is operating normally, they can lounge in their hammocks or sit and talk. When the boat stops during work hours they load heavy cargo off or onto the boat, repair the engine, dive under the boat to plug leaks or repair the drive shaft or propeller, and do other tasks. It is a Huckleberry Finn kind of life, seasoned with intense labor.

There is an inherent contradiction in the lives of these caboclo crews. In spite of their generosity and friendliness, many of them have violent backgrounds. Some crew members are fleeing from a city life that they never adjusted well to—failed marriages, debts, enemies, the police. In the isolation of the Amazonian tributaries, a violent land populated by violent men, a certain thickness of skin is required to endure.

Just as I began to sleep, Keren said she had to use the toilet. She and Shannon still had severe diarrhea. Countless times during this voyage I would need to help them use the chamber pot (which I had luckily thought to bring with us), covering them with a blanket for privacy, then carrying it and its contents through the crowd that gathered on the boat to stare at this sick American family, to the stern to empty and wash it in the boat's bathroom.

As I got back from cleaning the chamber pot, Shannon said, "I'm sorry, Daddy. I'm sorry."

"For what?" I asked.

I went near her and could tell by the smell that she had soiled herself. I looked and saw that she and her hammock were covered in diarrhea.

She was so ashamed and so sorry. I should have been watching her better. I got a bucket of water and hung a blanket up from the hammocks to give her a bit of privacy. Then I washed her off and helped her change clothes. I washed out her hammock as well as I could and gave her the blanket to lie on in the hammock so that she wouldn't feel the wetness. She was still apologetic. I then washed her clothes and hung them over the railing around the deck to dry.

The next day, Caleb and Kristene said that they had slept well. At lunchtime I tried to feed everyone. I sat Caleb and Kristene down on the bench against the railing around the deck. Then I got them each a small plate of beans and rice that was being served to the passengers. I turned to get something for myself and heard the sound of a plate falling and glass breaking. Caleb, only two years old, had dropped his plate. He was very apologetic. I got him some more and kicked all the glass and food over the side into the river. Then I asked Keren if she needed anything. She wanted a cold Coke, so I bought her one from the boat's snack bar, one deck up. After everyone had eaten, I went back to worrying.

The morning after we boarded the *recreio*, I approached the one-armed owner of the boat, Fernando. He wore the ubiquitous flip-flops and was bare-chested. About five feet nine inches tall, with a smallish build and a prosperous Brazilian's paunch, he hardly looked intimidating. But here he was the law.

Cesária and Godofredo had told me about Fernando. He was a hard case, with little sympathy for the poor, according to them. He would not go out of his way to help anyone. They said that some people were afraid of him and that his crew, about twenty hard-looking men, would do whatever he ordered them to. I thought about what I was going to say to him. I wanted to be eloquent in Portuguese and persuade him to do me a huge favor.

"Hello," I said. "My wife is very ill and I need to get her to a doctor as soon as possible. I will pay whatever it costs if you can take my family to Humaitá in the motorboat you are towing."

"I don't rent out the motorboat," he replied gruffly, barely looking at me.

"Well, then, I will pay whatever it costs for you to take the main boat itself straight to Humaitá and not stop to pick up anyone else." I didn't really care that many people depended on this boat for their own health and food needs and that I could be condemning others to a fate similar to Keren's if Fernando accepted my offer.

Fernando replied, "Look, comrade, if your wife is supposed to die, she will die. That's that. I won't speed up for you."

If he hadn't had a crew to back him up, I might have reacted violently. I went back to my family. I was impatient and tense—more than I could ever remember being. As I was thinking and praying about this situation, the boat slowed down. Then, as I stared, it came to a complete stop near a few houses, to pick up more passengers, I supposed. But then the motor stopped. Silence. I thought that there might be an engine problem. Then, incredulously, I watched the entire crew and Fernando leave the boat wearing identical soccer uniforms. At the top of a hill I could see a clearing. More men in different soccer uniforms were waiting. Most of the passengers also got off. For two fucking hours I thought of ways to kill these people for playing soccer while my wife and daughter were dying on their boat. I would have stolen the vessel and left them all there, but I couldn't operate it alone. I found the meanest and cruelest thoughts I've ever had bouncing around my brain. These were not the thoughts of a Spirit-filled missionary, I admit. They were thoughts worthy of my barroom-brawling cowboy dad.

Everyone eventually came back to the boat, laughing, flirting, and happy, ready to continue our journey to Humaitá. What was wrong with these people? I wondered. Were they totally devoid of any human sentiment? Years later, when the trauma of this trip was less raw, I began to understand the Brazilian perspective.

The hardship that I was experiencing, so out of the ordinary for me, was just life, just everyday misfortune to all the passengers on this ship. One did not panic in the face of life, however hard. One faced what there was and one faced it alone. In spite of the willingness of Brazilians to help, there is also a strong underlying sense, among caboclos at least, that one must handle one's own problems. Something like, "Although I will always be willing to help you, I don't want to ask you to help me."

The days on the *recreio* were the longest of my life. It was like being on a floating prison. I tried to relax by sitting on a bench close by Keren's hammock and watching the flora and fauna on the banks go by very slowly, as we pushed upriver at about six knots. The lack of privacy for Keren and Shannon, the constant staring of the other passengers, was hard on me. Even though people were mostly kind, it was hard being talked about in the third person constantly as though I wasn't even there.

"She is going to die, isn't she?" one woman asked another.

"Of course she is. That gringo was stupid to bring his family here. They have gotten malaria."

As I heard the common diagnosis that Keren and Shannon had malaria, I felt smug and superior to these people who had no idea that they really had typhoid fever.

"Her face is terribly sunburned."

"Look how white they all are!"

"I bet he has a lot of money."

And so it went, hour after mind-numbing hour.

Then, the third night out of the Auxiliadora, we rounded a bend in the Madeira and I saw a light show off the starboard side. I hadn't seen electricity for weeks. Humaitá's lights cut through the darkness of the jungle and reminded me that there was an entire world outside the Pirahãs, away from the Maici. Most urgently, they were evidence of civilization, of doctors. We began to slow and cut across the Madeira, more than a mile across here, to the city. It was about 3 a.m. The boat came up against the bank. There were some crumbled concrete steps, rendered useless by the erosion of the bank in the constant flow of the brown river. A narrow, springy plank was tossed across the four-foot-wide divide between the boat and the bank. No one offered to help me to carry my baggage or children. But I was feral in my urgency. I picked up some bags along with Kristene and Caleb and carried them across the plank to an abandoned structure at the top of the bank, near the road. I could see taxis waiting for passengers.

I told Kris, only four, "Wait right here. Do not move. Sit on the bags. Don't let anyone take our bags. I'm going to get Mommy and Shannon. You watch Caleb. Do you understand?"

Kristene had been sleeping soundly. It was now 3:30.

"Yes, Daddy," she said, rubbing her eyes and looking around to try to figure out where she was.

I ran back across the plank and took down all the hammocks. I laid

Keren on a bench on the boat and ran Shannon across the plank to Kris. She was shaking and moaning in pain. I returned and took Keren in my arms; she was even lighter than when we left. I carried her up the bank, straight to a taxi. The driver helped me throw the bags in the trunk of his car and I squeezed the kids and Keren in the backseat. In a few minutes we were on our way to the hospital.

The hospital, still standing, is at the edge of town. It was white then, with tile floors and simple brick-and-plaster walls. I took everything from the cab to the reception room. Lights dangled from wires in the ceiling. No one was behind the desk. The place seemed deserted. It was small, maybe fifty beds. But it was a hospital! I ran down the halls looking for help. I found a man in a white suit sleeping on an examining table.

I said, "My wife is sick. I think she has typhoid fever."

He arose slowly and replied, "Typhoid? Not much of that around here."

He walked with me to where my family was waiting. He took a look at Keren and noted her fever, and Shannon's. "Well," he said, "I think they have malaria. But we will see. I will do some slides."

He drew blood from Shannon's and Keren's fingers and made slides. Looking at them under the microscope, he started to chuckle.

"What are you laughing at?" I demanded indignantly.

"*Elas têm malária, sim. E não é pouco, não*" (They do have malaria. And not just a little bit).

He was laughing at my ignorance. And he was laughing because the level of malaria in Shannon's and Keren's bloodstreams, he told me, was higher than he had ever seen in his entire life, and he dealt with malaria every single day. No doubt this was because I had been so stupid and not begun malaria treatment right away in the village, I thought. The doctor got Keren and Shannon a room to themselves and started drips of intravenous chloroquine treatment. Krissy, Caleb, and I camped in their room with them. Keren woke up the next morning and asked weakly for some water, apparently improving a bit. Shannon seemed a bit better too and asked if I could find her a Coke. Keren then said she'd like something to hold her hair out of her face. Her hair at that time was waist length, and I had neglected to get anything from our village house to tie it with. I went out to the front desk, where two

nuns were working, since the hospital was a joint effort of the local
Catholic diocese and the government. I asked one of the nuns if they
had something to hold Keren's hair.

"*Olha, gente,*" she yelled out for everyone in the reception area to
hear, "*esse gringo acha que somos uma loja aqui. Ele quer algo para o
cabelo da mulher dele*" (Look, people, this gringo thinks we're a store.
He wants something for his wife's hair).

Since I had not come from a religious background I was unfamiliar
with the hatred that some Catholics have for Protestants and vice versa.
I was hurt by this response, as tired and disoriented as I was. I know
that poverty can make people suspicious of those who are not poor. I
seemed rich to this nun. And everyone assumed that as an American
I must also be a racist. I knew these social platitudes from books. But I
had never experienced them in the flesh. I had never been the victim of
prejudice myself, as I now was and would continue to be occasionally
during the next decades. I had no one to talk to here in Humaitá. Ironically, although everyone thought I was rich, we were almost out of
money. Kris, Caleb, and I had no place to sleep, since there were no beds
for us in the hospital. We dozed off a bit, sitting by Keren's and Shannon's beds, but I knew when I woke up that we had to get to Porto
Velho.

I found out that there was a bus to Porto Velho at 11:00 a.m. I decided
to take Kris and Caleb to the state capital and then return for Keren and
Shannon first thing the next morning. It was out of the question to take
Keren and Shannon on the bus. Keren could barely move with her
malarial pain, and Shannon was also aching terribly. They were being
fed, receiving intravenous fluids and medicine for malaria. I told Keren
and Shannon that we were leaving and that I would be back the next
morning.

"Please don't go, Daddy," Shannon sobbed. "I'm afraid without you
here."

Keren agreed that it was best for me to get everyone to Porto Velho, a
much larger city, as soon as possible. From there we could even get
them to the United States if necessary, since there was a commercial
airport. We both knew that I couldn't phone for help, since the mission
headquarters lacked a telephone. In 1979 phones were almost impossible to get in Brazil. A landline for a home in the city could cost more

than $10,000. So there was no way to make contact with the SIL missionary center, thirteen miles out of town.

I walked out of the hospital and down the street to try to find the bus station. Without the jungle shade, Humaitá was baking hot in the direct tropical sunlight. It was dusty and depressing, barely more than a clearing at the side of the Madeira River. The bus "station," I discovered, was a house off the main street, with a counter in the front room, just in front of a family watching television. I bought three tickets to Porto Velho with most of my remaining money. I returned for Kris and Caleb and we said goodbye to Shannon and Keren.

By this time I had had only about fifteen hours of sleep in over a week. I was thoroughly worn out, emotionally and physically at the end of my endurance. And I wasn't even thinking all that clearly. Kristene and Caleb and I got on the old rusty bus then running between Humaitá and Porto Velho and settled in as best we could for the nearly five-hour trip. I found enough change to buy us some water and snacks at the first stop and we tried to rest. When we arrived in Porto Velho it was nearly 4 p.m. I hailed a taxi and we got in wearily for this last leg of our trip. The cabdriver, like everyone else, stared at us—three dirty-looking white people with U.S. military duffel bags for luggage. I asked him to take us to the American colony, as the SIL missionary compound was known.

We drove on a jungle road that was surrounded by flora and fauna as wild as any along the Maici—I had seen a jaguar waiting just off the road myself while jogging during an earlier visit. When we arrived at the SIL center, I went to the house closest to the entrance to the compound. The missionaries there paid my taxi, then sent around a "phone chain" (the compound had a donated set of Bell telephones good only for calling between houses at the center). Soon all the missionaries there were praying for Keren and Shannon and offering me help. One man offered to drive right then to get them. I told him that they were too ill (and I had to sleep; I was about to fall down). I arranged for a nurse, Betty Kroeker, and a pilot, John Harmon, both of SIL, to fly back to Humaitá with me the next morning.

The three of us took off from the Porto Velho airport at 7:00 a.m. for the one-hour flight. John acted as though this were a routine trip, indicating that he thought I might be exaggerating the emergency. Betty

tried to reassure me. She had worked in major U.S. hospitals in emergency rooms and I knew that she was qualified for this task. As we were
nearly completing our descent to Humaitá's paved runway, John
buzzed the taxi stand in the center of town, a signal that a taxi was
needed at the runway out of town. By the time we landed, the taxi was
there with its doors open and the driver was waiting to help us with our
bags, smiling broadly. John stayed to watch over the plane while Betty
and I went to the hospital. I was extremely anxious and nervous, not
knowing at all what to expect. I didn't know how I could go on living if
anything happened to Shannon or to Keren. I had to stop thinking
about that or I could break down. I was tense, all of my body felt pulled
taut, and I was fighting back tears at times.

Pulling up to the hospital, I paid the driver and ran straight into
Keren's room, Betty just behind me. Keren and Shannon seemed OK,
though still very weak and, surprisingly, still feverish in spite of all the
chloroquine they'd been taking overnight. For the first time I noticed
how burned their faces were from the sun during our river trip. Their
skin was red and peeling. I asked if the ambulance could take them to
the runway. The administrator on duty said that they would indeed
send it out right away, so long as I could buy the gasoline. As we loaded
my daughter and wife into the back of the ambulance, I could see that
Betty's face was drawn and very serious. She said little to me. She began
injecting both Shannon and Keren with Plasil, an antinausea drug, and
giving them drops of Novalgina for their pain and fevers. As we pulled
up to the runway, I could see John nonchalantly reading something.
The ambulance backed up to the cargo door at the side of the Cessna
206. We opened the back and Betty climbed out. John was watching.
Then we started to pull Keren out. When John saw Keren, he suddenly
became all business and he turned immediately, working at a pace I had
never seen from him, taking out the backseats of the aircraft. We put
Keren in, then Shannon. John and Betty rigged their IVs to hook up
inside the plane. John said that we could not use seat belts for them,
they'd just have to lie in the back. And Betty would sit with them, without a seat belt herself. This defied all safety regulations and procedures,
something John otherwise never did. Within minutes we were in the air.

Arriving in Porto Velho, we took Keren to Betty's house and put her
in Betty's bed. Betty wanted to be able to watch Keren twenty-four

hours a day. We took Shannon to another house at the center, where another missionary nurse was waiting to care for her. Even as I write these words, tears of gratitude come to my eyes thinking of the kindness and professionalism of these missionary pilots, nurses, administrators, and others. I have never known kinder people in all my life. I suspect that I never will.

Betty sent me and her husband, Dean, to town to find a doctor.

"Look for Dr. Macedo," Betty urged. "He's good, I'm told."

Dean and I left and found Dr. Macedo where Betty said he would be, in his office on a small side street.

I explained to Dr. Macedo, "*Minha esposa tem malária. O senhor foi recomendado como um médico muito bom*" (My wife has malaria. You were recommended as a very good doctor).

Dr. Macedo was dark brown, very lean, and in his conversation he conveyed an obvious intelligence and confidence. He told me he had been the secretary of health for all of the territory (this was before its statehood) of Rondônia until recently. He said he would come with Dean and me forthwith. We made the drive that normally took thirty minutes in less than twenty, in spite of the rough condition of the dirt roads in the rainy season. As we walked into Betty's house, Dr. Macedo went straight back to Keren. He announced that her blood pressure was dangerously low and that she clearly had far too much malaria for outpatient care.

"We need to get her to the hospital right away," he said.

Betty had already been looking very concerned when we entered the bedroom. The doctor said that Keren needed blood, and urgently. Since she was O positive, donors would not be a problem. Many men at the center volunteered when they learned of this need by yet another phone chain. They were to go with Dr. Macedo back to town and I was to wait with Betty and Keren for the ambulance that Dr. Macedo would send when they got there.

"Look, this is very bad," Macedo told me after taking me aside. "Your wife has gotten here too late. She weighs about seventy-six pounds. The malaria is still strong in her blood. I think she may not live. If she has relatives, you should call them."

I just stared at him. He left. I turned to the nurse. "How is she, Betty, really?"

"We're losing her, Dan," Betty told me with tears in her eyes.

I told her that when we got to town, I would go to the phone company and call Keren's parents, Al and Sue Graham, who lived in Belém, where they had been missionaries for decades.

The ambulance arrived in an hour and Betty rode in the back of it with Keren. I followed along separately in another mission automobile, after checking on Shannon, who was in pain and still had a fever, but who was improving. I was numb. I didn't believe Keren could die. I had lost my mother at eleven years of age, when she was twenty-nine; my brother drowned when he was six and I was fifteen—isn't that surely enough for anyone? How could my wife die now? Once we got to town, they put Keren in a poorly lit room in a run-down private clinic in the center of Porto Velho. The nurses were just then trying to give her the donated blood. They had put it in an old freezer in the hall of the clinic, and as the ice-cold blood hit Keren's veins, she screamed with pain. They had started giving her intravenous quinine as well, and this caused her to need oxygen. I stayed for a couple of hours and then left Betty with Keren to return to stay with Shannon, Kris, and Caleb.

Keren's parents came to Porto Velho the next day from their home in Belém. Her mother stayed with us for six weeks to help as Keren began the hard road to recovery. After a couple of weeks of intensive care, the doctor assured me that Keren was going to make it, that she might even recover her full health. Sue Graham's presence was crucial; she worked tirelessly to help Keren and to provide a more normal home environment for my children on the SIL missionary compound. Shannon's recovery was a bit faster than Keren's, though not without setbacks.

One afternoon when Shannon felt well enough, I let her go bicycling with some friends around the compound. Just after they started I heard a bike fall and Shannon's voice say, "Owey," then she started crying. She came into the house with a gouge in her forehead that required stitches, and I realized as I looked at her thin arms and legs that she was still too weak for anything beyond short walks.

After Keren's mother left, I realized that Keren still needed her. So when Keren and Shannon were well enough, I sent them, along with Kristene and Caleb, to Belém to recover more fully with Sue and Al. I returned to the Pirahãs alone.

After nearly six months of rest and recuperation, Keren and Shannon were well enough that they and Kris and Caleb could return to the Pirahãs as well. They had gained weight and were once again in great physical shape. Keren was eager to face the challenge of the Pirahã language again.

Thus began our family's thirty-year commitment to the Pirahãs.

4 Sometimes You Make Mistakes

I realized when Keren and Shannon were near death with malaria that there were important things about the Pirahãs that I was not understanding or successfully appreciating. I was hurt that the Pirahãs didn't show more empathy for me and my situation.

It didn't occur to me then, caught up as I was in my own crisis, that the Pirahãs went through what I was now agonizing over on a regular basis. And their lot was worse than mine. Every Pirahã has seen a close family member die. They have seen and touched the bodies of their deceased loved ones and have buried them in the forest near their home. They had no medical doctor or hospital to turn to for help in most cases. When someone gets too ill to work among the Pirahãs, no matter how easily the disease might be treatable by Western medicine, there is a significant chance that the person will die. And the neighbors and family do not bring casseroles to a Pirahã funeral. If your mother dies, if your child dies, if your husband dies—you still have to hunt, fish, and gather food. No one will do this for you. Life gives death no quarter. No Pirahã can borrow a motorboat to take his family for help. And no one is likely to offer a Pirahã family help if they do appear in the nearest town looking for assistance. But neither would most Pirahãs accept help from a stranger.

The Pirahãs have no way of knowing that Westerners expect to live nearly twice as long as they do. And we not only expect to live longer, we consider it our right to do so. Americans in particular lack the Pirahãs' stoicism. It isn't that the Pirahãs are indifferent to death. A Pirahã father would paddle for days for help if he thought he could save a child. I have been awakened in the middle of the night by Pirahã men with desperate looks asking me to come right away to help a sick child or a sick spouse. The pain and concern on their faces are as deep as any I have ever seen. But I have never seen a Pirahã act as though the rest of the world had a duty to help him in his need or that it was necessary to suspend normal daily activities just because someone is sick or dying. This is not callousness. This is practicality. I had not learned this yet, though.

In the rainy season, river traders used to come up the Maici from the Marmelos daily in search of Brazil nuts, *sorva* (the sweet fruit of the couma tree), rosewood, and other jungle products. The routine was always the same. In the distance I heard the *putt-putt-putt* of their diesel engine. Sometimes they would go by without stopping, but not often. I dreaded their approach because they interrupted my research. And they often took my best language teachers away to work for them for days or even weeks at a time, slowing my progress considerably. I knew they were going to stop because just as they passed our house, I would hear the *ding* of the signal bell, the pilot letting the engine operator know when to slow the boat down. Then came another couple of *ding*s to stop the boat, as they allowed their slowing momentum against the Maici's current to bring them backward at the perfect angle and speed to dock in front of our house at the small log raft I had built as a combination quay and bathing platform.

For the arrival of most of these boats, I waited while it moored and the Pirahãs went running down to see what kind of *mercadorias* the trader might be carrying. I knew that eventually a Pirahã man would come to my house and say that the Brazilian wanted to talk to me.

I learned early on that it was considered rude to decline these invitations—never mind that three to six boats could stop on a busy day and each one took at least half an hour to tell me their business and visit. It wasn't that I minded the conversations with these men. On the contrary, I quite enjoyed talking with them and their families, who often accompanied them on their trading trips. They were tough pioneers, hard men by any standards, with names like Silvério, Godofredo, Bernar, Machico, Chico Alecrim, Romano, Martinho, Darciel, and Armando Colário.

They liked to talk to me for several reasons. First, I was the whitest man most of them had ever seen, and I had a longish red beard. Second, I talked funny. My Portuguese was closer to the São Paulo dialect than their own Amazonense dialect, rendered even less intelligible by American vowels scattered liberally through Portuguese words. Third, I had lots of medicine, and they knew I didn't charge for it if they were sick. Finally, they thought I was the Pirahã's *patrão*. After all, I was white and spoke the Pirahã language. That was enough proof that I was in charge for these traders, who, in spite of being fun to talk to, were uniformly racist—they thought of the Pirahãs as subhuman.

I used to try to convince them that the Pirahãs were just as human as they were.

"These people came here before you, from Peru, maybe five hundred years ago."

"What do you mean they came here? I thought they were just creatures of this forest, like the monkeys," the river men might reply.

It was common for them to compare the Pirahãs with monkeys. I suppose that lowering one variety of *Homo sapiens* down the scale of primates to the status of monkeys is standard among racists worldwide. For the river men, the Pirahãs talked like chickens and acted like monkeys. I tried hard to convince them otherwise, but to no avail.

Since they thought I was the Pirahãs' boss, it was common for the traders to ask me to have the Pirahãs work for them. But of course I was no *patrão*, and so I would tell them that they'd have to get the Pirahãs to agree on their own.

The Pirahãs communicated with them using gestures, a few stock Portuguese phrases that they had learned, and a number of words that both they and the traders knew from the *Lingua Geral*—"General Language," also known as "Good Tongue" (*Nheengatu*), a language based on Portuguese and Tupinamba (a now extinct but formerly very widespread indigenous language spoken along almost the entire coastline of Brazil).

One night at about nine o'clock, when the kids were tucked in and Keren and I had gone to bed, a boat I had not seen before came to the village. The Pirahãs yelled into my bedroom that the owner's name was Ronaldinho. Of course he wanted to see me, so I got up and went on board to talk to him. From the outset, his operation looked suspicious. There was not a single trade item in sight. Yet the boat was relatively large—over fifty feet long and twelve feet wide, with a board deck covering the hold.

I sat at one end of the empty vessel. Ronaldinho sat at the other end, with Pirahãs sitting around the sides of the deck.

"I want to know if I can take about eight men upriver with me to collect Brazil nuts," he said.

"You don't need to ask me. That is really none of my business. Ask the Pirahãs."

He winked at me as though we both knew that I was just saying this for effect. Then I added something that the director of the Porto Velho office of the Brazilian National Indian Foundation (FUNAI), Apoena Meirelles, had asked that I tell these traders.

"The only thing that the law requires is that the Indians agree to work for you and that you pay them the going market price for their produce, or at least minimum wage for their labor."

"But I have no money," Ronaldinho replied.

"Money would not even be appropriate for the Pirahãs. You can pay them in trade items," I suggested.

"OK," he murmured, unconvinced.

I looked around again. Perhaps some trade goods were under the deck, in the storage area called the *porão* in Portuguese.

"But you cannot pay them in *cachaça*" (sugarcane rum, pronounced ka-SHA-sa), I warned him. "The FUNAI director says that if you sell them alcohol, you can be punished with as much as two years in prison."

"Oh, I would never give them alcohol, Mr. Daniel," Ronaldinho promised. "Other traders do this, but thank God I am not one of those dishonest guys."

Bullshit, I thought, but I said only that I was going to bed.

"*Boa noite*," I said as I left.

"*Boa noite*," he replied.

I went up to my house and was quickly asleep, though my sleep was disturbed periodically by laughing from his boat. I was pretty sure that he was giving the Pirahãs cachaça, but I didn't want to play policeman. I was tired, and I was feeling a bit out of my depth.

Then, about midnight, I was awakened from a deep sleep by yelling.

The words that first impressed themselves on my senses were "I am not afraid to kill the Americans. The Brazilian says to kill them and he will give us a new shotgun."

"You're going to kill them, then?"

"Yes, I will shoot them while they are sleeping."

This discussion was coming from the jungle darkness less than a hundred feet from my house. Most of the men of the village were drunk on Ronaldinho's sugarcane cachaça. But Ronaldinho had done more than give them cachaça. He had urged them to kill me and my family, offering a brand-new shotgun to the man who would do the deed. I sat up in bed, Keren wide awake beside me.

This was just our second visit to the Pirahãs. We had been in the village continuously for seven months. I spoke their language well enough now to understand that they were talking about killing us. I understood that they were urging each other on. And I knew that something was likely to happen very soon if I didn't act. My children were asleep in their hammocks. Shannon, Kristene, and Caleb had no idea what kind of danger their parents had put them in.

I pulled back my mosquito net from our bed and, very unusually, left the house in the dark, with no flashlight to attract attention, wearing only the shorts and flip-flops that were lying by my bed. I stepped carefully through the jungle to the hut where the men were working up their emotions to kill us. Adding to my tension, I was afraid of stepping on a snake in the dark, even though I was only walking a few dozen yards.

I didn't know what to expect from the Pirahãs. I was so shocked by what they were saying that I no longer felt that I knew them. Maybe they would kill me as soon as they saw me. But I couldn't leave my family waiting for the Pirahãs to kill us.

I saw where they were—in the small house built originally by Vicenzo. Peering from the jungle darkness through the palm board slats into the house, I saw that they were sitting by the flickering light of a *lamparina*—a small kerosene lamp, common in Amazonia, which contains a few ounces of kerosene and a cloth wick emerging from a narrow aperture, looking something like illustrations of Aladdin's lamp in *The Arabian Nights*. These *lamparinas* give off a dull orange light in which people look eerie at night, their dully glowing faces standing out only barely from the surrounding blackness.

I caught my breath silently outside, trying to decide how to enter in the least confrontational way. Finally, I just walked inside with a big smile and said in my best Pirahã, "Hey, guys! How are you doing?"

I made small talk while I walked around the hut picking up arrows, bows, two shotguns, and a couple of machetes. The Pirahã men stared at me with dull alcohol-laden eyes, in silence. Before they could react, I was done. I walked out quickly and wordlessly into the dark, having successfully disarmed them. I was under no illusion that this made me or my family safe. But it did slightly reduce the immediate threat. I took the weapons to our house and locked them in the storeroom. The river trader who had given them the cachaça was asleep in his boat, still moored at the raft in front of my house. I decided to chase him off. First, though, I had to take care of my family.

I locked Keren and the children in our storeroom, the one room that had walls and a door. This was a dark room in which we had killed more than one snake, several rats, and lots of centipedes, cockroaches, and tarantulas. The kids had missed the entire episode so far and as we woke them up in their hammocks to move them to the storeroom they were groggy and half-conscious. They just lay down on the floor, without protest. I had Keren lock the door from the inside.

Then I walked down the riverbank toward the boat, anger building with every step. On the way, though, I was sobered by the realization that I had not seen my teacher Kóhoi or his shotgun. Almost at the exact second that I had this thought, I heard Kóhoi's voice from the bushes on the bank just behind me. "I am going to shoot you right now and kill you."

I turned toward the voice, fully expecting to receive the full blast of his 20-gauge shotgun in my face or torso as I did. He came toward me out of the bushes, unsteadily. But I could see with relief that he was not armed.

I asked, "Why do you want to kill me?"

"Because the Brazilian says that you do not pay us enough and he says that you told him he could not pay us if we worked for him."

We were talking in Pirahã, though he had originally threatened me in rudimentary Portuguese—*"Eu maTA boSAY"* (I kill you).

If I had not been able to speak Pirahã, I might not have survived the night. Kóhoi and I exchanged words in the Pirahãs' stacatto-sounding language (it sounds this way because of a consonant, the glottal stop, that Pirahã possesses and English doesn't). I struggled and focused as never before to put each thought across clearly to Kóhoi. I said, *"Xaói xihiabaíhiaba. Piitísi xihixóíhiaagá"* (The foreigner doesn't pay. Whiskey [he gives you] is cheap).

Kóhoi responded, *"Xumh! Xaói bagiáikoí. Hiatíihí xogihiaba xaói"* (Wow. The foreigner is stealing from us. The Pirahãs don't want him).

"It is the Brazilian who did not want to pay you," I continued. "All he wanted to pay you was bitter water" (as the Pirahãs called cachaça). "And that is because it costs him little. It would cost him more if he paid you with farinha, shotgun shells, sugar, milk, or other supplies, as I told him to."

The Pirahãs' comprehension of the Brazilian trader was distorted as well by their extremely limited knowledge of Portuguese. Only a few of them knew more than a handful of words and expressions. No one could be said to speak Portuguese outside of a small number of limited contexts.

We had continued to descend the bank as we talked. By this time Ronaldinho was looking out from under the roof of his boat cabin. He stared at me with surprise.

Suddenly, Kóhoi shouted at him, *"Pirahã maTA boSAY."*

Ronaldinho's expression changed and he disappeared momentarily. Then his boat motor cranked over and he had the engine running. He tried to pull away. But in his panic he had left the boat moored to the raft. He was going nowhere. A Pirahã was sleeping on the deck of his boat. Ronaldinho rolled the man off into the water and cut through the rope with a machete. Without saying a word he turned and his boat was sliding into the darkness, down the Maici.

Toucan, the man Ronaldinho pushed off the boat, emerged wet from the river, still barely awake. Then I heard Keren's voice. She had come out to the riverbank to see what I was doing. A few men, including Xahoábisi, the one who had talked the most about killing us, were pushing her from side to side, moving her closer and closer to the river-bank. I sprinted up the bank to Keren. I was no longer a missionary, a linguist, or even a nice person. I was ready to hurt someone. The men backed off, muttered incoherent cachaça-inspired words, and walked back into the darkness to the closest hut. I noticed that the village was completely dark. The women had thrown dirt on the fires that nor-mally burned constantly in each hut and had gone to the jungle to hide from their own husbands.

I told Keren to get back in the storeroom and she readily agreed. I walked up to the house with her, and as she entered the storeroom, I picked up one of the shotguns I had just taken from the Pirahãs. I checked to make sure that it was not loaded, and, in spite of my tired-ness, took a seat on a bench we had in our living room area to guard my family.

Several men started toward the house during the night, but as each man or group of men approached, I could hear others warn them, "Dan's got lots of weapons now." By this time most men were coming not to harm us but to ask me for trade items and canned meat. They knew that they were intimidating and wanted to take advantage of this to demand food. All were still very belligerent—not only with me now, but also with each other.

Suddenly they began to lose interest in us, arguing with each other. Xahóápati, another one of my main language teachers, came to me to say that he was sorry that people had threatened us. He spoke in slurred, drunken Pirahã: "*Ko Xoo. Hiaitíihí hi xaaapapaaaai baáááábikoí. Baía . . . baía . . . baía . . . baía, baíaisahaxá. Ti xaaóó-*

píhíabíííígá" (Hey Dan. The Pirahãs have baaad headsssss now. Don't, uh, don't, uh, don't fear. I am not maaaad).

His shorts were oozing diarrhea, much of which was running down his legs. The right side of his face was coated in wet snot. Xabagi was now trying to start a fight with a teenager, just outside our house, brandishing a machete.

I saw an arrow streak by the front of my house as one unknown Pirahã shot at another Pirahã whose face I did not recognize in the dark, missing him. He was standing just at the corner of Kóhoi's house, about twenty feet upriver from my house. No one shot arrows at me.

I finally got too tired. In spite of the danger, at about 4 a.m., I retreated to the storeroom, where I hoped to sleep for an hour or two. I could hear Pirahãs coming into our house and fighting, in the back of the house, in the front of the house, and in front of the storeroom door. But I was too tired to react usefully. I just wanted to sleep.

At dawn we emerged cautiously from the storeroom. We were all aching and stiff from sleeping on boards. In the early morning light we saw blood spattered on the walls and little pools of blood on the floors in every room of the house. The white sheets on our bed had blood smears in various places. I saw men walking by with soiled shorts, bloody faces, bruises on their cheeks, black eyes, and other testosterone-alcohol prizes. Shannon and Kristene were afraid when they saw the blood; Caleb was too young to understand what was going on. But no one came toward us. Men wobbled by, purposely steering wide of our house.

Later in the day, after they had slept off most of their drunkenness, the Pirahã men came into our house to apologize, most of the women standing outside, shouting out suggestions for what the men should say to us.

Kóhoi spoke for the men: "We're sorry. Our heads get really bad when we drink and we do things that are bad."

No kidding, I thought.

After what we had been through, I wasn't sure whether to believe them. But they did seem sincere. And the women were shouting to Keren and me now, saying, "Don't leave us. Our children need medicine. Stay here with us. There are lots of fish and game to eat here and the Maici has beautiful water."

In the end we all agreed with their sensible view that they should not kill us, because we were their friends.

"Look, you guys can drink or do anything you want," I said. "This is Pirahã land. This is not my jungle. I am not the boss here. The Pirahãs are the bosses here. This is their land. But you scared my children. If you want me here, you cannot threaten to kill me and scare my children. OK?"

"OK!" they replied as a chorus. "We will not scare you or kill you."

In spite of the Pirahãs' apology and assurances that this would never happen again, I knew that I had to get to the bottom of what had transpired the night before. I needed to understand why they would have even talked about killing my family. I was a guest of the Pirahãs. If I had done something to offend them to the point that they would contemplate killing me, then I would have to figure out what the offense was and avoid committing it in the future.

I decided to talk to a few of the men about this incident in more detail. Xahoábisi seemed angry with me and grew sullen each time I approached his house. I needed to talk to him, to find out what I had done wrong.

One day I took a thermos of sweet coffee, a couple of cups, and some cookies to Xahoábisi's hut.

"Hey, tell the dogs not to be mad at me!" I called to him in the traditional Pirahã way of approaching someone else's home. "Would you like some coffee? I put a lot of sugar in it! And I have some cookies."

Xahoábisi smiled and told me I could come to his hut. He grunted to his dogs, about six ratlike little curs that were nonetheless ferocious and fearless (I have seen these fifteen-pound dogs attack wildcats and boars to protect their masters), and they sat at his feet. Snarling and growling, they made no move to eat me just yet. I gave him some coffee and a cookie.

"Are you mad at me?" I asked.

"No," he replied, after he sipped his coffee. "The Pirahãs are not angry with you." (It is common for individual Pirahãs to phrase their opinions as coming from the group, even if this is just their own opinion.)

"Well, the other night you seemed really angry."

"I was angry. I am not angry now."

"Why were you angry?"

"You told Brazilians not to sell us whiskey."

"Yes," I admitted. "The FUNAI said no one should sell whiskey here. Your women told me not to let anyone sell whiskey to you." (The Pirahãs knew the FUNAI somewhat, from different representatives who came by occasionally. They had observed that the FUNAI exerted some sort of vague authority over Brazilians in the region.)

"You are not a Pirahã," he declared. "You do not tell me that I cannot drink. I am a Pirahã. This is the Pirahãs' jungle. This is not your jungle." Xahoábisi's emotions were rising a bit now.

"OK," I responded, wishing that the Pirahãs had an expression that literally meant "I'm sorry." I continued, "I will not tell you what to do. This is not my jungle. But my children were afraid when the Pirahãs got drunk. I was afraid too. I won't stay here if you want me to leave."

"I want you to stay," Xahoábisi replied. "The Pirahãs want you to stay. But don't tell us what to do!"

"I won't tell you what to do," I promised, ashamed that I had given this impression to him.

We talked a bit more about lighter topics, such as fishing, hunting, children, and river traders. Then I got up and returned with my coffee cups and empty thermos to my house, about fifty feet away. I felt chastened and embarrassed. I realized that I had nearly disastrously misinterpreted the Pirahãs' perception of my role among them. I had thought that they saw me, the missionary, as a protector and authority figure. The wives of the men who drank the most, Xíbaihóíxoi (wife of Kóhoibiíihíai), Xiabikabikabi (wife of Kaaboogí), Báígipóhoái (wife of Xahoábisi), and Xiako (wife of Xaikáibaí), had told me that the previous missionaries, Arlo Heinrichs and Steve Sheldon, would not allow whiskey to be sold.

Later, when I checked with Arlo and Steve, they chuckled and told me that they never told the Pirahãs or Brazilian river traders in the area what they could or couldn't do. Apparently the women had told me this because they didn't want their husbands to drink and they believed that I was their only hope of preventing this. But of course this was ultimately none of my business. I wasn't the village constable. By glibly going along with the women's request, I had put my life and my family's lives in danger. And I had jeopardized my good relationship with the Pirahã men. I didn't understand these people well.

A few weeks later, another river trader gave them a large quantity of cachaça. I discovered this after the trader left the village, because all the men disappeared. A couple of hours later I started hearing the men laughing, then yelling and talking about how brave and tough they were, one Pirahã saying to another the equivalent of "I can kick your ass." They talked pretty much like drinking men anywhere in the world. My cowboy dad's behavior when he was drunk was largely indistinguishable from the Pirahãs'.

This wasn't much comfort, though. I just didn't have it in me to endure another round of being the target of drunken bravado. Since it was early afternoon, Keren and I decided to pack overnight supplies in our boat and spend the night upriver at Aprígio's house, about a fifteen-minute motorboat trip away. Aprígio and his family were Apurinã Indians. Their parents had been brought to the Maici more than sixty years before by the Brazilian government to help contact the Pirahãs. While we were packing, Kóhoi suddenly walked into our house with an armful of shotguns, bows, and arrows.

"Here," he said with a smile, alcohol slurring his speech. "Now you don't need to be afraid. You have the guns."

I appreciated the gesture in one sense. But the Pirahãs were clearly conflicted by our being there when they were drinking. We decided to go to Aprígio's anyway to reduce the tension for the Pirahãs and the danger for us. The Pirahãs' drinking and violence were problems for us that we had not anticipated, and they seemed recent in Pirahã history—the previous missionaries told us later that they had never noticed a severe drinking or violence problem among the Pirahãs. But the village had been "missionary free" for nearly three years before our arrival, almost four if we didn't count my family's first abortive stay in 1979 or my ten-day stay a couple of years prior. So things had changed without the missionaries' inhibiting presence.

I had avoided thinking much about their culture, I suppose, because of my initial disappointment with it. The Pirahãs didn't wear feathers, enact elaborate rituals, paint their bodies, or show other exotic outward cultural manifestations like so many other Amazonian groups. I had not yet realized how unusual the Pirahãs were culturally, as well as linguistically. Their culture was subtle but powerful in its conservative values and in the way that it shaped their language. But because I still hadn't recognized this, I indulged in self-pity, thinking that I could have been working with "interesting people." On many days, the men didn't do anything I could see but sit around the graying embers of a fire, talking, laughing, farting, and pulling baked sweet potatoes out of the coals. Occasionally, they supplemented this routine by pulling one another's genitals and laughing as though they were the first earthlings to engage in something so clever. I had hoped to see villages like those that I had studied in anthropology classes, such as Yanomami villages with their open huts built around a village clearing and Gê villages arranged like a wagon wheel, with houses at the ends of the spokes. It seemed to me that Pirahã villages had no organization. They were overgrown with grass, which attracted bugs and snakes. Why couldn't they at least clear the brush and garbage out of their villages? I have seen Pirahãs sleep while covered with hundreds of migrating cockroaches and I have heard them snore contentedly with tarantulas crawling over them.

There had to be more to this way of life than what my superficial observations were revealing. I determined to proceed with my analysis of their culture as professionally as I was able. I went about this by observation and questioning. First, I observed their daily lives, family relations, house construction, village plan, children's enculturation, socialization, and so on, following what anthropological field guides I could get my hands on. Next, I decided to look more deeply into their beliefs in the spirit world, their myths, and their religion. Then I wanted to look at their social power structures. Finally, I wanted to come up with a theory of Pirahã identity based on my observations. At this time I had only minimal training in anthropology, so I was largely groping in the dark.

5 Material Culture and the Absence of Ritual

From the time I first met the Pirahãs I wanted to understand their culture better. I thought I would begin simple, with their material culture, rather than, say, with their beliefs and moral values. Since the majority of their time in the village was spent in their huts, I wanted to see one built. I got my chance one day when Xaikáibí decided to build a new hut. The hut he was building is the more substantial of two types of hut that the Pirahãs make, called *kaii-ii* (daughter-thing).

Pirahã homes are remarkably simple. In addition to the "daughter-thing" they also make a *xaitaii-ii* (palm-thing), a less substantial construction. The "palm-thing," used mainly for shade on the beach, consists simply of sticks to support a roof covered with just about any kind of broad leaves, though palm leaves are most commonly used. These are made only to provide shade for children. Adults will just sleep on the sand and sit in the bright sun all day, occasionally putting some branches vertically in the sand in front of themselves for shade. The "daughter-thing" is sturdier, even though both types of houses blow over in storms. Although it takes a strong storm to blow over a "daughter-thing," a gust of wind is sufficient to topple some "palm-things."

Pirahã houses reveal important distinctions between their culture and ours. When I think of Pirahã houses, I am often reminded of Henry David Thoreau's suggestion in *Walden* that all a person really needs is a large box that he can carry around to protect himself from the elements. The Pirahãs don't need walls for defense, because the village is the defense—every member of the village will come to the aid of every other member. They don't need houses to display wealth, because all Pirahãs are equal in wealth. They don't need houses for privacy,

because privacy is not a strong value—though if privacy is needed for
sex, relieving oneself, or anything else, the entire jungle is around, or
one can leave the village in a canoe. Houses don't need heating or cooling, because the jungle provides a nearly perfect climate for lightly
clothed human bodies. Houses are just a place to sleep with moderate
protection from the rain and sun. They are places to keep one's dogs
and the few belongings that a family has. Each house is a rectangle
formed by three rows of three poles each, with the center row higher to
allow for the roof to be raised in the middle.

Xaikáibaí began constructing the *kaii-ii* with the supports that hold
the roof and the sleeping platform. He first cut six poles of rot-resistant
wood approximately ten feet long. The Pirahãs know many tree species;
this one is called *quariquara* in Portuguese and *xibobiihi kohoaihiabisi*
(ants don't eat) in Pirahã. He laid the poles out near the place he wanted
to build on, then dug a hole with his machete and hands and worked
each pole by hand about two feet into the ground. He then joined the
poles at the top with other poles laid across the width of the house, to
bind the vertical poles together. The horizontal poles were tied to the
vertical poles with vines that had been split for greater flexibility.

The vertical poles in the ground were of two lengths. Four of the
poles were roughly of equal length. The poles in the center of each end
of the structure were one to two yards taller than the other poles. All
poles were spaced two or three feet apart. The end poles were notched
at their tops to support longer horizontal poles that spanned the length
of the house.

Next Xaikáibaí began to put on the thatch roof. He gathered the
thatch at groves several miles away on the other side of the river. The
thatch comes from the young, yellow sprouts of a species of palm
the Pirahãs call *xabíisi*. Several tiring trips were necessary to cut, bundle, and transport the thatch to canoes and the village. When the thatch
was collected together near his hut-in-progress, he "opened" it. In this
process the young palm leaves, about three yards in length, are pulled to
one side of the shoot. These are then laid across the upper perpendicular poles in bundles of three or four and fastened to the poles by vine or
bark. Xaikáibaí next placed these palm leaf bundles every six inches
ascending from the bottom of the roof structure to the central shaft at
the top. The result of his labor was a rainproof and cool roof. Thatch

also muffles the sound of the rain. Thatch has disadvantages, however. When dry, it is very flammable. And it provides an excellent home for varmints. It also needs to be replaced every few years.

Xaikáibaí was almost done with his hut. To complete it, he built a small raised platform at one end inside the hut. The frame for the platform was built from sturdy wood poles. The platform itself was made from the trunks of small *paxiuba* palm trees, each split in half, laid inner side down on the frame, and tied into place with vines.

This was to be his sleeping platform and was four feet wide or so. Pirahã huts are cool, relatively sturdy, and—when the embers of a fire are glowing at one end—homey. I often sat on the sleeping platform beside a Pirahã, talking about the day's fishing or other work, as I listened for new words and grammar in this relaxing environment. It is hard not to nod off while the Pirahãs are talking, they are so laid-back, even when the conversation is about things like the jaguar someone saw the last time they went hunting.

I knew already that their material culture is among the simplest known. They produce very few tools, almost no art, and very few artifacts. Perhaps their most outstanding tools are their large, powerful bows (over two yards in length) and arrows (two to three yards long). A bow takes about three days to make—one day to find one of the half-dozen types of acceptable bow wood and two days to shape and scrape the bow. While the man is working on the bow itself, his wife, mother, or sister makes the bowstring from soft tree bark, rolled tightly along her outer thigh. Then each arrow takes approximately three hours to make—finding the arrow shaft material, heating it in the fire and straightening it, and making the proper tip from bamboo (for shooting big game), sharpened hardwood (for monkeys), or a long, narrow piece of wood with a sharpened nail or bone on the end (for fish). The feathers and tip are tied on with homespun cotton. I have seen wild pigs skewered by these arrows—entering near the rectum and protruding out the throat.

Of the few artifacts they make, none are permanent. For example, if they need to carry something in a basket, they will weave a basket on the spot from wet palm leaves. After one or two uses these baskets become dried out and fragile, and they are abandoned. Using the same skills they already demonstrated in making these disposable baskets,

they could make longer-lasting baskets, simply by selecting more durable material (such as wicker). But they don't, I concluded, because they don't want them. This is interesting. It indicates an interest in making things as you go.

Other material artifacts include necklaces. The Pirahãs make them to ward off spirits and to look more attractive. Women, girls, and babies of both genders wear necklaces. Women make these necklaces from seeds and homespun cotton string, decorating them further with teeth, feathers, beads, beer-can pull tabs, and other objects. The necklaces rarely show symmetry and are very crude and unattractive compared to the artifacts of other groups in the region, such as the Tenharim and Parintintin, known for beautiful feather headdresses, jaguar-tooth necklaces, fine woven baskets and strainers, and tools for manioc processing. And for the Pirahãs, necklaces are decorative only secondarily, their primary purpose being to ward off the evil spirits the Pirahãs see almost daily. They also like feathers and bright colors on the necklaces to make them visible to spirits so that the spirits are not startled—like wild animals, spirits are more likely to attack when startled. Pirahã adornment has an immediate function and involves little planning or concern for classical aesthetic values such as symmetry. Clearly, they could make lasting ornamentation but they choose not to.

The Pirahãs can make canoes out of bark—called *kagahói*—but they rarely do, preferring to steal or trade for the sturdier dugout and board canoes made by Brazilians, called *xagaoas*. Inasmuch as the Pirahãs depend on these sturdier canoes for their fishing, transportation, and recreation on the river, it has always fascinated me that they do not make them. And they never have enough to go around for all the families in the village. Although canoes are said to be possessed by individuals of the village and hence are not, properly speaking, community property, in practice each canoe owner loans out his canoe either to a son or son-in-law or to someone else in the village. Using someone's canoe carries the expectation that any fish caught while using that canoe will be shared with the canoe's owner. Acquiring new canoes for the village is always difficult for the Pirahãs, so it didn't surprise me when one day they turned to me for help.

"Dan, can you buy us a canoe? Our canoes are rotten," the men said to me one day out of the blue, as they sat in my house drinking coffee.

"Why don't you make a canoe?" I asked.

"Pirahãs don't make canoes. We don't know how."

"But I know you can make a bark canoe; I have seen you do that," I rejoined.

"Bark canoes don't carry weight. One man, some fish, no more. Only Brazilian canoes are good. Pirahã canoes are no good."

"Who makes canoes around here?" I asked them.

"At Pau Queimado they make canoes," the men answered, nearly in unison.

It appeared that they didn't make dugout canoes because they didn't know how, so I decided to help them learn. Since the best canoe masters in the area lived at the village of Pau Queimado, several hours away by motorboat on the Marmelos River, I decided to try to contract one of these men to spend about a week with the Pirahãs to teach them how to make canoes the Brazilian way. The main canoe builder at Pau Queimado, Simprício, agreed to teach them.

When he arrived, the Pirahãs all gathered (enthusiastically) to learn from him. As per our agreement, Simprício let the Pirahãs do the labor, supervising rather than building the canoe directly and instructing them carefully as they worked. After about five days of intense effort, they made a beautiful dugout canoe and showed it off proudly to me. I bought the tools for them to make more. Then a few days after Simprí-cio left, the Pirahãs asked me for another canoe. I told them that they could make their own now. They said, "Pirahãs don't make canoes" and walked away. No Pirahã has ever made another *xagaoa* to my knowl-edge. This taught me that Pirahãs don't import foreign knowledge or adopt foreign work habits easily, if at all, no matter how useful one might think that the knowledge is to them.

Pirahãs have the knowledge to preserve meat—when they are about to embark for a place where they expect to encounter Brazilians, they salt meat (if they have salt) or smoke it, to preserve it. But among them-selves they never preserve meat. I haven't seen another Amazonian group that doesn't salt or smoke meat routinely. The Pirahãs consume everything as soon as it is hunted or gathered. They preserve nothing for themselves (leftovers are eaten until they are gone, even if the meat begins to turn rancid). Baskets and food are short-term projects.

One reason I find Pirahã views of food interesting is that the subject seems less important in some sense to them than it is in my own cul-ture. Obviously they have to eat to live. And they enjoy eating. When-ever there is food available in the village, they eat it all. But life is full of priorities for all of us, and food is ranked differently by different peo-ples and different societies. The Pirahãs have talked to me about why they don't hunt or fish some days when they are hungry. Instead, they might play tag or play with my wheelbarrow, or lie around and talk.

"Why aren't you fishing?" I asked.

"Today we will just stay home," someone answered.

"Aren't you hungry?"

"Pirahãs aren't eating every day. *Hiatíihí hi tigisáaikof*" (Pirahãs are hard). "*Americano kóhoibaai. Hiaitíihi hi kohoaihiaba*" (Americans eat a lot. Pirahãs eat little).

Pirahãs consider hunger a useful way to toughen themselves. Miss-ing a meal or two, or even going without eating for a day, is taken in stride. I have seen people dance for three days with only brief breaks, not hunting, fishing, or gathering—and without any stockpiled food.

How much non-Pirahãs eat relative to Pirahãs is made obvious by Pirahã reactions to food consumption when they visit the city. Pirahãs in the city for the first time are always surprised by Western eating habits, especially the custom of eating three meals a day.

For their first meal outside of the village, most Pirahãs eat greedily—large quantities of proteins and starch. For the second meal they eat the same. By the third meal they begin to show frustration. They look puzzled. Often they ask, "Are we eating *again*?" Their own practice of eating food when it is available until it is gone now conflicts with the circumstances in which food is always available and never gone. Often after a visit to the city of three to six weeks, a Pirahã will return as much as thirty pounds overweight to the village, rolls of fat on their belly and thighs. But within a month or less, they're back to normal weight. The average Pirahã man or woman weighs between 100 and 125 pounds and stands five feet to five feet four inches tall. They are lean and tough. Some of the men remind me of Tour de France cyclists in their fitness. The women tend to carry a bit more weight than men, but are also fit and strong.

Pirahãs eat fish, bananas, wild game, grubs, Brazil nuts, electric eels, otters, caimans, insects, rats—any sort of protein, oil, starch, sugar, or other foodstuff they can hunt, fish, or gather from their environment—though they avoid reptiles and amphibians, for the most part. Their diet is perhaps 70 percent fish, fresh from the Maici, often mixed with farinha (which the Pirahãs have learned to make over the years from contact with outsiders) and washed down with clear Maici River water.

Because different fish can be caught at different times of the day and night, Pirahã men can be found out fishing at any time. This means that there is less differentiation between day and night, aside from visibility. A Pirahã man is as likely to be found fishing at 3 a.m. as at 3 p.m. or 6 a.m. I have many times traveled the river at night and shined my spotlight at favorite fishing spots to see Pirahã men sitting in their canoes catching fish. One method of fishing at night is to shine a flashlight into the water to attract fish and then arrow them. Four to six hours per day will usually supply a family with enough protein for the twenty-four-hour period. But if there are sons in the family of sufficient age, then the males will rotate the fishing responsibilities on different days. If someone catches fish at 3 a.m., then that is when it will be eaten. Everyone will get up to eat as soon as it is brought in.

Gathering, which is mainly the women's job, takes perhaps twelve hours per week for a family of four, a fairly typical family size among the Pirahãs. Gathering and fishing together, then, takes about fifty-two hours per week, divided among father, mother, and children (and grandparents on occasion), so that no one needs to spend more than fifteen to twenty hours per week "working"—though these activities are enjoyable to the Pirahãs and hardly fit any Western concept of labor.

The people also rely on imported machetes for butchering, building, making bows and arrows, digging manioc out of the ground, and so on. They trade for these when possible. They gather machetes, files, hoes, and axes at the beginning of each dry season so that they can clear and plant their fields with manioc. Manioc, one of the most widely consumed foods in the world, is indigenous to the Amazon and is an ideal source of starch. It grows as long as it is in the ground, meaning that an abandoned field a couple of years old can harbor manioc tubers in excess of three feet in length. Manioc contains cyanide, so consuming the raw tuber is fatal, and bugs and animals avoid it. Only humans can eat it because it requires an elaborate process of soaking, draining, and straining to get rid of most of the cyanide.

Preparing and planting fields is a relatively new development, one that Steve Sheldon worked hard to introduce. But tilling the fields relies on the possession of foreign tools, which the Pirahãs have no way of acquiring in most villages. I noticed that in spite of how important these tools are to them, the Pirahãs do not take good care of them. Children throw new tools in the river; people leave the tools in the fields; and often they trade tools away for manioc meal when outside traders make their way in.

A pattern was emerging: they had no method for food preservation, neglected tools, and made only disposable baskets. This seemed to indicate that lack of concern for the future was a cultural value. It certainly wasn't laziness, because the Pirahãs work very hard.

I was fascinated that things as important and difficult to come by as tools were treated so cavalierly by the Pirahãs. After all, the only way for them to acquire goods from the outside world is by collecting jungle produce and bartering with the riverboat traders. Only a few villages are able to do this, because no traders travel very far up the Maici—there are too few natural products to make it worth their while. So other Pirahã groups trade with the Pirahãs with the tools and these implements make their way eventually to all the villages along the Maici.

There were many other aspects of Pirahã material culture that supported my growing belief that planning for the future is less important for the Pirahãs than enjoying each day as it comes. As a result they invest no more effort in something than is necessary for minimal function.

Pirahãs take naps (fifteen minutes to two hours at the extremes) during the day and night. There is loud talking in the village all night long. Consequently, it is often very difficult for outsiders to sleep well among the Pirahãs. I believe that the Pirahãs' advice not to sleep because there are snakes is advice that they literally follow—sleeping too soundly in the jungle can be dangerous. The Pirahãs warned me about snoring, for example. "Jaguars will think a pig is nearby and come to eat you," they told me cheerfully.

When I tell people about the simplicity of the Pirahãs' material culture, they often become curiously concerned. After all, we define success in industrialized cultures at least partially as the ongoing improvement of our technology. But the Pirahãs show no such improvement, nor a desire for it.

How does it happen that Pirahã culture is so materially simple? Some people have suggested to me that their culture may be the result of the trauma of contact with European cultures in the eighteenth century. It is true that European contact with native peoples of the Americas, whether indirect (as with the transmission of disease or the acquisition of trade items) or direct (face-to-face), was traumatic for most indigenous peoples. In many cases this trauma led to cultural disintegration and loss of knowledge and cultural specializations and marginalization of whole populations. It would be a serious error to suppose that a cultural trait produced by this sort of "contact trauma" fairly reflected a natural state of the culture.

On the other hand, even if such trauma were responsible for cultural change, after a certain amount of time we would have to describe the culture in its current state. England's current state is undoubtedly a result of earlier stages, but it can no longer be described in terms of the code of chivalry. The evidence from records of the Mura and Pirahã for

nearly three hundred years since contact was first made in 1714 strongly
supports the conclusion that Pirahã culture has changed little since
contact with Europeans. Curt Nimuendaju, for example, in his paper
"The Mura and Pirahã," concludes:

> [The Pirahã tribe] has evidently always occupied its present
> habitat between lat. 6° 25′ and 7° 10′ S., along the lower Maicy
> river. . . . The Pirahã have remained the least acculturated
> Mura tribe, but they are known only through a short word list
> and unpublished notes obtained by the author during several
> brief contacts in 1922, when efforts were being made to pacify
> the Parintintin. (Handbook of South American Indians
> [U.S. Department of State and Cooper Square Publishers,
> 1963], pp. 266–67)

Nimuendaju goes on to discuss several aspects of Pirahã material
culture, citing older sources as well, all of which corroborate his contemporary findings, which are identical for the most part to my own.

Not everything needs to be linked to specific cultural values, though.
Pirahã clothes—or lack thereof—are also simple, but of course in the
Amazonian heat, not much commentary is needed to explain why peo-
ple use minimal covering on their bodies.

In addition to the possessions and artifacts mentioned, a Pirahã
family will usually have an aluminum pot or two for cooking, perhaps
a spoon, a couple of knives, one or two other small artifacts from the
outside world, and an indigenous handheld cotton spinner.

This book could have been called The Water People, since the river is
so vital to their social and physical lives. Pirahã villages are as close to
the river as they can build them. In the dry season (piiáiso, "shallow
water"), when large beaches of soft white sand emerge from the receding Maici River, they move their settlements to the largest of the
beaches, where they sleep directly on the sand with little or no shelter at
all, except for an xaitaí-ií or two for infants during the day. At this time
of year, when food is plentiful and the nights are for the most part
colder than in the rainy season, the entire community (swelling to fifty
to one hundred people on a single beach) sleeps and eats together,
although family members sleep near one another at night.

Pirahã villages can sustain greater numbers in the dry season because there is less water and hence a higher concentration of fish in what remains of the river. For Indians who live deeper in the jungle, the dry season is a time of hunger because the game leave the central forest in search of water. For Indians like the Pirahãs who live on the banks of major rivers, the dry season is a time of plenty.

I remember once coming upon a group of Pirahãs on a beach. Just downriver from the beach was a tree leaning over the water, anchored to the bank by a few roots that had not yet been torn loose. The trunk was perhaps one foot above the water. A Pirahã man, Xahoaogií, was nearby. I thought that the leaves on the tree looked as though something heavy had pressed on them. I had an idea.

"Who sleeps here?" I asked.

"I do," he responded sheepishly.

Apparently he had no fear of falling into the river from a bed only eight inches wide. No fear of anacondas, caimans, or other animals that could easily have reached up and bitten him or pulled him off into the river.

In the rainy season (*piiodbaíso,* "deep water"), villagers distribute themselves by nuclear families, each family occupying its own house. As I noticed during my first day in the village, the houses in the rainy season are built in a line along the river, well hidden in jungle growth, with houses usually ten to fifty paces apart. These rainy season villages are smaller than summer villages, usually consisting of one elderly couple and their adult sons or daughters, along with their spouses and children. Houses of a village need not be on the same side of the river and occasionally close relations build their houses on opposite banks.

Ritual is a set of prescribed actions with symbolic significance for the culture. Pirahã culture is remarkable to some Westerners, as indeed it was to me early on in my life among them, for its relative lack of ritual. There are areas where we might expect ritual behavior, but we do not find clear cases of it.

When someone dies, he or she is buried. The Pirahãs never abandon bodies of deceased Pirahãs to the elements, but always bury them. This is an area where we can expect some ritual, though there is little that we can describe with this term here. I have witnessed several deaths among them. There are some loosely followed traditions surrounding burial, but no ritual. Occasionally, the dead are buried in a sitting position with many of their belongings placed beside them (never more than a dozen or so small objects, since the Pirahãs accumulate so little materially in the course of their lives). Often they bury their dead in a prone position. Very rarely, if there are boards and nails (left by a river trader or by me), they might try to make a Western-style coffin. I have only seen them try to make a coffin once, for a young baby, when a Brazilian river trader happened to be present when the baby died.

If the deceased is large, he or she will more likely be buried sitting because this requires less digging (according to the Pirahãs themselves). The dead are buried almost immediately. One or two close male relatives will usually dig the grave, preferring spots near the bank of the river, with the effect that in a couple of years the grave has been washed away by erosion. The corpse is placed in the hole. Then, after the possessions are added, green sticks are crisscrossed above the body, securely wedged into the hole. Over these are placed banana leaves or similar broad leaves. Then the grave is filled with dirt. Rarely, in imitation of Brazilian graves they have seen, they will place a cross, with carvings that imitate the writing they have observed on Brazilian crosses.

Most aspects of burials are subject to variation, however, and I have not seen any two burials exactly alike. The ad hoc nature of the burials, plus the fact that they are a logical solution to the indelicacy of leaving a rotting corpse above ground, leads me to avoid interpreting them as ritualistic, though others might disagree.

Sex and marriage also involve no ritual that I can see. Although Pirahãs are reluctant to discuss their own intimate sexual details, they have done so in general terms on occasion. They refer to cunnilingus and fellatio as "licking like dogs," though this comparison to animal behavior is not intended to denigrate the act at all. They consider animals good examples of how to live. Sexual intercourse is described as eating the other. "I ate him" or "I ate her" means "I had sexual intercourse with him or her." The Pirahãs quite enjoy sex and allude to it or talk about others' sexual activity freely.

Sex is not limited to spouses, though that is the norm for married men and women. Unmarried Pirahãs have sex as they wish. To have sex with someone else's spouse is frowned upon and can be risky, but it happens. If the couple is married to each other, they will just walk off in the forest a ways to have sex. The same is true if neither member of the couple is married. If one or both members of the couple are married to someone else, however, they will usually leave the village for a few days. If they return and remain together, the old partners are thereby divorced and the new couple is married. First marriages are recognized simply by cohabitation. If they do not choose to remain together, then the cuckolded spouses may or may not choose to allow them back. Whatever happens, there is no further mention of it or complaint about it, at least not openly, once the couple has returned. However, while the lovers are absent from the village, their spouses search for them, wail, and complain loudly to everyone. Sometimes the spouses left behind asked me to take them in my motorboat to search for the missing partners, but I never did.

Perhaps the activity closest to ritual among the Pirahãs is their dancing. Dances bring the village together. They are often marked by promiscuity, fun, laughing, and merriment by the entire village. There are no musical instruments involved, only singing, clapping, and stomping of feet.

The first time I saw a dance I was impressed by how much everyone enjoyed themselves singing, talking, and walking around in a circle. Kóhoi invited me to dance with them.

"Dan, you want to dance with us tonight?"

"I don't know how to dance like Pirahãs," I said, hoping to get out of this. I am a terrible dancer.

"Steve and Arlo danced with us. Don't you want to dance like a Pirahã?" Kóhoi insisted.

"I'll try. But don't laugh."

During the dance, a Pirahã woman asked me, "Do you only lie on top of one woman? Or do you want to lie on others?"

"I just lie on one. I don't want others."

"He doesn't want other women," she announced.

"Does Keren like other men?"

"No, she just wants me," I responded as a good Christian husband. Sexual relations are relatively free between unmarried individuals and even between individuals married to other partners during village dancing and singing, usually during full moons. Aggression is observed from time to time, from mild to severe (Keren witnessed a gang rape of a young unmarried girl by most of the village men). But aggression is never condoned and it is very rare.

Pirahãs have told me about a dance in which live venomous snakes are used, though I have never seen one of these (such dances were corroborated, however, by the eyewitness account of the Apurinã inhabitants of Ponto Sete, before the Pirahãs dispersed them). In this dance, the regular dancing is preceded by the appearance of a man wearing only a headband of *buriti* palm and a waistband, with streamers, made entirely of narrow, yellow *paxiuba* palm leaves. The Pirahã man so dressed claims to be Xaítoii, a (usually) evil spirit whose name means "long tooth." The man comes out of the jungle into the clearing where the others are gathered to dance and tells his audience that he is strong, unafraid of snakes, and then tells them about where he lives in the jungle, and what he has been doing that day. This is all sung. As he sings, he tosses snakes at the feet of the audience, who all scramble away quickly.

These spirits appear in dances in which the man playing the role of the spirit claims to have encountered that spirit and claims to be possessed by that spirit. Pirahã spirits all have names and personalities, and their behavior is somewhat predictable. Such dances might be classified as a weak form of ritual, in the sense that they are witnessed and imitated and clearly have value and meaning to the community. As rituals they are intended to teach the people to be strong, to know their environment, and so on.

The relative lack of ritual among the Pirahãs is predicted by the immediacy of experience principle. This principle states that formulaic language and actions (rituals) that involve reference to nonwitnessed events are avoided. So a ritual where the principal character could not claim to have seen what he or she was enacting would be prohibited. Beyond this prohibitive feature, however, the idea behind the principle is that the Pirahãs avoid formulaic encodings of values and instead transmit values and information via actions and words that are original in composition with the person acting or speaking, that have been witnessed by this person, or that have been told to this person by a witness. So traditional oral literature and rituals have no place.

Pirahãs laugh about everything. They laugh at their own misfortune: when someone's hut blows over in a rainstorm, the occupants laugh more loudly than anyone. They laugh when they catch a lot of fish. They laugh when they catch no fish. They laugh when they're full and they laugh when they're hungry. When they're sober, they are never demanding or rude. Since my first night among them I have been impressed with their patience, their happiness, and their kindness. This pervasive happiness is hard to explain, though I believe that the Pirahãs are so confident and secure in their ability to handle anything that their environment throws at them that they can enjoy whatever comes their way. This is not at all because their lives are easy, but because they are good at what they do.

They like to touch to show affection. Although I have never seen kissing among the Pirahãs, there is a word for it, so they must do it. But they all touch one another frequently. In the evenings, as it got dark, they loved to touch me too, especially little children, who would stroke my arms, hair, and back. I didn't look at them when they did this, because that would have embarrassed them.

Pirahãs are patient with me. They are stoic with themselves. They are caring for the elderly and the handicapped. I noticed an old man in the village, Kaxaxái (Alligator), who walked funny and was unable to fish or hunt. He gathered a little firewood each evening for the people. I asked a man why he gave food to Kaxaxái, who never gave him anything in return. "He fed me when I was young. Now I feed him."

The first time the Pirahãs brought me something to eat, roasted fish, they asked me, *"Gíxai soxóá xobáaxáaí. Kohoaipi?"* (Do you already know how to eat this?) It is a great phrase, because if you really don't want something, it gives you a way out without causing offense. All you have to say is "No, I don't know how to eat this."

The Pirahãs seemed peaceful. I felt no aggression toward me or other outsiders, unlike in so many other new cultures I had entered over the years. And I saw no aggression internal to the group. Although, as in all societies, there were exceptions to the rule, this is still my impression of the Pirahãs after all these years. The peaceful people.

As is the case at the village of Xagíopai, known to Brazilians as Forquilha Grande—"Big Fork"—because the Maici branches into a dead-end oxbow lake at that point, sisters will often bring their husbands to live around their parents. In other villages, though, such as the village of Pentecoste near the mouth of the Maici, men bring wives to their parents' village. Thus one village can be matrilocal, but another patrilocal. Or neither—in some villages no pattern is discernible. This flexibility is probably based on the laissez-faire nature of Pirahã society as well as the Pirahãs' minimalist kinship system.

The Pirahãs have only the following kinship terms, constituting one of the simplest kinship systems in the world:

baíxi—parent, grandparent, or someone to whom you wish to express submission temporarily or permanently. Pirahã call me baíxi when they want something from me; they sometimes refer to river traders as baíxi; adults can call other adults baíxi if they want something, such as fish, from them. Young children can call other children baíxi if they want something from them. This term is gender-neutral. Sometimes the expression ti xogií (my big) is used instead of baíxi. It can also be used as a term of affection for the elderly. If it becomes necessary to distinguish a woman or a male parent, one can say ti baíxi xipóihií (my female parent) and so on. Context will often determine whether biological parents are being referred to. When it doesn't, it probably isn't necessary to draw that distinction anyway.
xahaigí—sibling (male or female). This can also refer to any Pirahã of the same generation and, in some contexts, to any Pirahã at all if he or she is being contrasted with outsiders, as in "What did the xahaigí say to the Brazilian?"
hoagí or hoísai—son. Hoagí is the verb "to come" and hoísai means "the one that came."
kai—daughter.

There is one more term, *piihí,* which has a wider range of meanings, including "child with at least one deceased parent," "stepchild," and "favorite child."

That's it. Although some anthropologists who do not speak Pirahã have proposed additional terms, all those proposals that I am aware of result from the misanalysis of entire phrases. The most usual error is to analyze possessive forms of the terms above as though they were separate kinship terms. So, for example, one anthropologist proposed that the phrase *ti xahaigí* means "uncle," but in fact it just means "my sibling."

Anthropologists have long believed that the more complex the kinship system, the more likely it is that there will be kinship-based restrictions on whom to marry, which relative to live close to or with, and so on. But the inverse necessarily holds as well—the fewer the number of kinship terms, the smaller the number of kinship-related restrictions there will be in a society. This has an interesting effect in Pirahã. Since they lack any word for cousin, unsurprisingly there is no restriction against marrying a cousin. And, perhaps because *xahaigí* is ambiguous, I have even seen men marry their half sisters.

The effect of the apparently universal incest taboo prohibits only a small number of sexual couplings among the Pirahãs, such as full sibling with full sibling and grandparent or parent with child.

There is more to this kinship system than meets the eye, however. Some of the kinship terms label concepts that are broader than mere kinship. I mentioned already the use of *baíxi* to refer to either authority or kinship.

The concept of *xahaigí* is interesting as well. It seems to express more than kinship. It expresses a value of community. Because this word is genderless and numberless, it can refer to a man, a woman, women, men, or a mixed group. Although Pirahã mostly live in nuclear families, there is a strong sense of community and mutual responsibility for the well-being of other community members. *Xahaigí* names and strengthens this sense of community by labeling the community's members.

The most important connotation of *xahaigí* is this sense of belonging, of family and brotherhood. This feeling is marked among the three hundred or so living Pirahãs. Even though they may be separated by miles of river, every person in every village follows the news of all other villages and individual Pirahãs. It is impressive how fast news travels the 240-plus miles of the Maici along which the Pirahãs are scattered. The crucial part of the *xahaigí* concept is that each Pirahã is important to every other Pirahã. A Pirahã will always defend or take the side of another Pirahã over any non-Pirahã, no matter how long he or she has known the latter. And no foreigner, not even I, can expect to be called *xahaigí* by all Pirahãs (some do now refer to me as *xahaigí*, but most do not, even some of my best Pirahã friends).

Another example of *xahaigí* is seen in the treatment of children and the elderly. A father of one family will feed or care for another child, at least temporarily, if that child is abandoned, even for a day. Once an older man got lost in the jungle. For three days the entire village searched for him, with little food or sleep. They were very emotional when they found him, safe but tired and hungry, carrying a sharpened pole for protection. They called him their *baíxi* and hugged him and smiled, giving him food as soon as they reached the village. This also illustrates their sense of community.

The Pirahãs all seem to be intimate friends, no matter what village they come from. Pirahãs talk as though they know every other Pirahã extremely well. I suspect that this may be related to their physical connections. Given the lack of stigma attached to and the relative frequency of divorce, promiscuousness associated with dancing and singing, and post- and prepubescent sexual experimentation, it isn't far off the mark to conjecture that many Pirahãs have had sex with a high percentage of the other Pirahãs. This alone means that their relationships will be based on an intimacy unfamiliar to larger societies (the community that sleeps together stays together?). Imagine if you'd had sex with a sizable percentage of the residents of your neighborhood and that this fact was judged by the entire society as neither good nor bad, just a fact about life—like saying you've tasted many kinds of food.

My entire family noticed daily the striking differences between the Pirahãs' and our own concepts of family. One morning I watched a toddler walk unsteadily toward the fire. As he got closer, his mother, two feet away, grunted at him. But she made no effort to pull him away.

He teetered and then fell, just beside the hot coals. He blistered his leg and butt and howled with pain. His mother jerked him up by one arm and scolded him.

I watched this and wondered why this mother, whom I knew to be loving with her children, would scold her toddler for hurting himself, especially since she had not warned him about the hot coals, so far as I knew. This in turn raised a larger issue: how did the Pirahãs view childhood? What were their goals for child raising? I began a deeper reflection on this by recalling my observation that the Pirahãs don't talk baby talk to their children. Children are just human beings in Pirahã society, as worthy of respect as any fully grown human adult. They are not seen as in need of coddling or special protections. They are treated fairly and allowance is made for their size and relative physical weakness, but by and large they are not considered qualitatively different from adults. This can lead to scenes that to Western eyes can seem strange or even harsh. Since I find myself predisposed to agree with much of the Pirahãs' view of parenting, I often don't even notice child-rearing behavior that other outsiders find shocking.

As an example, I recall how a colleague of mine was surprised by the adult treatment of Pirahã children. Peter Gordon, a psychologist at Columbia University, and I were in a Pirahã village together in 1990 interviewing a man about the spirit world. While we were talking we had set up a video camera to record our interactions with the people. That evening as we watched bits of the video, we noticed that a toddler about two years old was sitting in the hut behind the man we were interviewing. The child was playing with a sharp kitchen knife, about nine inches in length. He was swinging the knife blade around him, often coming close to his eyes, his chest, his arm, and other body parts one would not like to slice off or perforate. What really got our attention, though, was that when he dropped the knife, his mother—talking to someone else—reached backward nonchalantly without interrupting her conversation, picked up the knife, and handed it back to the toddler. No one told him not to cut himself or hurt himself with the knife. And he didn't. But I have seen other Pirahã children cut themselves severely with knives. Many times Keren or I had to put sulfa powder on cuts to reduce the chances of infection.

Any baby who cuts, burns, or otherwise hurts itself gets scolded (and cared for too). And a mother will often answer a baby's cry of pain in such circumstances with a growl of disgust, a low guttural "*Ummm!*" She might pick it up by an arm and angrily (but not violently) set it down abruptly away from the danger. But parents do not hug the child or say things like "Poor baby, I'm so sorry, let Mommy kiss it and make the boo-boo better." The Pirahãs stare with surprise when they see non-Pirahã mothers do this. They even think it is funny. "Don't they want their children to learn to take care of themselves?" the Pirahãs ask me.

But there is more to it than wanting children to become autonomous adults. The Pirahãs have an undercurrent of Darwinism running through their parenting philosophy. This style of parenting has the result of producing very tough and resilient adults who do not believe that anyone owes them anything. Citizens of the Pirahã nation know that each day's survival depends on their individual skills and hardiness.

When a Pirahã woman gives birth, she may lie down in the shade near her field or wherever she happens to be and go into labor, very often by herself. In the dry season, when there are beaches along the Maici, the most common form of childbirth is for the woman to go alone, occasionally with a female relative, into the river up to her waist, then squat down and give birth, so that the baby is born directly into the river. This is cleaner and healthier, in their opinion, for the baby and the mother. Occasionally, women's mothers or sisters accompany them. But if a woman has no female relatives in her village, she may be forced to give birth alone.

Steve Sheldon told me about a woman giving birth alone on a beach. Something went wrong. A breech birth. The woman was in agony. "Help me, please! The baby will not come," she cried out. The Pirahãs sat passively, some looking tense, some talking normally. "I'm dying! This hurts. The baby will not come!" she screamed. No one answered. It was late afternoon. Steve started toward her. "No! She doesn't want you. She wants her parents," he was told, the implication clearly being that he was not to go to her. But her parents were not around and no one else was going to her aid. The evening came and her cries came regularly, but ever more weakly. Finally, they stopped. In the morning Steve learned that she and the baby had died on the beach, unassisted.

Steve recorded a story about this incident, repeated here. This text is valuable for two reasons. First, it recounts a tragic incident that provides insight into Pirahã culture. In particular it tells us that the Pirahãs let a young woman die, alone and without help, because of their belief that people must be strong and get through difficulties on their own.

Second, it is important for our understanding of Pirahã grammar. Note the relative simplicity of the structure (not the content) of the sentences, which lack any sign of one sentence or phrase appearing inside another.

The Death of Xopísi's Wife, Xaogíoso
Recorded by Steve Sheldon

Synopsis: This story tells of the death of Xopísi's wife, Xaogíoso. She died in the early morning, while giving birth to a baby. She was all alone giving birth at the river's edge when she died. Her sister, Baígipóhoasi, did not help her at all. Xabagi (an older village man who occasionally helps in childbirth) called to someone (the woman's son-in-law), but he did not respond or go see her before she died. Xopísi, her husband, was down the river fishing for piranha when the death occurred, so there was no one watching after her.

1. *Xoii hiaigíagásai. Xopísi hiabikadhaaga.*
   Xoii spoke. Xopísi is not here.

2. *Xoii hiaigiagaxai Xaogíosohoagi xioaakaahaaga.*
   Xoii then spoke. Xaogíoso is dead.

3. *Xaigia hiaitibíi.*
   Well, he was called.

4. *Ti hi giaitibíigaoai Xoii. Hoihiai.*
   I called Xoii. The only one.

5. *Xoii hi aigia ti gaxai. Xaogíosohoagi ioabaahoihoi, Xaogíoso.*
   I thus spoke to Xoii. Xaogíoso has died, Xaogíoso.

6. *Xoii xiboaipaihiabahai Xoii.*
   Xoii did not go to see her on the floating dock.

7. *Xaogíosohaogi xioaikoi.*
   Xaogíoso is really dead.

8. *Ti xaigía aitagobai.*
   Well, I am really fearful.

9. *Xoii hi xaigiagaxaisai. Xitaíbígaí hiaítisi xaabahá.*
   Xoii then spoke. Xitaíbígaí did not tell about it.

10. *Hi gaxaisi xaabahá.*
    He said she did not tell.

11. *Xaogíosohoagi xihoisahaxaí.*
    Xaogíoso, do not die!

12. *Ti xaigíagaxaiai. Xaogíosohoagí xiahoaga.*
    I then spoke. Xaogíoso has become dead.

13. *Xaabaobaha.*
    She is no longer here.

14. *Xoii hi xi xobaipaihiabaxai.*
    Xoii did not go to see her on the floating dock.

15. *Xopísi hi Xiasoaihi hi gixai xigihí.*
    Xopísi, you are Xiasoaihi's husband.

16. *Xioaíxi Xaogíoso.*
    Xaogíoso is dead.

17. *Ti xaigíai hi xaitibíigaópai. Xoii xiobáipápaí.*
    Well, I called to Xoii. Go see her.

18. *Xaogíosogoagi xiahoagái.*
    Xaogíoso has become dead.

19. *Xaabaobáhá.*
She is no longer here.

20. *Xaogíosohoagí hi xaigía kaihiagóhaaxá.*
Xaogíoso dropped (gave birth to) her child.

21. *Xoii ti xaigíagáxaiai. Xoii hi xioi xaipihoaipái. Xoii hi xobágátaxaíhiabaxaí.*
I said to Xoii. Xoii gave her medicine. Xoii did not go see her again.

22. *Xoii hi xaigíagáxai. Hoagaixóxai hi gáxisiaabáhá Hoagaixóxai.*
Xoii then spoke. Hoagaixóxai said nothing, Hoagaixóxai.

23. *Xaogíoso xiaihidbahíoxoi.*
Xaogíoso is very, very sick.

24. *Xi xaipihoaipaáti xi hiabahá.*
The medicine was not given to her.

25. *Hi xai hi xahoaihiabahá gíxa pixáagixi.*
He did not tell anyone, the younger one.

26. *Xaogíoso hi xábahíoxoisahaxaí.*
Xaogíoso, don't get bad.

27. *Hi gáaisiaabahá.*
He did not say anything.

28. *Hi xabaasi hi gíxai kaisahaxaí.*
You did nothing for the people.

29. *Xabaxaí hoihaí.*
All alone she went.

This story is, once again, interesting at various levels. From the linguistic perspective, the most relevant property is the simplicity of the sentence structure. On the other hand, this Pirahã story, like all others, does show relatively complex relationships between ideas in sentences. Some ideas of the story occur inside of other ideas, even though neither the sentences nor the grammar proper show this. So, for example, there are four broad divisions of subtopics in the text. Lines one through five introduce the story and the participants. Lines six through fourteen discuss the neglect of responsibility of the dead woman's husband. Lines fifteen through nineteen repeat neglect of responsibility by others. And another round of lamentation of neglect is given in lines twenty until the end. And of course all of the lines form a single story in which every line plays its part. So all sentences in the story are found *within* the story in both the sense of their appearance on the page and in their cognitive grouping—that is, the speaker thinks that they all belong and structures the story to reflect this perception.

These groupings of sentences are not grammatical groupings in the sense that syntacticians would accept, but they are rather groupings of ideas. They reveal thinking processes. This central device of placing thoughts inside other thoughts mirrors one that many linguists consider to be part of grammar—recursion. And yet the Pirahã text groupings are not part of grammar, even though they are found in all Pirahã stories. So the device in question, putting things inside of other things, such as phrases in phrases or sentences in sentences, is independent of grammar, contrary to what many, but by no means all, linguists have thought.

While to many nonlinguists this may seem like an arcane theoretical point, it is at the heart of one of the biggest rifts in modern linguistics. If recursion is not found in the grammar of all languages, but it is found in the thought processes of all humans, then it is part of general human intelligence and not part of a "language instinct" or "universal grammar," as Noam Chomsky has claimed.

Culturally the story is interesting because the speaker seems to be attempting to come across as guiltless. The neglect of the woman is presented as though it were bad, as many Westerners would think as well, and yet neither the teller of the story nor anyone else went to her aid. This suggests that the value of letting everyone pull their own weight, even in very dangerous circumstances, is shown in overt behavior even when it is not supported in words. Like members of other cultures, the Pirahãs often make a distinction between values in speech and values in practice.

An experience of my own was even more shocking to me. A young mother named Pokó gave birth to a beautiful baby girl. Pokó and the baby were doing very well. My family and I left the village to rest in Porto Velho, returning two months later. When we arrived back in the village, Pokó and some other Pirahãs, as usual, were living in our house. But Pokó was emaciated. She clearly had some illness, but we didn't know what. She was close to death, nearly skeletal. Her cheeks were sunken, her legs and arms were bone-thin, and she was so weak that she could barely move. Since she had no milk her baby was also very ill. Other mothers would not nurse Pokó's baby since they needed the milk, they said, for their own babies. Pokó died just a couple of days after our return. Since we had no radio, we had no way of calling for help for her. But her baby survived.

We asked who would care for Pokó's daughter.

"The baby will die. There is no mother to nurse her," we were told.

"Keren and I will take care of the baby," I volunteered.

"OK," the Pirahãs responded, "but the baby will die."

The Pirahãs know death and dying when they see it. I understand this now. But I was committed to helping that baby.

Our first problem was to feed the child. We made some diapers for the baby out of old sheets and towels. We tried to give it a bottle (we always kept baby bottles in the village for possible infant sicknesses), but it would not suck. It was almost comatose. I determined not to let this baby die. I thought of a way to get milk into it. We mixed up some powdered milk with sugar and a bit of salt and warmed it. I had a couple of squeeze bottles of Right Guard deodorant (deodorant is commonly sold in plastic squeeze bottles in Brazil). I emptied them and washed them out. I pulled out the plastic tubes from each and washed those out too. Then I filled a Right Guard bottle with some of our baby "formula." I connected two of the tubes, wrapping them in medical tape where they were joined. Then I inserted one of them into the Right Guard bottle with the milk. Carefully and slowly we then worked the other tube down the baby's throat. The baby showed only slight discomfort. With equal care I squeezed slowly on the Right Guard bottle and got quite a bit of milk into the baby's stomach.

Within an hour the baby seemed more energetic. We fed it every four hours, day and night. For three days we got almost no sleep, working to save this baby. It seemed to be coming around. With each feeding, the baby moved more energetically, cried more loudly, and even had a bowel movement. We were ecstatic. One afternoon we felt we could leave the baby and go jogging on the airstrip. So I asked the father of the baby if he could watch the baby until we got back from the airstrip. We went and jogged, feeling that we were making a tangible and important contribution to at least one Pirahã's well-being.

But the Pirahãs were certain that the baby would die for three reasons. First, it was near death already. They believed that when a person gets emaciated to a certain point, a point this baby had passed, the person would not survive. Second, they also believed that for a baby this sick to survive it needed to be cared for by a Pirahã mother—one that would nurse it. And this was not going to happen, because the baby's mother had died and no other mother would allow her own baby to go hungry in order to feed another woman's baby. Finally, they did not believe that our medicine could compensate for these first two conditions, so my efforts to feed the baby were, to the Pirahãs, just prolonging its misery and causing it unnecessary pain.

When we returned from our jog, several Pirahãs were huddled in a corner of our house, and there was a strong smell of alcohol in the air. Those in the huddle looked conspiratorial and stared at us. Some seemed angry, others ashamed. Others just stared down at something on the ground that they were all surrounding. As I approached, they parted. Pokó's baby was on the ground, dead. They had forced cachaça down its throat and killed it.

"What happened to the baby?" I asked, almost in tears.

"It died. It was in pain. It wanted to die," they replied.

I just picked up the baby and held it, with tears now beginning to stream down my cheeks.

"Why would they kill a baby?" I asked myself in confusion and grief.

We made a small wooden coffin from some old crating I had brought in. Then the father and I dug a grave about one hundred yards upriver on the bank of the Maici, next to where Pokó was buried. We put the baby in the grave, threw dirt over it, in front of the three or four other Pirahãs who had come to see the burial. Then we bathed in the river, to remove the clay and dirt that had clung to us. I went back to my house and brooded.

The more I thought about this incident, though, the more I came to realize that the Pirahãs, from their perspective, did what they thought was best. They weren't simply being cruel or thoughtless. Their views of life, death, and illness are radically different from my Western ideas. In a land without doctors, with the knowledge that you have to get tough or die, with much more firsthand direct experience with the dead and dying than I had ever had, the Pirahãs could see death in someone's eyes and health before I could. They felt certain that this baby was going to die. They felt it was suffering terribly. And they believed that my clever milk tubes contraption was hurting the child and prolonging its suffering. So they euthanized the child. The father himself put the baby to death, by forcing alcohol down its throat. I knew of other babies that had survived their mother's death, but they had all been in robust health when they were orphaned.

The Pirahãs' view that children are equal citizens of society means that there is no prohibition that applies to children that does not equally apply to adults and vice versa. There certainly is no age-based prejudice that children should be "seen but not heard." Pirahã children are noisy and rambunctious and can be as stubborn as they choose to be. They have to decide for themselves to do or not do what their society expects of them. Eventually they learn that it is in their best interests to listen to their parents a bit. One young boy, Paitá, whom I particularly liked, was the son of my good friend Kóxoí—a man so relaxed and laid-back that I found it hard to stay awake around him, a smiling man, never out of sorts, even when he was dying from what might have been tuberculosis. Kóxoí's son illustrates well the general status of Pirahã children.

One afternoon I saw Paitá coming down the path. He was about three years old. Paitá was always filthy, reminding me of Pig-Pen from the *Peanuts* comic strip. He tilted his head when he looked at you, and grinned and laughed freely. His feet and legs were covered in mud, since the path was so wet. But what attracted my attention was that this little three-year-old was smoking a fat cigarette, hand-rolled. His father

no doubt had rolled it for him—strong, hard tobacco rolled in notebook paper. And Paitá was wearing a dress.

As the father came along the path, not far behind Paitá, I asked,
laughing, "What is your son doing?" I was referring to the cigarette.

Kóxoí responded, "Oh, I like to dress him in girl's clothes."

For Kóxoí, the unusual aspect of his son's appearance had nothing to
do with smoking. Even if the Pirahãs had known about the long-term
health effects of tobacco use, it would not have affected whether they
gave it to their children. First, no Pirahã smokes enough for it to present any significant health risk—they only have access to tobacco every
couple of months and can never get more than about a day's supply.
Second, if an adult can take the "risk" of smoking, a child can too. Of
course, the dress was evidence that children are treated somewhat differently from adults. But these differences do not include prohibitions
against engaging in activities more commonly associated with adults in
Western society.

Once a trader gave the tribe enough cachaça for everyone to get
drunk. And that is what happened. Every man, woman, and child in the
village got falling-down wasted. Now, it doesn't take much alcohol for
Pirahãs to get drunk. But to see six-year-olds staggering with slurred
speech was a novel experience for me. To the Pirahãs, though, everyone
must share in the hardships of life, and everyone is likewise entitled to
share in the enjoyable things of life.

A child born into a Pirahã family inherits a set of relationships that
is not too different from those of a child born into many European
societies. The biggest difference, of course, is that Pirahã children roam
about the village and are considered to be related to and partially the
responsibility of everyone in the village. But on a day-to-day basis,
most Pirahãs have nuclear families that include the stable presence of a
father, a mother, and siblings (full, half, and adopted). Parents treat
their children with much affection, talk to them respectfully and frequently, and rarely discipline them.

As in most hunter-gatherer societies, there is some specialization
among Pirahã parents and sexes. Women are the primary gatherers of
jungle products, tubers, and other food from their gardens. Men hunt,
chop trees, and clear jungle gardens. Mothers are the primary care-
givers for the children, but fathers often stay at home and care for the

children while the mothers go to the field or the jungle to gather fruits, to hunt small game with dogs, to collect firewood, or to go fishing. (Interestingly, women only fish with hooks and line and only hunt using dogs to kill small game, while men also use the bow and arrow to fish and hunt. The bow and arrow is a male-only tool.)

Pirahã parenting involves no violence, at least in principle. But my model of parenting did. It is worth contrasting the two here because ultimately I have come to believe that the Pirahãs have a healthier attitude in many ways than I did at the time. I was a young father—Shannon was born when I was nineteen. And because of my immaturity and Christian parenting framework, I thought that corporeal punishment was appropriate and useful, following the biblical injunction that to spare the rod was to spoil the child. Shannon, as my oldest child, often suffered the worst of this phase of my life. In the village one day, she said something to me that I thought entitled her to a spanking. I got a switch and told her to meet me in the bedroom. She started yelling that she didn't need a spanking. The Pirahãs came quickly, as they always did when we sounded angry.

"What are you doing, Dan?" a couple of women asked.

"I'm, uh, well . . ." Hmm. I didn't have an answer. What the hell *was* I doing?

Anyway, I felt the weight of the Bible and so I told Shannon, "OK, no spanking here. Meet me at the end of the airstrip and pick another switch along the way. I will meet you there in five minutes!"

As Shannon started out of the house, Pirahãs asked her where she was going.

"My dad is going to hit me on the airstrip," she replied with a mix of irritation and glee, knowing what the effect of her words would be.

Pirahã children and adults came running behind me when I left. I was defeated. No more spankings around the Pirahãs. Pirahã mores won out. Shannon was smug and delighted with her victory.

What effect does a Pirahã upbringing have on a child? Pirahã teenagers, like all teenagers, are giggly and can be very squirrelly and rude. They commented that my ass was wide. They farted close to the table as soon as we were sitting down to eat, then laughed like Jerry Lewis. Apparently the profound weirdness of teenagers is universal.

But I did not see Pirahã teenagers moping, sleeping in late, refusing to accept responsibility for their own actions, or trying out what they considered to be radically new approaches to life. They in fact are highly productive and conformist members of their community in the Pirahã sense of productivity (good fishermen, contributing generally to the security, food needs, and other aspects of the physical survival of the community). One gets no sense of teenage angst, depression, or insecurity among the Pirahã youth. They do not seem to be searching for answers. They have them. And new questions rarely arise.

Of course, this homeostasis can stifle creativity and individuality, two important Western values. If one considers cultural evolution to be a good thing, then this may not be something to emulate, since cultural evolution likely requires conflict, angst, and challenge. But if your life is unthreatened (so far as you know) and everyone in your society is sat-isfied, why would you desire change? How could things be improved? Especially if the outsiders you came into contact with seemed more irritable and less satisfied with life than you. I asked the Pirahãs once during my early missionary years if they knew why I was there. "You are here because this is a beautiful place. The water is pretty. There are good things to eat here. The Pirahãs are nice people." That was and is the Pirahãs' perspective. Life is good. Their upbringing, everyone learn-ing early on to pull their own weight, produces a society of satisfied members. That is hard to argue against.

It is interesting to me that in spite of a strong sense of community, there is almost no community-approved coercion of village members. It is unusual for a Pirahã to order another Pirahã about, even for a par-ent to order about a child. This happens occasionally, but it is generally frowned upon or discouraged, as indicated by the remarks, expres-sions, and gestures of others watching. I cannot recall having seen an adult intervene to stop another adult from violating community norms.

One day I decided to ask one of my main language teachers, Kaa-boogí, if he would work with me. I walked to his house. Coming up the path, I noticed that Kaaboogí's brother Kaapási had been drinking cachaça. I heard Kaapási yell for Kaaboogí's little white dog to stop barking. A few steps later, only fifty feet from Kaapási's hut, I saw him raise his shotgun and shoot his brother's dog in the stomach. The dog yelped and jumped, bleeding profusely, its intestines hanging from the hole torn in its abdomen. It fell to the ground twitching and whimpering. Kaaboogí ran to it and picked it up. His eyes watered as the dog died in his arms. I feared that he would shoot one of Kaapási's dogs or attack Kaapási himself.

The village stared at Kaapási and Kaaboogí—quiet except for the yelping of dogs. Kaaboogí just sat holding his dog, tears in his eyes.

"Are you going to do anything to Kaapási?" I asked.

"What do you mean?" said Kaaboogí, puzzled.

"I mean, what are you going to do to him for shooting your dog?"

"I will do nothing. I won't hurt my brother. He acted like a child. He did a bad thing. But he is drunk and his head is not working well. He should not have hurt my dog. It is like my child."

Even when provoked, as Kaaboogí was now, the Pirahãs were able to respond with patience, love, and understanding, in ways rarely matched in any other culture I have encountered. The Pirahãs are not pacifists. They are by no means perfect. But peace is valued among them, at least peace with other Pirahãs. They see themselves as a family—a family in which every member feels obliged to protect and care for every other member. This is not to say that they never violate their own norms. All groups do. But this simply highlights the norm of helping one another and its relative rarity cross-culturally.

At the same time, the Pirahãs are individualistic with regard to their own and their family's survival. They and their family come first. They won't let another Pirahã starve to death or suffer if they can help, but the person receiving help has to obviously need it—to be suffering from some physical ailment or to be too young or old to care for himself and to be able to be helped (not considered too far gone to help, for example). Otherwise, each one carries his own load. If a man cannot provide food and shelter for his wife and children, his family will likely abandon him for a better provider. If a woman is lazy and won't get firewood, manioc from the jungle garden, or nuts from the forest, she will be left, at least as soon as her age begins to erase her beauty or fertility.

But there is still a sense of belonging that permeates the values of all Pirahãs. The Pirahãs see immediately that outsiders lack this quality. They see Brazilians cheat and mistreat other Brazilians. They see American parents spank their children. Most puzzling to them, they have heard that Americans fight huge battles to kill large numbers of other peoples and that Americans and Brazilians even kill other Americans and Brazilians.

Kóhoi once said, "My father told me that he saw his father go to kill other Indians. But we do not do this now. It is bad." There are other interesting concepts in Pirahã culture, though some are less momentous than their view of violence and war.

For example, marriage and other relations in Pirahã are partially subsumed to the concept of *kagi*. This term was very hard for me to nail down. If a Pirahã sees a plate of rice and beans (that either I or a Brazilian trader or government worker has brought into the village, since they do not grow these themselves), they might call it rice with *kagi*. If I showed up in a Pirahã village with my children, the Pirahãs might say, "Here's Dan with *kagi*." Or the Pirahãs might use the same term if I had showed up with my wife: "Dan arrived with *kagi*." If a person goes to hunt with their dogs, they would say, "He went hunting with *kagi*." So what on earth does *kagi* mean? And how is it related to marriage? Well, although no easy translation works, it means something like "expected associate." The expectation and the association are determined by cultural familiarity and cultural values. Your spouse is the person that by habit is expected to be with you. Like rice and beans, hunter and dog, parent and child, marriage is a correlation between culturally linked beings. There is no cultural pressure, however, to keep the same *kagi*.

Again, couples initiate cohabitation and procreation without ceremony. If they are unattached at the time, they simply begin to live together in the same house. If they are married, they first disappear from the village for two to four days, while their former spouses call for and search for them. Upon their return, they begin a new household or, if it was just a "fling," return to their previous spouses. There is almost never any retaliation from the cuckolded spouses against those with whom their spouses have affairs. Relations between men and women and boys and girls, whether married or not, are always cordial and often marked by light to heavy flirting.

Sexually it is the same. So long as children are not forced or hurt, there is no prohibition against their participating in sex with adults. I remember once talking to Xisaoxoi, a Pirahã man in his late thirties, when a nine- or ten-year-old girl was standing beside him. As we talked, she rubbed her hands sensually over his chest and back and rubbed his crotch area through his thin, worn nylon shorts. Both were enjoying themselves.

"What's she doing?" I asked superfluously.

"Oh, she's just playing. We play together. When she's big she will be my wife" was his nonchalant reply—and, indeed, after the girl went through puberty, they were married.

Marriage itself among the Pirahãs, like marriage in all cultures, comes with sets of mores that are enforced in different ways. People often ask me, for example, how the Pirahãs deal with infidelity in marriage. So how would this couple, the relatively old man and the young girl, deal with infidelity? They would deal with it like other Pirahãs, in what I take to be a very civilized fashion.

The solution or response to infidelity can even be humorous. One morning I walked over to my friend Kóhoibiíihíai's home to ask him to teach me more of his language. As I approached his hut, everything looked pretty normal. His wife, Xíbaihóíxoi, was sitting up and he was lying down with his head in her lap.

"Hey, can you help me learn Pirahã words today?" I inquired.

He started to raise his head to answer. Then I noticed that Xíbaihóíxoi was holding him by the hair of his head. As he tried to raise his head, she jerked his head back by the hair, picked up a stick at her side and started whacking him irregularly on the top of his head, occasionally hitting him in the face. He laughed hard, but not too hard, because she jerked his hair every time he moved.

"My wife won't let me go anywhere," he said, giggling.

His wife was smirking but the grin disappeared right away and she struck him harder. Some of those whacks looked pretty painful to me. Kóhoi wasn't in the best position to talk, so I left and found Xahoábisi, another good language teacher. He could work with me, he said.

As we walked back to my house together, I asked, "So what is going on with Kóhoibiíihíai? Xíbaihóíxoi is holding down his head and hitting him with a stick."

"Oh, he was playing with another woman last night," Xahoábisi chortled. "So this morning his woman is mad at him. He can't go any-where today."

The fact that Kóhoi, a strong man and a fearless hunter, would lie like that all day and allow his wife to whack him at will (three hours later I revisited them and they were in the same position) was clearly partly voluntary penance. But it was partly a culturally prescribed rem-edy. I have since seen other men endure the same treatment.

By the next day, all seemed well. I didn't hear of Kóhoi playing around with women again for quite a while after that. A nifty way to solve marital problems, I thought. It doesn't always work, of course. There are divorces (without ceremony) among the Pirahãs. But this form of punishment for straying is effective. The woman can express her anger tangibly and the husband can show her he is sorry by letting her bang away on his head at will for a day. It is important to note that this involves no shouting or overt anger. The giggling, smirking, and laughter are all necessary components of the process, since anger is the cardinal sin among the Pirahãs. Female infidelity is also fairly common. When this happens the man looks for his wife. He may say something mean or threatening to the male who cuckolded him. But violence against anyone, children or adults, is unacceptable to the Pirahãs.

Other observations of Pirahã sexuality were a bit more shocking to my Christian sensibilities, especially when they involved clashes between our culture and Pirahã values. One afternoon during our sec-ond family stay among the Pirahãs, I walked out of the back room of our split-wood and thatched-roof home on the Maici into the central area of the house, which had no walls and in practice belonged more to the Pirahãs than to us. Shannon was staring at two Pirahã men lying on the floor in front of her. They were laughing, with their shorts pulled down around their ankles, each grabbing the other's genitals and slap-ping each other on the back, rolling about the floor. Shannon grinned at me when I walked in. As a product of sexophobic American culture, I was shocked. "Hey, don't do that in front of my daughter!" I yelled indignantly.

They stopped giggling and looked up at me. "Don't do what?"

"*That*, what you're doing, grabbing each other by the penis."

"Oh," they said, looking rather puzzled. "He doesn't like to see us have fun with each other." They pulled their pants up and, ever adaptable to new circumstances, changed the subject and asked me if I had any candy.

I never really needed to tell Shannon or her siblings much about human reproduction, death, or other biological processes. They got a pretty good idea of all that from watching the Pirahãs.

Pirahã families are more familiar territory for Westerners. Parents and children are openly affectionate—hugging, touching, smiling, playing, chatting, and laughing with one another. This is one of the most immediately perceivable traits of Pirahã culture. I have always been challenged to be a more patient person, watching the Pirahãs. Parents do not strike their children or order them about, except under duress. Infants and toddlers (until about four years of age or the time they are weaned—when active life begins) are pampered and given much open affection.

Mothers wean their children when a new child is born—usually when the previous offspring is three or four years old. Weaning is traumatic for the child for at least three reasons: loss of adult attention, hunger, and work. Everyone must work; everyone must contribute to the life of the village. The child recently stopped from nursing will have to enter this adult world of work. In addition to talking and laughter, one frequently hears the sound of children screaming and crying at night. This is almost always caused by weaning. Once when a visiting doctor was with me among the Pirahãs, he woke me up.

"Dan, that baby sounds like it's in pain and very ill."

"It's all right," I assured him, and tried to get back to sleep.

"No, it's not all right! It's sick. If you won't go with me, I'll go alone," he insisted.

"Fine," I said, "let's go see it." But I thought that this doctor was nosing around when he ought to be sleeping.

We walked out to the hut where the baby was screaming. He shone his flashlight in. A little boy of about three was sitting up screaming, while his parents and siblings apparently slept.

"How can they sleep through that racket?" the doctor asked.

"They're only pretending to be asleep," I responded. "They don't want to talk to us right now about this child."

"Well, I want to make sure he's OK," the doctor insisted. "Ask them if he is."

I called to Xooi, the father. "Xooi, is the child sick?"

No answer.

"They don't want to talk," I said.

"Ask them, please!" the doctor demanded. He was pissing me off.

"Xooi, is the child sick?" I repeated.

With exasperation in every movement and syllable, Xooi looked up at me and said gruffly, "No, he wants to suck his mother's tit."

I translated.

"He's not sick?" the doctor asked, unsure as to whether to believe Xooi or not.

"No, he isn't. Let's go to bed."

We returned to our hammocks.

The weaned child is no longer the baby, no longer treated as special compared to other children. Instead of sleeping next to Mom, the child stays with its siblings a few significant feet away from the parents on the sleeping platform. Newly weaned toddlers experience hunger, like all Pirahãs except nursing babies. But, again, minor hunger is not considered a hardship for the Pirahãs. When children first enter this adult world they are shocked.

The child is no longer hand-fed and pampered by its parents. Within just a few years, boys are expected to fish while fathers, mothers, and daughters work in the field or go gathering or hunting.

Children's lives are not unpleasant. They play with toys if they have them and they especially like dolls and soccer balls (though no one in the village knows how to play soccer—they just like the balls). Kóxoí and Xiooitaóhoagí impressed me because they were the only parents I knew who always asked for toys for their children when I asked if I could bring them something from the city. The people can make spinning tops, whistles, toy canoes, and carved dolls, but they never do unless asked by outsiders. It isn't clear, therefore, that these objects are truly indigenous to the Pirahãs. They could be borrowed or merely the vestiges of older practices now fading out of current relevance.

There is one exception to this, however. Frequently, after a plane has just visited the village, the Pirahã boys collect balsa wood and make model planes.

Everyone loves the planes that visit them from time to time. They have seen three types that I am aware of in the history of the people: an amphibious floatplane, a pontoon floatplane, and a Cessna 206. The amphibious aircraft lands on its belly in the river and its single engine is placed above the cabin. The other two have single engines installed at the front of the aircraft. When the planes come the boys make balsa-wood models of them, carved handily with machetes and occasionally painted red with urucum dye (a seed pod with red seeds and red oil inside) or, more rarely, painted with the model maker's blood, from a thumb or finger purposely punctured.

I have observed boys from villages that did not actually see the plane show up a couple of days later with model planes, having learned of the visit from boys that did witness the plane's visit and based their models on the models of the eyewitnesses. These models, usually twelve to twenty-four inches long and five or six inches high, are built according to an interesting accumulated experience. The models usually have two propellers, rather than the single propeller of the monomotor planes that are the only ones that have ever visited them. One propeller is placed above the cabin section and the other propeller at the nose of the model. This is an amalgam of the two types of planes that the Pirahãs have seen.

My investigations into Pirahã culture required spending long periods of time among them. Perhaps our longest visit was in 1980, when we spent almost the entire year in the village. At the beginning of this period, I saw that the palm-thatched roof on our large hut and our palm-wood floor needed to be replaced. It was in bad shape because while we were away from the village the Pirahãs liked to sleep in the loft where I had my study. They enjoy stargazing, so they would push holes in the thatch, ruining the roof.

But this thatch problem turned out to be the beginning of my entry into the real world of the Pirahãs, the jungle, where my evaluation of them would become more positive. I would come to see them as one of the most resourceful and clever groups of survivalists anywhere in the world. As I saw them in the jungle, I came to realize that the village was just their drawing room, a place to relax. And you can't understand people just watching them at leisure. The jungle and the river are the Pirahãs' office, their workshop, their atelier, and their playground.

Upon seeing the condition of my roof, I asked the Pirahãs if they would help me gather more thatch for the roof and more *paxiuba* palm wood for patching holes in my floor (where holes had been burned by Pirahãs building cooking fires in our house). I had not been deep into the jungle yet, in spite of living for months among the Pirahãs. So I had unknowingly missed opportunities to get to know them much better than I currently did.

To be a good linguist requires not only hours at the desk but also many hours with the people. I decided to go with the Pirahãs to the jungle for roof materials, in order to help them, learn from them, and participate in their activities.

So I prepared to set out. I hooked two full, one-quart military surplus canteens to my military surplus gunbelt, as well as a long Mexican "Acapulco" machete. The five Pirahã men, carrying nothing but one ax and a few machetes among them, laughed at my long sleeves, long pants, boots, hat, canteens, and enormous machete. But off we went, down the path, my companions laughing and conversing, I clanging with every step, as canteens and machete banged into one another and I tried unsuccessfully not to jam the handle of the machete into my private parts as it bumped against tree trunks.

After about thirty minutes, the jungle grew taller and darker, the brush less dense. The air became cooler. Mosquitoes began to buzz. And I heard more of my favorite Amazonian sound, the falsetto *hwe hwioo* of the screaming piha bird. Here I noticed a change in my traveling companions. The Pirahãs' hands were folded across their chests, crossing each other like a large letter X, even as they walked at a pace that required me to jog occasionally. They wasted no space with their bodies. They walked lightly and surely.

As we came to a stream, our way across was a lichen-covered log. The Pirahãs walked on it without a moment's hesitation. I walked two feet out on the log, slipped, and fell into the stream. Coming out of it almost as fast as I had gone in (such streams have many dangerous creatures, such as stingrays, anacondas, and small caimans), scampering up the bank gracelessly, I found the trail and caught up. The Pirahãs acted as though they had barely noticed my fall—in any case it was my embarrassment and they were too kind to exacerbate it by offering to help. They laughed when I caught up, just to show me that it was no big deal, nothing to be ashamed of (of course, *they* would never have fallen, nor would any of their children, dogs, grandparents, or disabled). We came eventually to a stand of *paxiuba*. I helped chop the palm trunks. I noticed quickly that for all my size and strength, the Pirahãs cut more deeply with every swing. They were better with the ax, more efficient in their movements. I was soaking in perspiration and had already drained one of my canteens. The Pirahãs' bodies were completely dry. They had drunk nothing at all.

After the men agreed that we had all we could carry back in a single trip we tied the palm wood and thatch into bundles. We each then grabbed a bundle or two and began walking the several miles back to the village. The path had seemed obvious on the way out, but now I felt a bit uncertain of the direction and began to hold back, watching the Pirahãs carefully. They smiled and stopped. "You go at the head," they snickered. "You take us back." I tried. But I kept taking the wrong turn, getting us into exitless brush cul-de-sacs. This was very entertaining to the Pirahãs. In spite of the delays I was causing, they were quite happy to allow me to continue to lead. No one was in a hurry. As I found a more obvious main path, we settled into walking and my load began to weigh me down. With every step the palm wood on my back bumped against overhanging branches or tree trunks, and I tripped on exposed tree roots and slipped on slimy leaves in the path. I was winded and tired. I was surprised that the Pirahãs did not seem tired at all, however. In the village the Pirahã men avoided carrying heavy things. When I asked them for help in carrying boxes or barrels and such, they were always reluctant to respond. When they did help, they could barely lift things that I could carry with ease. I had just assumed that they were weak and lacked endurance. But I was wrong. They didn't normally carry foreign objects and they didn't like to display their ignorance of how to handle them. Nor did they particularly like me to ask them for help in what they considered my own work. Neither endurance nor energy had anything to do with it.

As we walked, I realized that I was getting very tired and again per-spiring profusely. I was wondering if I could make it back to the village with this load. My thoughts were interrupted by Kóxoí, who came up alongside of me, smiled, and then reached and took my bundle of palm wood onto his shoulder, adding it to his own load. "You don't know how to carry this" was all he said. He was taking onto his shoulder per-haps fifty pounds extra. Fifty pounds is a heavy load when walking sev-eral miles down a narrow, jungle path surrounded by low-hanging vegetation. But he now carried at least one hundred pounds. And I knew he felt the weight. By working and sweating together, laughing at our own difficulties and errors, the Pirahãs and I cemented friendships through these jungle trips.

Another aspect of Pirahã culture that I wanted to understand in my initial attempt to sketch their principal cultural values was coercion—how the Pirahã society got its members to do what it thought they should do.

A widespread belief is that most American Indians have chiefs or other kinds of indigenous authority figures. This is incorrect. Many American Indian societies are by tradition egalitarian. The day-to-day lives of people in such societies, many more than is usually realized, are free of the influence of any leaders. There are various reasons for the misinformed notion that most indigenous peoples of the Americas naturally have monarchical structures.

First, we tend to project the values and mechanisms of our own soci-eties and ways of doing things onto other societies. Since it is difficult for us to imagine our own society without leaders of one sort or another, especially people with the power to enforce societal rules, per-haps it is also difficult for us to imagine that there are old and well-functioning societies without such rules.

Second, the views of many Westerners are heavily influenced by Hollywood and other fictional depictions of these societies. Movies rarely portray Indian societies without the dynamic personalities of chiefs.

Finally, and perhaps most important, Western societies prefer that American Indians have leaders that they can do business with. It is nearly impossible, for example, to gain access to Indian lands or even to cede lands to them legally without a representative. What has often happened, as in the Xingu region of Brazil and elsewhere in the Americas, is that chiefs have been invented and vested with, in many cases, the artificial power to be the legal representatives of "their" people, in order to facilitate economic access to Indian possessions.

One reason for the idea that all tribes have chiefs is the universal fact that societies entail control—and centralized control is easier for most people to understand than the kind of diffuse control and power that is found in many American Indian communities. Émile Durkheim, the French pioneer of sociology straddling the late nineteenth and early twentieth centuries, wrote convincingly that coercion is fundamental to the constitution of society. The members of any society are bound together by group values and limits and the majority of a society's members stay within the boundaries of their values (criminals and the insane being two of the more obvious counterexamples—the marginalized members of society, the transgressors).

Well, the Pirahãs do constitute a society. Therefore, if Durkheim and other sociologists—indeed, common sense—are on the right track, then there has to be a way to keep people in line, some way to assure uniformity of behavior. Such behavior, after all, is beneficial to society and to the individuals that constitute the society. It brings, among other things, security of expectations. So how does Pirahã society manifest coercion?

There is no "official" coercion in Pirahã society—no police, courts, or chiefs. But it exists nonetheless. The principal forms I have observed are ostracism and spirits. If someone's behavior is abnormal in a way that bothers the majority, he or she will be ostracized by degrees. An older man, Hoaáípi, whom I met at the beginning of my career among the Pirahãs, was unusual in that he and his wife lived alone, separated from the other Pirahãs by a considerable distance. When he paddled down to see me the first of the two times I ever saw him, he came without Western goods, in a *kagahói* rather than a Brazilian canoe, wearing only a loincloth. This meant that he was outside the normal relationships of trade and social intercourse that almost all Pirahãs participate in with one another. When he arrived, he was stared at more than I was. And he had a fresh arrow wound from another Pirahã, Tíigíi. He didn't want medicine for the arrow wound, but he did want some coffee and sugar, which I happily gave him, as a fair exchange for being able to meet him. Although he seemed like a sweet old man to me, the Pirahãs did not want him around. They said that he was mean. I have no idea to this day what they meant exactly, but I do know that he was the first, but not the last, Pirahã I saw who had been ostracized.

Another effective form of ostracism, much less dramatic but more common, is to exclude someone from food sharing for a while. Such exclusion can last for a day or a few days, but rarely longer. I had many men come to me to say that so-and-so was mad at them for one reason or another so they couldn't use a canoe to fish, or that no one would share with them. They next either asked me to intervene, which I did not, or asked for food, which I often gave them, trying to avoid any impression of getting involved in a village dispute.

Spirits can tell the village what it should not have done or what it should not do. Spirits can single out individuals or simply talk to the group as a whole. Pirahãs listen carefully and often follow the exhortations of the kaoáíbógí. A spirit might say something like "Don't want Jesus. He is not Pirahã," or "Don't hunt downriver tomorrow," or things that are commonly shared values, such as "Don't eat snakes." Through spirits, ostracism, food-sharing regulation, and so on, Pirahã society disciplines itself. It has very little coercion by the standards of many other societies, but it seems to have just enough to control its members' aberrant behavior.

My children's experience living as a minority within an Amazonian culture taught them to "see" the world in a different way and contributed to their development. When they first saw the Pirahãs, all my children exclaimed that they were the ugliest people that they had ever seen. Pirahãs rarely bathe with soap (they don't have any), the women don't brush their hair (they lack brushes), and the average Pirahã child's skin is encrusted with dirt, snot, and blood. But after they had come to know the Pirahãs, my children's attitudes changed. Almost a year later, when a visiting Brazilian military officer commented that the Pirahãs were ugly, my children got furious. "How can anyone call the Pirahãs ugly?" they wondered. They had forgotten their own judgments and now thought of the Pirahãs as beautiful people. They learned to think simultaneously like Americans, Pirahãs, and Brazilians. Shannon and Kristene made friends quickly and began to leave early in the mornings with Pirahã girls their age, when they didn't have study assignments, and canoe up or down the Maici, returning only in late afternoon with berries, nuts, and other jungle delicacies.

My children also learned about the Pirahãs' ability to cope with danger from nature. Shannon and I once went with the men to hunt an anaconda. Kóhoibiíihíai, a good friend as well as language instructor, asked us to travel with him and his brother, Poióí, to a spot about four minutes upriver in my motorboat. When we got there, he told me to cut the engine so he could paddle us near the bank. I did what he asked and Kóhoi and Poióí both paddled silently to a spot just beneath some overhanging trees on the right bank of the river. Kóhoi turned to me and Shannon and asked, "Do you see its hole there just under the water?"

"No," we replied. I didn't see a thing.

"Watch!" he said.

At this, Kóhoi took his bow, like all Pirahã bows about two yards in length, and probed under the water for a few seconds.

"That will make it mad." He giggled. "See it?" he asked.

"No," I responded. Neither Shannon nor I could see a thing other than murky water, since it was still the rainy season.

"See the dirt!" Kóhoi exclaimed. "It's moving now."

I did see a small swirl of mud in the water. Before I could remark, Kóhoi had stood in the boat and drawn his bow. *Thwang! Thwang!* Two arrows were fired into the water within a second of each other.

Almost immediately a ten-foot-long anaconda burst through the surface of the river, thrashing, with long Pirahã arrows through its head and body.

"Help me pull it in," Kóhoi said to me and Poióí, who was grinning widely.

"What are we going to do with this?" I asked him, even as I pulled on the snake's body, trying to grab its tail to help hoist it aboard, while Shannon stared openmouthed. I knew that the Pirahãs don't eat anacondas, so I couldn't figure out why we were putting this writhing mass in my boat.

"We're going to take it to scare the women," Kóhoi said, laughing.

We took it back to the village. Once we got back, I noticed the snake start to move again. So I beat it over the head with a paddle to make sure it was dead, breaking the paddle in the process. This caused Kóhoi and Poióí to laugh out loud. Imagine worrying about a snake with an arrow in its head. Then, after removing the arrows, we placed the snake near the bank where the women went to bathe.

"That will scare them!" Kóhoi and Poióí laughed as they ran up the bank.

I moored the boat and removed the outboard, and Shannon and I climbed the bank to the village. Shannon ran ahead to tell her mother and siblings what we had seen.

The attempt to scare the women didn't work, though. They had seen us coming with the snake, and as soon as we got up the bank, the women ran down and pulled the snake out of the water, holding it up and laughing.

Pirahã humor like this works because of their strong sense of community. They can show sarcasm, play practical jokes like the anaconda at the river's edge, and so on, because they are knitted together tightly in a community of trust (not complete trust—there is, after all, stealing and unfaithfulness—but mainly trust that each member of the community will understand each other member of the community and share the same values).

And this sense of community, xahaigí, is built on the nuclear family, where most values and the language are first learned. Families are central to Pirahã society. Every one of the Pirahãs is, in a sense, a brother or sister of all other Pirahãs. But their closest ties by far are with their nuclear family.

The Pirahãs' relationship to nature is fundamental to under-standing them. Understanding this relationship is as important to gaining a full picture of their values and overall culture as understanding their material culture and their sense of community. As I began to study how the Pirahãs relate to nature in more detail, I dis-covered that concepts and words for the environment help to define their perspective on how nature fits together and how it is related to human beings. Two terms, *bigí* and *xoí*, are telling in this regard and help us comprehend the Pirahã worldview.

I learned something about *bigí* one day just after a rain. First, I recorded the phrase *bigí xihoíxaagá* as a description of wet or muddy ground. Then I pointed up to the cloudy sky to get the phrase for *cloudy sky*. The speaker just repeated *bigí xihoíxaagá*—the same phrase he had just given me for *muddy ground*. I thought I must be missing some-thing. Ground and sky are two very different things. So I tried again with several other speakers. Everyone gave me the same answer. It is possible, of course, that I was getting a nonresponsive answer from all my teachers, along the lines of "You are an idiot" or "You're pointing." But I was fairly confident that this was not the case.

These concepts are important in various ways. Especially interesting is their contribution to our understanding of sickness among the Pirahãs. I learned this early on when Kóhoibiíihíai and I were talking about his daughter, Xíbií. I was trying to explain to him why she had malaria. I was starting to talk about mosquitoes and blood.

"No, no," Kóhoi stopped me in midsentence. "Xíbií is sick because she stepped on a leaf."

"What? *I* stepped on a leaf. I'm not sick," I answered, puzzled by his account of Xíbií's malaria.

"A leaf from above," he said, increasing the enigma for me.

"What leaf from above?"

"A bloodless one from the upper *bigí* came to the lower *bigí* and left a leaf. When the Pirahãs step on leaves from the upper *bigí*, it makes them sick. They are like our leaves. But they make you sick."

"How do you know it is a leaf from the upper *bigí*?" I inquired.

"Because when you step on it you get sick."

I questioned Kóhoi further about this and then spoke with several other Pirahãs about it. It turns out that for the Pirahãs the universe is like a layer cake, each layer marked by a boundary called *bigí*. There are worlds above the sky and worlds beneath the ground. I recognized this as similar, though not identical, to the beliefs of the Yanomami, who also believe in a layered universe.

Just as *bigí* has a wider scope of meaning than I initially imagined possible, so did another major environmental term, *xoí*. Originally, I believed that *xoí* simply meant "jungle," because that is its most common use. Then I realized that it in fact labels the entire space between *bigís*. That is, it can refer to "biosphere" or "jungle," somewhat like our word *earth*, which can refer either to our planet or to just the soil on the planet's surface. If you go into the jungle you say, "I am going into the *xoí*." If you tell someone to remain motionless, as when sitting in a canoe or when a stinging insect lands on them, you say, "Don't move in the *xoí*." If it is a cloudless day you can say, "The *xoí* is pretty." So the word is broader than merely "jungle."

These terms were revelations to me about different ways to conceive of the environment. But bigger surprises were in store.

One of the first was the apparent lack of counting and numbers. At first I thought that the Pirahãs had the numbers one, two, and "many," a common enough system around the world. But I realized that what I and previous workers thought were numbers were only relative quantities. I began to notice this when the Pirahãs asked me when the plane was coming again, a question they enjoy asking, I eventually realized, because they find it nearly magical that I seem to know the day that the plane is arriving.

I would hold up two fingers and say, "*Hoi* days," using what I thought was their term for two. They would look puzzled. As I observed more carefully, I saw that they never used their fingers or any other body

parts or external objects to count or tally with. And I also noticed that they could use what I thought meant "two" for two small fish or one relatively larger fish, contradicting my understanding that it meant "two" and supporting my new idea of the "numbers" as references to relative volume—two small fish and one medium-size fish are roughly equal in volume, but both would be less than, and thus trigger a different "number," than a large fish. Eventually numerous published experiments were conducted by me and a series of psychologists that demonstrated conclusively that the Pirahãs have no numbers at all and no counting in any form.

Before carrying out these experiments, however, I already had experiential evidence supporting the lack of counting in the language.

In 1980, at the Pirahãs' urging, Keren and I began a series of evening classes in counting and literacy. My entire family participated, with Shannon, Kristene, and Caleb (nine, six, and three at that time) sitting with Pirahã men and women and working with them. Each evening for eight months we tried to teach Pirahã men and women to count to ten in Portuguese. They wanted to learn this because they knew that they did not understand money and wanted to be able to tell whether they were being cheated (or so they told us) by the river traders. After eight months of daily efforts, without ever needing to call the Pirahãs to come for class (all meetings were started by them with much enthusiasm), the people concluded that they could not learn this material and classes were abandoned. Not one Pirahã learned to count to ten in eight months. None learned to add 3 + 1 or even 1 + 1 (if regularly writing or saying the numeral 2 in answer to the latter is evidence of learning). Only occasionally would some get the right answer.

Whatever else might be responsible for the Pirahãs' lack of acquiring the skill of counting, I believe that one crucial factor is that they ultimately do not value Portuguese (or American) knowledge. In fact, they actively oppose some aspects of it coming into their lives. They ask questions about outside cultures largely for the entertainment value of the answers. If one tries to suggest, as we originally did, in a math class, that there is actually a preferred response to a specific question, this is unwelcome and will likely result in a change of conversational topic or simple irritation.

As a further example of this, I considered the fact that Pirahãs would "write stories" on paper, which I gave them for this purpose at their request. These inscriptions consisted of a series of identical, repetitive, usually circular marks. But the authors would "read" the stories back to me, telling me something about their day, about someone's sickness, and so on—all of which they claimed to be reading from their marks. They might even make marks on paper and say Portuguese numbers, while holding the paper for me to see. They did not care at all that their symbols were all the same, nor that there are such things as correct and incorrect written forms. When I asked them to draw a symbol twice, it was never replicated. They considered their writing to be no different from the marks that I made. In classes, we were never able to train a Pirahã to draw a straight line without serious "coaching," and they were never able to repeat the feat in subsequent trials without more coaching. Partially this was because they see the entire process as fun and enjoy the interaction, but it was also because the concept of a "correct" way to draw is profoundly foreign.

These were interesting facts, which I began to suspect could be linked to a larger fact about the Pirahã culture. I just had no idea yet what this larger fact might be.

I next noticed, discussing this with Keren and with Steve Sheldon and Arlo Heinrichs, that the Pirahãs had no simple color words, that is, no terms for color that were not composed of other words. I had originally simply accepted Steve Sheldon's analysis that there were color terms in Pirahã. Sheldon's list of colors consisted of the terms for black, white, red (also referring to yellow), and green (also referring to blue).

However, these were not simple words, as it turned out. They were phrases. More accurate translations of the Pirahã words showed them to mean: "blood is dirty" for black; "it sees" or "it is transparent" for white; "it is blood" for red; and "it is temporarily being immature" for green.

I believe that color terms share at least one property with numbers. Numbers are generalizations that group entities into sets that share general arithmetical properties, rather than object-particular, immediate properties. Likewise, as numerous studies by psychologists, linguists, and philosophers have demonstrated, color terms are unlike other adjectives or other words because they involve special generalizations that put artificial boundaries in the spectrum of visible light.

This doesn't mean that the Pirahãs cannot perceive colors or refer to them. They perceive the colors around them like any of us. But they don't codify their color experiences with single words that are inflexibly used to generalize color experiences. They use phrases.

No numbers, no counting, and no color terms. I still didn't understand all this, but the accumulation of evidence was beginning to give me a better idea, especially as I studied more Pirahã conversations and longer narratives.

Then I found out that Pirahã also lacks another category of words that many linguists believe to be universal, namely, quantifiers like *all, each, every,* and so on.

To appreciate this fact, it would be useful to look at the closest expressions Pirahã has to these quantifiers (I have put the quantifierlike words from Pirahã and English in boldface):

> *Hiaitíihí hi ogixáagaó pió kaobíi*
> "**The bulk of** the people went to swim/went swimming/are swimming/bathing, et cetera." (Literally, "the *bigness* of the people . . .")

> *Ti xogixáagaó itii isi ogió xi kohoaibaaí, koga hói hi hi Kóhoi*
> *hiaba*
> "We ate **most** of the fish." (Literally, "My bigness ate [at] a
> bigness of fish, nevertheless there was a smallness we did not
> eat.")

This latter sentence is the closest I have ever been able to get to a sentence that would substitute for a quantifier like *each*, as in *Each man
went to the field*.

> *Xigihí hi xogiáagaó xoga hápií. Xaikáibaísi, Xahoáápati pío,*
> *Tíigi hi pío, ogiáagaó*
> (Literally, "The **bigness/bulk** of men all went to the field,
> Xaikáibaísi, Xahoáápati, Tíigi their **bigness** went.")

> *Gátahai hóihii xabaxáigio aoaagá xagaoa koó*
> "There were (a) few cans in the foreigner's canoe." (Literally,
> "Smallness of cans remaining associated was in the gut of
> the canoe.")

However, there are two words, usually occurring in reference to an
amount eaten or desired, which by their closest translation equivalents,
"whole" (*báaiso*) and "part" (*gíiái*), might seem to be quantifiers:

> *Tíobáhai hi báaiso kohoaisóogabagaí*
> "The child wanted/wants to eat the **whole** thing." (Literally,
> "Child muchness/fullness eat is desiring.")

> *Tíobáhai hi gíiái kohoaisóogabagaí*
> "The child wanted/wants to eat a **piece** of the thing." (Liter-
> ally, "Child that there eat is desiring.")

Aside from their literal meanings, there are reasons for not interpreting these two words as quantifiers. First, they can be used in ways
that real quantifiers could not be. The contrast in the following examples shows this. Someone has just killed an anaconda. Kóhoi utters the
first sentence. Then someone takes a piece of the snake before it is sold

to me. Kóhoi utters the second sentence, in which *báaiso* (whole) is still used in Pirahã. This would not be acceptable in English.

> *Xáoói hi paóhoa'aí xisoí báaiso xoaboíhaí*
> "The foreigner will likely buy the entire anaconda skin."

> *Xaió hi báaiso xoaobáhá. Hi xogió xoaobáhá*
> "Yes, he bought the whole thing."

To understand why this exchange is important for showing that Pirahã has no quantifiers, let's first compare it with the English equivalent. Imagine that someone, a store owner perhaps, says to you, "Sure, I'll sell you *all* the meat."

You then pay him the money for the entire piece of meat.

But then the store owner takes away a piece of the meat in front of you before wrapping and giving you the rest. Do you think the store owner did something dishonest? If you do it is because the word *all* in English, when used precisely, means that there is nothing left over, that every bit of something or every member of a set of entities is affected. English speakers, and others with a word like *all*, would not describe what just happened as the store owner selling *all* the meat—only, perhaps, a large portion of it. Linguists and philosophers refer to these properties of quantifier words as their truth conditions. Truth conditions are the circumstances under which speakers will admit that a word is used correctly or not. It is true that these can vary. So a child might say, "All the kids are coming to my party," but neither they nor their parents actually believe that all children in the world, the country, the state, or the city will be coming—just a number of the child's friends. In this sense, the child is not using *all* in its most precise meaning, but he or she is using it in an equally acceptable way. The point is that the truth conditions in Pirahã never include the precise, quantifierlike meaning of *all* (where *all* means "every single entity in a set") for any word in their language.

We see this because in the example above a Pirahã will always repeat, in spite of taking away a piece of the anaconda skin, that "he bought the whole anaconda skin." If the word really meant "all" this would not be possible. So Pirahã lacks quantifiers.

This accumulation of discoveries about Pirahã culture challenged me to look in more detail at some of the less obvious values of their society. I went about this mainly by studying their stories.

Pirahã conversations and stories took up most of my time in the village, since they clearly embodied the beliefs and values of the society as a whole, revealing these in ways that I could not learn nearly as well by simply observing the culture. The subjects of their stories were also revealing—the people do not talk about unexperienced events, such as long past or far future events, or fictional topics.

One story that I have always enjoyed is the story told to me by Kaaboogí, the day that he killed a panther (a black jaguar), perhaps weighing as much as three hundred pounds (my estimate is based on the size of the head and the fact that four Pirahãs could not carry the entire body back to the village). He brought its head and paws to the village in a basket for me to see.

In the original telling of the story, immediately after his presentation of the head and paws, there were more details. He told me that he was out hunting and that his dog got a scent and ran ahead. Then he heard his dog yelp and suddenly stop. He ran to see what had happened and saw half of his dog on one side of a log and half on the other side of the log. As he approached to look more closely, he saw a black blur out of the corner of his right eye. He carried with him a 28-gauge single-shot shotgun that I had bought him the year before. He turned and fired with this pathetically small weapon and some of the buckshot went into the panther's eye. The panther fell to the side and started to get up. Since the shotgun didn't eject shells automatically, Kaaboogí quickly knocked the spent shell out with a stick and reloaded—he had three shells with him. He fired again and broke the panther's leg. Then he shot and killed it. The head of this panther was much larger than mine and the paws were large enough to completely cover my hand. The claws were about half as long as my fingers. The canines, when extracted with their roots, were more than three inches long, solid ivory.

When I got Kaaboogí to sit down to tell me the story for the tape recorder, he told it as it is on the following pages. In presenting the story here, I have removed most of the technical linguistic details so that it flows better. Talking to people from very different cultures, as this story shows, involves much more than merely getting the word meanings right. One can translate every word well and still have a hard time understanding the story. This is because our stories include unstated assumptions about the world that are made by our culture. I numbered the sentences to simplify following the story.

Killing the Panther

1. *Xakí, xakí ti kagáihiaí kagi abáipí kodi.*
   Here the jaguar pounced upon my dog, killing him.

2. *Ti kagáihiaí kagi abáipí kodi. Xaí ti aiá xaiá.*
   There the jaguar pounced on my dog, killing him. It happened with respect to me.

3. *Gaí sibaíbiabdbdopiiá.*
   There the jaguar killed the dog by pouncing on it.

4. *Xi kagi abáipísigiaí. Gaí sii xísapikobdobiíhaí.*
   With respect to it, the jaguar pounced on the dog. I thought I saw it.

5. *Xaí ti xaiá xakí Kopaíai kagi abáipáhai.*
   Then I, thus the panther, pounced on my dog.

6. *Xaí Kopaíai kagi abáipá haii.*
   Then the panther pounced on my dog.

7. *Xaí ti gáxaiá. Kopaíai xáaga háia.*
   Then I spoke. That this [is the work of] a panther.

8. *Xaí kopaí ti gái. Xaki xisi xísapi kobabáopiíhaí.*
   Then I spoke with respect to the panther. Here is where it went. I think I see [where it went].

9. *Mm ti gáxaiá. Xakí xísaobogáxaiá xai.*
   Uh, I said. The jaguar then jumped up on the log.

10. *Giaibaí, kopaíai kági abáipáháii.*
    As for the dog, the panther pounced on it.

11. *Kopaíai xíbaikoaísaagáhai.*
    The panther killed the dog by hitting it.

12. *Xaí kapágobaósobáíbáohoagáixiigá xaí.*
    Then when I had gunshot the jaguar it began to fall.

13. *Kaapási xaí. Ti gáí kaapási kaxáowí kobáaátahaí.*
    To Kaapási I spoke. Throw a basket [to me].

14. *Xí kagihoi xóbáaátahaí. Kagi abáipí.*
    Throw me a basket. [It is] to put the dog into.

15. *Sigiáihí xaí báóhoipaí. Xisao xabaabo.*
    The cat is the same. It pounced on the dog.

16. *Kopaíai xisao xabaabáhátaío. Xaí xabaabáátaío.*
    The panther pounced on the dog. Thus it caused him to
    be not.

17. *Xí kagigía xiowi hi áobísigío. Kagigía xiowi.*
    Put the jaguar into the same basket with the dog.

18. *Hi aobisigío xabaabátaó. Hi agía sóxoa.*
    Put it in with the dog, he caused the dog to be not. He
    has therefore already [died].

19. *Xísagía xíigáipáó. Kagihoi xoáobáhá xaí.*
    You have the jaguar parts in the basket. Put the basket on
    your head.

20. *Giaibáihi xaí xahoaó xitaógixaagahá xai.*
    The dog then at night smelled him for sure then.

21. *Kagi xí gií bagáihí kagi abáboitaá híabá.*
It is right on top of the dog. It pounced on the dog and killed him.

22. *Kagi aboíboítaásogabaisai. Xóóagá.*
It wanted to pounce on the dog. It really wanted to.

23. *Xaí ti gáxaiá xaí Kaapási hi ísi hi . . .*
Then I was talking, then Kaapási he, animal, he . . .

24. *Káapí xoogabisahaí. Kapáobíigaáti.*
Don't shoot from far away. Be shooting down on it.

25. *Xi ti boítáobíhaí. Xíkoabáobáhátaío xísagía.*
I moved quickly down toward the action onto the trunk, [I] killed it, thus it changed [died].

26. *Xí koabáobíigáhátaio. Xíkahápií hiabahátaio.*
It was dying. It wasn't able to leave therefore.

27. *Xigíxai xí koabáobáátaio. Xaí koabáobíigá.*
OK, then, it thus came to die. Then it was coming to die.

28. *Xaí Kaapási, xigía xapáobísáihí.*
Then Kaapási, OK, he shot it.

29. *Xaí sagía koábáobái. Xisagía sitoáopáó kahápitá.*
Then the animal thus changed and was dying. The animal stood up. It went away again.

30. *Koábáobáisaí.*
Its dying was lingering.

31. *Ti xagíá kapaigáobítahaí. Xitoíhió xíáihíxaí.*
I therefore shot it again, breaking its elbow.

32. *Ti í kapaigáobítahaí. Xaí ti giá kapáobíso.*
Then I shot it again. I then shot it again then.

33. *Koabái. Koabáigáobihaá xaí. Xisaitaógi.*
It came to die. It came to die. It had thick fur [a Pirahã way of saying that it was tough].

34. *Xí koaií. Hi abaátaíogíisai. Xisaitaógi.*
It intended thus to die. He did not move. It is really tough.

35. *Koaí hi abikwí. Gái xáowíí, xáowí gíxai, kobaihiabikwí.*
He had not died. [I said] "That foreigner, you [Dan] the foreigner, have not seen [a jaguar] dead."

36. *Xaí pixái xí kaapíkwí pixáixíiga.*
Then right away, [I] moved it, right then.

37. *Xaí báóhoipaí so Xisaitaógi sowá kobai.*
Then cats, Xisaitaógi [Steve Sheldon] has already seen.

38. *Xakí kagáihiáí, so kopaiai, Xisaitaógi hi í kobaihiabiigá.*
Here jaguars [he has seen], only panthers Steve Sheldon has not yet seen.

39. *Pixái soxóá hiaittíhí kapíkwí pixáixíiga.*
Now, the Pirahãs have just now shot [a jaguar], right now.

40. *Xaí hiaittíhí baaiowí. Baóhoipaí Kopaíaihi. Xigíai.*
Then the Pirahãs are intensely afraid of panthers. OK, I'm done.

This story about the panther that Kaaboogí killed is interesting in many respects. We know that it is a complete story because it starts by introducing the principal character immediately, the jaguar. And it ends with *xigíai*, a Pirahã word meaning literally "it is combined," and used generally for "OK." In this situation it means that the story is finished.

To non-Pirahã ears, the story can seem massively repetitive in many places, as in the number of lines at the beginning that repeat that the panther killed the dog. This repetition has a rhetorical purpose, however. First, it expresses excitement. But it also serves to ensure that the hearer can tell what is going on in spite of the fact that there is a lot of noise in the background, including many other Pirahãs talking simultaneously. And the repetition is also "stylish" for the Pirahãs—they *like* stories that have lots of repetition.

"Killing the Panther" is a typical text in that it is about immediate experience. This is a crucial parameter circumscribing all Pirahã stories. After noticing that Pirahã stories are always about immediate experience, I learned a new word that turned out to be the key to understanding many of the facts that were so puzzling about the Pirahãs.

The word is *xibipíío* (I-bi-PEE-o). The first time I remember hearing this word was in descriptions of the arrival of a hunter back from the jungle. As Xipoógi, perhaps the best Pirahã hunter, walked out of the jungle into the village, several Pirahãs exclaimed, "*Xipoógi hi xibipíío xaboópai*" (Xipoógi he *xibipíío* arrives).

I next noticed the word when Kóhoibiíihíai arrived home in his canoe from a fishing trip downriver, just outside the mouth of the Maici, on the Marmelos River. Upon seeing him round the bend in the river and come into sight, a child yelled excitely, "Kóhoibiíihíai is *xibipíío* arriving!"

But I heard this expression most frequently when planes landed and took off from the village. The first time I heard it in this context, I woke up in the morning, excited to see the plane after several weeks with my family in the village. I yelled to Kóhoibiíihíai, "Hey Ko! The plane will be here when the sun is straight above us!" He shouted back from his hut, upriver from mine, "I like to see the plane!" Then he turned and bellowed out to the other Pirahãs of the village, "Dan says that the plane is coming today." As noon approached, all the Pirahãs in the village began to listen. There were several false reports of the plane coming, mainly from children. "There it is!" they shouted, only to start giggling and admit that they hadn't seen or heard anything. Finally, minutes before I heard the plane, a shout went up from almost the entire village simultaneously: *"Gahióo, hi soxóá xaboópai"* (The plane already comes). Then people ran to the nearest clearing and strained their eyes to try to be the first to see the plane as it appeared in the clouds. Everyone shouted almost simultaneously, "Here comes the plane! *Gahióo xibipíío xaboópai.*"

When the plane left, they shouted a similar expression, *"Gahióo xibipíío xopitaha,"* as it disappeared over the horizon, heading back to Porto Velho.

Such observations gave me an initial guess as to the word's meaning. It meant something like "just now," as in "He is just now arriving," or "The plane is just now leaving." This guess seemed to work pretty well, and I began to use the word in my own speech. Pirahãs appeared to understand what I was saying whenever I used the word.

Then one night Xaikáibaí and Xabagi, an old man who had recently moved to our village from an upriver Pirahã village, came to my house. I had just extinguished my kerosene lamp a few minutes before their visit and didn't want to bother with it again. So instead I switched on my flashlight. But while we were talking, the batteries of my flashlight began to go out. I went to the kitchen and got some matches, just as the batteries bit the dust. In the pitch-black night, I continued talking to Xaikáibaí and Xabagi. Xabagi suddenly dropped a couple of fishhooks that I had just given them. I used my matches to help us search for the precious fishhooks on the floor. The match began to flicker. The men commented, "The match is *xibipíío*-ing." I heard this word used this way on another night about the flames of a campfire that were beginning to go out. In these contexts, the Pirahãs were not using the word as an adverb.

Whoa! It doesn't mean "just now," I realized one afternoon. It is used to describe the situation in which an entity comes into sight or goes out of sight! So, I thought, when someone comes around a bend in the river, they are just coming into sight. And this explains why the Pirahãs use the word when things go out of sight too, like the plane disappearing on the horizon.

I still felt that I was missing something, though. There must be a more general cultural concept that includes both *coming into sight* and its opposite, *going out of sight*. I recalled that *xibipíío* could be used to describe someone talking when he or she just became audible or just left audibility, as when I talked mornings on my two-way radio with SIL members in Porto Velho, letting them know that my family was all right, ordering supplies, and so on.

Pirahãs overhearing me talking might say of a man's voice coming over the radio for the first time that morning, "The foreign man is *xibipíío* talking."

When a canoe came around a bend in the river, whatever Pirahãs happened to be around the village at the time came running out to the edge of the bank to see who it was. This just seemed like natural curiosity to me about who might be coming to their village. But one morning as Kóhoibiíihíai was leaving to fish, I noticed that a group of children were giggling and staring at him as he paddled. At the precise moment that he disappeared around the bend, they all shouted in unison "*Kóhoi xibipíío!*" (Kóhoi disappeared!) This scene was repeated every time someone came or left—at least some Pirahãs would comment, "He disappeared!" And the same when they returned around the bend. The disappearing and appearing, not the identity of the person traveling, were what interested the Pirahãs.

The word *xibipíío* seemed to be related to a cultural concept or value that had no clear English equivalent. Of course, any English speaker can say, "John disappeared," or "Billy appeared just now," but this is not the same. First, we use different words, hence different concepts, for appearing and disappearing. More important, we English speakers are mainly focused on the identity of the person coming or going, not the fact that he or she has just left or come into our perception.

Eventually, I realized that this term referred to what I call experiential liminality, the act of just entering or leaving perception, that is, a being on the boundaries of experience. A flickering flame is a flame that repeatedly comes and goes out of experience or perception.

This translation "worked"—it successfully explained to me when it was appropriate to use the word *xibipíío* (and a useful working translation is the best a researcher can hope for in this type of monolingual situation).

The word *xibipíío* therefore reinforced and gave a positive face to the pervasive Pirahã value I had been working on independently. That value seemed to be to limit most talk to what you had seen or heard from an eyewitness.

If my hypothesis was correct, then knowledge about *bigí* beings in other layers, spirits, and so on, must come from information supplied by living eyewitnesses. As counterintuitive as it might sound initially, there *are* purported eyewitnesses to the layered universe. The layers themselves are visible to the naked eye—the earth and the sky. And the inhabitants of the layers are also seen, because these other beings traverse the upper boundary, that is, come down from the sky and walk about our jungle. The Pirahãs see their tracks from time to time. The Pirahãs even see the beings themselves, lurking as ghostly shadows in the jungle darkness, according to the eyewitness accounts.

And the Pirahãs can traverse a *bigí* in their dreams. To the Pirahãs, dreams are a continuation of real and immediate experience. Perhaps these other beings travel in their dreams too. In any case, they do traverse the boundaries. Pirahãs have seen them.

One morning at three o'clock a group of Pirahãs was sleeping, as usual, in the front room of our tribal house. Xisaabi, one of the group, suddenly sat up and started singing about things he had just seen in the jungle, in his dream. "*TiI hiOxiaI kaHÁpiI. BAaxaIxAagaHA*" (I went up high. It is pretty) and so on, recounting a trip to the upper ground, the sky, and beyond. The singing woke me up but I wasn't bothered because it was hauntingly beautiful, echoing back from the opposite bank of the Maici, a full moon shining brightly, illuminating him clearly. I got up and walked to where Xisaabi was singing and sat down a few feet behind him. There were Pirahã men, women, and children, perhaps twenty or more, sleeping all around us on the *paxiuba* floor. No one was moving but Xisaabi. The moon was bright silver just above the silhouette of the trees, casting its pale light across the smooth surface of the Maici. Xisaabi faced the moon, looking across the water, and ignored me, though he clearly heard me sit down behind him. He had an old blanket gathered around him, covering his head, but not his face, and sang loudly, unconcerned that there were people sleeping, or at least pretending to be asleep, all around him.

The next day I talked to Xisaabi about his dream. I began by asking him, "Why were you singing in the early morning?"

"I *xaipípai*," he answered.

"What is *xaipípai*?"

"*Xaipípai* is what is in your head when you sleep."

I came eventually to understand that *xaipípai* is dreaming, but with a twist: it is classified as a real experience. You are an eyewitness to your dreams. Dreams are not fiction to the Pirahãs. You see one way awake and another way while asleep, but both ways of seeing are real experiences. I also learned that Xisaabi had used musical speech to discuss his dream because it was a new experience and new experiences are often recounted with musical speech, which exploits the inherent tones of all Pirahã words.

Dreams do not violate *xibipíío*, as I was beginning to refer to the cultural value of talking mainly about immediately experienced subjects. In fact, they confirm it. By treating dreaming and being awake as conforming to immediacy of experience, the Pirahãs could deal with problems and issues that to us would involve an explicitly fictitious or religious world of beliefs and spirits in terms of their direct and immediate experience. If I dream about a spirit that can solve my problems and my dreaming is no different from my conscious observations, then this spirit is within the bounds of my immediate experience, my *xibipíío*.

As I tried to absorb the implications of all of this, I wondered if there might be other applications of *xibipíío* in the culture or the language. Specifically, I began to rethink some of the unusual aspects of Pirahã culture and asked myself if these could be explained by the concept of immediate experience represented by *xibipíío*. I thought first about the expression of quantities in Pirahã.

I believed that immediacy of experience might explain the disparate gaps and unusual facts about Pirahã that had been accumulating in my thoughts and notebooks over the months. It would explain the lack of numerals and counting in Pirahã, because these are skills that are mainly applied in generalizations beyond immediate experience. Numbers and counting are by definition abstractions, because they entail classifying objects in general terms. Since abstractions that extend beyond experience could violate the cultural immediacy of experience principle, however, these would be prohibited in the language. But although this hypothesis seemed promising, it still needed to be refined.

In the meantime, I remembered other facts that seemed to support the value of immediate experience. For example, I recalled that the

Pirahãs don't store food, they don't plan more than one day at a time, they don't talk about the distant future or the distant past—they seem to focus on *now*, on their immediate experience.

That's it! I thought one day. The Pirahã language and culture are connected by a cultural constraint on talking about anything beyond immediate experience. The constraint, as I have developed my conception of it, can be stated as follows:

> *Declarative Pirahã utterances contain only assertions related directly to the moment of speech, either experienced by the speaker or witnessed by someone alive during the lifetime of the speaker.*

In other words, the Pirahãs only make statements that are anchored to the moment when they are speaking, rather than to any other point in time. This doesn't mean that once someone dies, the Pirahãs who spoke to him will forget everything he reported to them. But they rarely talk about it. Occasionally they will talk to me about things that they have heard that were witnessed by someone now dead, but this is rare, and generally only the most experienced language teachers will do this, those who have developed an ability to abstract from the subjective use of their language and who are able to comment on it from an objective perspective—something rare among speakers of any language in the world. So this principle has occasional exceptions, but only in very rare circumstances. In the day-to-day life of the people it is almost never violated.

This means that they will use the simple present tense, the past tense, and the future tense, since these are all defined relative to the moment of speech, but no so-called perfect tenses and no sentences that fail to make assertions, such as embedded sentences.

In an English sentence like *When you arrived, I had already eaten,* the verb *arrived* is situated relative to the moment of speech—it precedes it. This type of tense is fully compatible with the immediacy of experience principle. But the verb *had eaten* is not defined relative to the moment of speech, but relative to *arrived.* It precedes an event that is itself located in time relative to the moment of speech. We could just as easily have said *When you arrive tomorrow, I will have eaten,* in which case *eaten* is still before your arrival, though you will arrive *after* the moment of speech, that is, after the time that we are talking. Therefore, by the immediacy of experience principle, the Pirahãs do not have tenses like this, the perfect tenses of our grammar school days.

By the same token, neither will Pirahã allow sentences like *The man who is tall is in the room*, because *who is tall* makes no assertion and is not relative to the moment of speech per se.

The immediacy of experience principle accounts as well for Pirahã's simple kinship system. The kinship terms do not extend beyond the lifetime of any given speaker in their scope and are thus in principle witnessable—a grandparent can be seen in the normal Pirahã lifespan of forty-five years, but not a great-grandparent. Great-grandparents are seen, but they are not in everyone's experience (every Pirahã sees at least someone's grandparents, but not every Pirahã sees a great-grandparent), so the kinship system, to better mirror the average Pirahã's experience, lacks terms for great-grandparents.

This principle also explains the absence of history, creation, and folklore in Pirahã. Anthropologists often assume that all cultures have stories about where they and the rest of the world come from, known as creation myths. I thus believed that the Pirahãs would have stories about who created the trees, the Pirahãs, the water, other living creatures, and so on.

So I would ask speakers questions like Who made the Maici River? Where did the Pirahãs come from? Who made trees? Where did the birds come from? and so on. I borrowed and purchased linguistic anthropology books on field methods and followed these very closely to attempt to record the kinds of tales and myths that I thought every culture had.

But I never had any luck. I asked Steve and Arlo. I asked Keren. No one had ever collected or heard of a creation myth, a traditional story, a fictional tale, or in fact any narrative that went beyond the immediate experience of the speaker or someone who had seen the event and reported it to the speaker.

This seemed to make sense to me in light of immediacy of experience. The Pirahãs do have myths in the sense that they tell stories that help bind their society together, since they tell stories about witnessed events from their particular vantage point almost every day. Repetitions of the stories recorded in this book, such as the jaguar story, the story of the woman who died in childbirth, and others count as myths in this sense. But the Pirahãs lack folktales. So "everyday stories" and conversations play a vital binding role. They lack any form of fiction. And their myths lack a property common to the myths of most societies, namely, they do not involve events for which there is no living eyewitness. The latter is at once a small and a profound difference. It is a small difference in the sense that the Pirahãs do have stories that bind their culture together, like all other human societies. But it is a profound difference because of the "evidentiary twist" imposed by the Pirahãs on their myths—there must be an eyewitness alive at the time of the telling.

I sat with Kóhoi once and he asked me, after hearing about my god, "What else does your god do?"

And I answered, "Well, he made the stars, and he made the earth." Then I asked, "What do the Pirahãs say?"

He answered, "Well, the Pirahãs say that these things were not made."

The Pirahãs, I learned, have no concept of a supreme or creator god. They have individual spirits, but they believe that they have seen these spirits, and they believe they see them regularly. When we looked into it, we saw that these aren't invisible spirits that they're seeing. They are entities that take on the shape of things in the environment. They'll call a jaguar a spirit, or a tree a spirit, depending on the kinds of properties that it has. *Spirit* doesn't really mean for them what it means for us, and everything they say they have to evaluate empirically.

As an example of this, consider the following story about an encounter with a jaguar, a story originally recorded by Steve Sheldon. Some Pirahãs interpret the story as about an animal only. But most understand it as an encounter with a spirit jaguar.

Xipoógi and the Jaguar
Informant: Kaboibagi
Recorded and transcribed by Steve Sheldon

Synopsis: Xitihoixoí, the one who is attacked by the jaguar, is only mentioned once by name, but everyone knows who he is. The jaguar struck and scratched him but otherwise he escaped unharmed.

1. *Xipoógi xahaigá xobabíisaihíai.*
   Xipoógi heard a brother call.

2. *Hi gáxaisai Xitahá. Xibigai soóxiai xísoi xaitísai.*
   He spoke, Xitahá's parent. What did the parent yell?

3. *Xipoógi gaigói. Hi xáobáopábá.*
   Xipoógi spoke. Go see.

4. *Hi gásaihíai Xipoógi. Xi baóhoipaíi xaitísai.*
   He spoke, Xipoógi. It is a jaguar.

5. *Hi gásai Xipoógi. Gí hóiiigopápí.*
   He spoke, Xipoógi. Throw your bow.

6. *Xí soxoá hí xabáií boáhoipáii Xitihoixoí.*
   The jaguar already grabbed Xitihoixoí.

7. *Hi gásaihíai. Boaí gí tipápí.*
   She spoke. Boai, you go [too].

8. *Hi xobaaopiíhaí.*
   You go see.

9. *Hi baóhoipaíoi aitísai.*
   The jaguar roared.

10. *Hi gásai. Xi káopápá baóhoipaíi.*
    She spoke. The jaguar went far.

11. *Xi soxoá híabáipí.*
    It has already grabbed him.

12. *Xí kagi xohoabá. Hi xaii ísi xioi boiigahápisaihíai.*
    Perhaps it ate the partner dog [*kagi*]. He took the dog with him.

13. *Hi xaigíagáxaisahai xipoíhió. Kaxaó xi baóhoipaíi kagi xaígióiigahápi.*
The woman spoke. Let's go; the jaguar may get away.

14. *Hi xaigía kagi xáobáha. Kagi xahápi. Hi giopaí oóxiai.*
He may have seen the dog partner. The dog partner left. The dog went into the jungle.

15. *Xísaigía hi xaigía hi gáxaisai. Híaigí xiigapí tagasága. Xií sokaopápaá.*
He spoke. Bring your machete. Sharpen the arrows.

16. *Hi baiaí hí xaagahá xipoíhió.*
The woman was afraid.

17. *Hi xaógaahoisaabai.*
He had become tired.

18. *Xi higí sóibáogíso.*
It hit him in the face then.

19. *Hi xoabahoísaihíai.*
It bit him.

20. *Hi xaigía hi xapiságaitáo.*
It scratched his arm.

21. *Hi boásoa gaitáopáhátaí.*
It scratched his shoulder.

22. *Hi gásaihíai kahiabáobíi.*
He [Itahoixoi] said, the arrows are all gone.

The claim that the Pirahãs see spirits is no more remarkable than similar claims by many Americans, to take but one example, who believe that prayers are answered, that they talk to God, and that they

see visions and spirits. Contacts with the numinous are claimed to
occur regularly around the world. For those of us who believe that such
spirits do not exist, it is absurd that they can be seen. But that is simply
our perspective.

Throughout history people have claimed to see these supernatural
entities. The Pirahãs are not that much different, if at all. In the pro-
logue, I gave one example of how the Pirahãs are eyewitnesses to spirits, and I have suggested that these spiritual encounters fall under the
principle of immediacy of experience. But the Pirahãs encounter many
kinds of spirits.

The kind of spirit most commonly spoken of is the *kaoáíbógí* (fast
mouth). This spirit is responsible for a range of good and bad things
that happen to the Pirahãs. It can kill them or give them useful advice,
depending on its whim. The *kaoáíbógí* belong to one of the two sets of
animate, humanoid creatures that populate the Pirahãs' world. The
first type are the *xíbiisi* (bloods), entities that have blood—like the
Pirahãs themselves, or foreigners, though the Pirahãs are not always
sure that all Americans have blood, because they are so white. But all
spirits, including the *kaoáíbógí*, are beings *xíbiisihiaba* (without blood;
literally, "no blood").

The other kinds of spirits are known by different terms, but the
generic term is *kapioxiai* (it is other). Again, people with blood in their
veins are *xíbiisi*. You can tell *xíbiisi* generally by the color of their skin—
their blood makes their skin dark. Those without blood, all spirits, are
generally light-skinned and blond. So dark-skinned peoples are
humans and light-skinned peoples are traditionally not humans,
though the Pirahãs will concede that some white people may in fact be
xíbiisi—mainly because they have seen me and a couple of other white
people bleed.

But there are lingering doubts that surface occasionally. After I had
worked with them for over twenty-five years, one night a group of
Pirahã men, sipping coffee with me in the evening, asked out of the
blue, "Hey Dan, do Americans die?"

I answered them in the affirmative and hoped that no one would
seek empirical verification. The reason for the question seemed to be
that Americans' life expectancy is much longer than the Pirahãs'. Arlo

Heinrichs still sends them pictures of himself and his wife, Vi, from time to time. Both of them look strong, healthy, and vibrant, even though they are in their seventies. This is fascinating to the Pirahãs.

Pirahãs occasionally talked about me, when I emerged from the river in the evenings after my bath. I heard them ask one another, "Is this the same one who entered the river or is it *kapioxiai*?"

When I heard them discuss what was the same and what was different about me after I emerged from the river, I was reminded of Heraclitus, who was concerned about the nature of identities through time. Heraclitus posed the question of whether one could step twice into the same river. The water that we stepped into the first time is no longer there. The banks have been altered by the flow so that they are not exactly the same. So apparently we step into a different river. But that is not a satisfying conclusion. Surely it is the same river. So what does it mean to say that something or someone is the same this instant as they were a minute ago? What does it mean to say that I am the same person I was when I was a toddler? None of my cells are the same. Few if any of my thoughts are. To the Pirahãs, people are not the same in each phase of their lives. When you get a new name from a spirit, something anyone can do anytime they see a spirit, you are not exactly the same person as you were before.

Once when I arrived in Posto Novo, I went up to Kóhoibííihíai and asked him to work with me, as he always did. No answer. So I asked again, "*Ko Kóhoi, kapiigakagakaisogoxoihí?*" (Hey Kóhoi, do you want to mark paper with me?) Still no answer. So I asked him why he wasn't talking to me. He responded, "Were you talking to me? My name is Tiáapahai. There is no Kóhoi here. Once I was called Kóhoi, but he is gone now and Tiáapahai is here."

So, unsurprisingly, they wondered if I had become a different person. But in my case their concern was greater. Because if, in spite of evidence to the contrary, I turned out not to be a *xíbiisi*, I might really be a different entity altogether and, therefore, a threat to them. I assured them that I was still Dan. I was not *kapioxiai*.

On many rainless nights, a high falsetto voice can be heard from the jungle near a Pirahã village. This falsetto sounds spiritlike to me. Indeed, it is taken by all the Pirahãs in the village to be a *kaodíbógí*, or fast mouth. The voice gives the villagers suggestions and advice, as on how to spend the next day, or on possible night dangers (jaguars, other spirits, attacks by other Indians). This *kaodíbógí* also likes sex, and he frequently talks about his desire to copulate with village women, with considerable detail provided.

One night I wanted to see the *kaodíbógí* myself. I walked through the brush about a hundred feet to the source of that night's voice. The man talking in the falsetto was Xagábi, a Pirahã from the village of Pequial and someone known to be very interested in spirits. "Mind if I record you?" I asked, not knowing how he might react, but having a good idea that he would not mind.

"Sure, go ahead," he answered immediately in his normal voice. I recorded about ten minutes of his *kaodíbógí* speech and then returned to my house.

The next day, I went to Xagábi's place and asked, "Say, Xagábi, why were you talking like a *kaodíbógí* last night?"

He acted surprised. "Was there a *kaodíbógí* last night? I didn't hear one. But, then, I wasn't here."

Very puzzling, I thought.

Peter Gordon and I were among the Pirahãs conducting experiments on Pirahã numerosity (linguistic and psychological expression and control of numerical concepts). Peter wanted to ask the Pirahãs about their spirits because he was interested in trying to situate his findings in his own understanding of Pirahã culture. Xisaóoxoi, the man with whom we were speaking, suggested, "Come tonight after dark. There will be spirits here." Peter and I said that we would come and then we continued working.

Afterward we returned to our campsite facing the village on the other side of the Maici. We planned to bathe, then have a dinner of canned meat. But we were pleasantly surprised by a man returning in his canoe from fishing, who rescued us from the canned meat by offering to trade a large peacock bass for a can of sardines, which we agreed to with alacrity.

Peter rolled the fish in a batter of eggs and oatmeal and roasted it on a rack of green wood over our campfire. After a bath and a nice dinner of burned clumpy oatmeal mixed with fish skin and white bass meat

(Peter's recipe didn't turn out well), we crossed back over to the village to see the spirits. I wasn't sure what to expect, because I had never been invited to see a spirit before.

It was dark, the sky resplendent with stars and a clear view of the Milky Way. Large river frogs were croaking. Some Pirahãs were seated on logs facing the jungle. Peter and I took our seats near them and Peter set up his Sony professional Walkman recorder, with a high-quality external microphone. Several minutes elapsed. Pirahã children were laughing and giggling. Little girls looked at us and again at the jungle, through the slightly spread fingers of their hands clasped across their faces.

After some delay, which I could not help but ascribe to the spirits' sense of theatrical timing, Peter and I simultaneously heard a falsetto voice and saw a man dressed as a woman emerge from the jungle. It was Xisaóoxoi dressed as a recently deceased Pirahã woman. He was using a falsetto to indicate that it was the woman talking. He had a cloth on his head to represent the long hair of a woman, hanging back like a Pirahã woman's long tresses. "She" was wearing a dress.

Xisaóoxoi's character talked about how cold and dark it was under the ground where she was buried. She talked about what it felt like to die and about how there were other spirits under the ground. The spirit Xisaóoxoi was "channeling" spoke in a rhythm different from normal Pirahã speech, dividing syllables into groups of two (binary feet) instead of the groups of three (ternary feet) used in everyday talking. I was just thinking how interesting this would be in my eventual analysis of rhythm in Pirahã, when the "woman" rose and left.

Within a few minutes Peter and I heard Xisaóoxoi again, but this time speaking in a low, gruff voice. Those in the "audience" started laughing. A well-known comical spirit was about to appear. Suddenly, out of the jungle, Xisaóoxoi emerged, naked, and pounding the ground with a heavy section of the trunk of a small tree. As he pounded, he talked about how he would hurt people who got in his way, how he was not afraid, and other testosterone-inspired bits of braggadocio.

I had discovered, with Peter, a form of Pirahã theater! But this was of course only my classification of what I was seeing. This was not how the Pirahãs would have described it at all, regardless of the fact that it might have had exactly this function for them. To them they were seeing spirits. They never once addressed Xisaóoxoi by his name, but only by the names of the spirits.

What we had seen was not the same as shamanism, because there was no one man among the Pirahãs who could speak for or to the spirits. Some men did this more frequently than others, but any Pirahã man could, and over the years I was with them most did, speak as a spirit in this way.

The next morning when Peter and I tried to tell Xisaóoxoi how much we enjoyed seeing the spirits, he, like Xagábi, refused to acknowledge knowing anything about it, saying he wasn't there.

This led me to investigate Pirahã beliefs more aggressively. Did the Pirahãs, including Xisaóoxoi, interpret what we had just seen as fiction or as fact, as real spirits or as theater? Everyone, including Pirahãs who listened to the tape later, Pirahãs from other villages, stated categorically that this was a spirit. And as Peter and I were watching the "spirit show," I was given a running commentary by a young man sitting next to me, who assured me that this was a spirit, not Xisaóoxoi. Moreover, based on previous episodes in which the Pirahãs doubted that I was the same person and their expressed belief that other white people were spirits, changing forms at will, the only conclusion I could come to was that for the Pirahãs these were encounters with spirits—similar to Western culture's seances and mediums.

Pirahãs see spirits in their mind, literally. They talk to spirits, literally. Whatever anyone else might think of these claims, all Pirahãs will say that they experience spirits. For this reason, Pirahã spirits exemplify the immediacy of experience principle. And the myths of any other culture must also obey this constraint or there is no appropriate way to talk about them in the Pirahã language.

One might legitimately ask whether something that is not true to Western minds can be experienced. There is reason to believe that it can. When the Pirahãs claim to experience a spirit they have experienced *something,* and they label this something a spirit. They attribute properties to this experience, as well as the label *spirit.* Are all the properties, such as existence and lack of blood, correct? I am sure that they are not. But I am equally sure that we attribute properties to many experiences in our daily lives that are incorrect. A man might claim that the bearded five-foot-nine-inch fellow he saw at the mall was Ringo

Starr, when in fact it was just me that he saw. And we talk about the beliefs and desires of our dogs as though we had evidence for them. When my dog sees me rise and go to the laundry room at 4:30 p.m., he gets up and wags his tail. I could say that he *knows* that I keep his food in there and that he *believes* I am about to feed him. But this could be little more than a response to a certain stimulus, rather than beliefs and knowledge on the part of my dog (though I believe he knows and believes).

But if all Pirahã myths must exemplify immediacy of experience, then the scriptures of many world religions, such as the Bible, the Koran, the Vedas, and so on, could not be translated or discussed among the Pirahãs, because they involve stories for which there is no living eyewitness. This is the main reason that no missionary for nearly three hundred years has had any impact on the Pirahãs' religion. The stories of the Abrahamic religions lack living eyewitnesses, at least as I practiced religion when I was religious.

Joaquim, like the other residents of the Apuriná Indian settlement of Ponto Sete on the Maici, had arisen early and gone about his tasks—tending his jungle garden and small manioc field, looking for signs of game for a possible evening hunting trip, and fishing in the clear Maici water upriver from his home. Like others at "Sete," Joaquim was broader and stronger-looking than the Pirahãs. His Tupi and Apuriná lineage endowed him with a muscularity that contrasted with the Pirahãs' intense leanness. With broad, strong feet from a lifetime without shoes, his powerful toes could grip the path securely, giving him greater stability than Westerners in expensive hiking footwear. He was a shy man, very quiet, about thirty years old, who smiled frequently, but always held his hand to his mouth when he did so in order to hide his missing front teeth. He purloined cups (plastic, nonbreakable cups are a favorite and hard-to-come-by item) from me from time to time when he thought I would not notice. He laughed at the Pirahãs as inferior. But he was after all a man who had faced the same hardships and environment as they, accumulating much more materially than they have—a fact that, while irrelevant to the Pirahãs, was clearly important to him. But he and the others at Ponto Sete believed that they and the Pirahãs were good friends. The Apurinãs at Sete always treated the Pirahãs well.

What Joaquim could not have known was that one village of Pirahãs did not accept him or any of the Sete residents as either close friends or as having legitimate claims to the land they occupied. The material differences between his way of life and Pirahã culture only distanced him further from the Pirahãs, and this village considered him an inferior interloper.

The Apurinãs made the tragic discovery of these Pirahãs' real estimation of them by a very indirect route. It began with a feud that developed between the Apurinãs and the Colário family, a group of traders that did business with them and the Pirahãs.

The Colários, ostensibly evangelical Christians of the Assembly of God denomination, enjoyed dealing with the numberless, preliterate Pirahãs who would accept exchange goods in a volume far below market value for Brazil nuts, latex, *sorva, kopaiba*, and other jungle products. But they discovered that the Apurinãs followed market prices closely on their short-wave radio, prices that the Brazilian channel Radio Nacional announced daily.

One day the Apurinãs warned the Colários, who operated three boats, not to return to Ponto Sete, because they were cheats. When Darciel Colário defied this ban and returned, the Apurinãs opened fire on his boat with their shotguns. They destroyed many of his trade goods and shot holes in the cabin on his boat. Colário escaped injury by hiding behind his stove. He managed to turn his boat around without standing up and exposing himself to the blasts of shotgun pellets and beat a hasty retreat down the Maici. The Apurinãs thought that they had taught him a good lesson.

But the Colários were not successful river traders because they were pushovers. They were not going to take this lightly. Armando Colário referred to all Indians as *bichinhos*, little animals, and would certainly want revenge against these subhumans who had attacked his son. And his son Darciel's ethics were no different from his father's. I had myself threatened Darciel because he got the Pirahãs drunk and encouraged them to steal from me. I walked onto his boat the next time he came and told him that if he came up the Maici again I would throw him off, burn his boat in front of him, and let him swim back (intemperate braggadocio from a twenty-seven-year-old missionary). After I left the Maici to return to UNICAMP, the Colários put their plan for revenge into action.

Darciel and Armando decided to enlist the Pirahãs to help them teach the residents of Sete a lesson. They found some willing Pirahãs, a group of hotheaded teenagers led by Túkaaga (a name borrowed directly from the Portuguese *tocandeira*, a large stinging ant), son of Xopísi, the most prominent Pirahã at the village of Coatá, just down-

river from Sete. Darciel legitimized these teenagers' desire for adventure and their desire to show their toughness by giving them a new shotgun to drive off the residents of Sete. Darciel and his family wanted unfettered access to the Brazil nuts, hardwoods, and other jungle products near the Apurinãs' settlement, and many Pirahãs wanted that land free from competitors for fish and game. And the Colários also wanted revenge.

On the fateful day, Armando Apurinã, along with his oldest son, Tomé, and their wives, were upriver, just under a day's journey by canoe, to fish and hunt. Joaquim and his Pirahã brother-in-law, Otávio (Toíbaitií in Pirahã, the only Pirahã to marry an outsider), had remained at the village. While Otávio fished, Joaquim and his wife went to collect manioc and firewood. This is hard work. Manioc tubers are firmly attached to the soil and can be more than eighteen inches in length. Hard tugging and sometimes chopping are necessary to get each root out of the soil. The roots are then tossed into a large woven wicker basket. When the basket holds thirty to forty pounds of manioc, it is raised and secured around the head via a tumpline. Along with his burden of manioc, Joaquim collected some thirty pounds of firewood, which he carried in his arms, at right angles to and even with his abdomen. Walking back home he was so overladen that he was unable to look carefully from side to side as most men in the jungle would naturally do. But that was OK, Joaquim reasoned, because he knew the path well and there were unlikely to be any major predators this close to the village.

He had no way of knowing that lying silently in wait along the path was Túkaaga, with his new 20-gauge shotgun, accompanied by his friends Xowágaii and Bixí, two other teenagers from Coatá. None of these boys had ever harmed a human being. But they were all skilled hunters and expert killers of animals. As Joaquim and his wife neared them, talking about whether to fish or hunt after putting the manioc in the river to soak, Túkaaga waited and tensed. Joaquim's wife passed by, then Joaquim came into view. When he was about ten feet away, Túkaaga shot him in the midsection.

Blood spurted from Joaquim's crotch, thighs, and belly. The force of the blast, combined with the weight of the tumpline and the firewood in his arms, threw him violently to the ground. As Joaquim cried out in agony, his wife and her sister, Otávio's wife, Raimunda, ran to the sound of the shot. Raimunda took one look at Joaquim and went running to find Otávio to come help, while Joaquim's wife did what she could to stop the bleeding, stuffing mud and leaves into the wounds. Otávio helped get Joaquim to his hut, out of the hot sun, then paddled for all he was worth upriver to find Tomé and his father-in-law.

Joaquim was in agony this entire time, the 20-gauge shot having perforated his side and front and torn out chunks of flesh. He didn't die until evening. Tomé, Armando, and their wives received the news from Otávio that Joaquim had been shot by unknown assailants around the same time that Joaquim died. Tomé and Armando started back at once in separate canoes. They thought that the likely attackers were either the Colários or Parintintin Indians, but they had no suspicions of the Pirahãs at all. Tomé was stronger and more aggressive than anyone on the Maici River, including all the Pirahãs and river traders. Everyone who knew his temper walked softly around him. The muscles in his arms and legs were as well defined and as impressive as many a professional bodybuilder's. He could work all day with an ax, hunt all night, and fish the next day, never losing any sign of vigor. He rowed downriver furiously, without letting up. About midnight he was approaching Sete. He wanted to first check on Joaquim, not knowing he had already died, and set out right afterward to hunt down the cowards who had shot his brother-in-law without warning.

Boom! The shot rang out and echoed down the banks of the Maici. As Tomé and his wife rounded the last bend in the river before their village, their way lit only by starlight reflecting dimly off the surface of the Maici, someone fired at them. Tomé took most of the buckshot in his shoulder and back. He was blown out of the canoe into the river, along with his canoe paddle. As he began to sink to the depths of the Maici, his wife, Nazaré, struck by only a few pellets from the blast, quickly grabbed him by the hair and held his head above water. She grabbed an aluminum pan from the bottom of the canoe and, leaning forward to maintain a firm grasp on Tomé's hair, managed to paddle them to the shore using the pot in her left hand. Again, the Pirahã teenagers led by Túkaaga did not wait to see the results. They left immediately, running through the darkness back to their village, Coatá.

Armando, close behind, pulled his son out of the water. Of the four men who had lived at Sete, one had been murdered (Armando learned on arrival that Joaquim was dead) and one was severely wounded. Not knowing what to do, the survivors went downriver immediately after burying Joaquim, to Coatá, to seek protection from Otávio's people, the Pirahãs. For three days, Armando, Otávio, Tomé, and their wives stayed at Coatá with the Pirahãs, not knowing that they were guests of the families of their murderers. Neither did they comprehend that the Pirahãs at Coatá in fact despised Armando, Tomé, and the Apurinã women. Months later, Xopísi, the main man at Coatá, told me, laughing, that they didn't finish off the Apurinã men from Sete because they were in the middle of the village and Pirahãs could have been hurt. And they did not want to harm Otávio, unless he accidentally got in the way.

Tomé was in very serious condition, but a trader arriving to buy Brazil nuts was persuaded to take him to the hospital in Manicoré, about a two-day trip downriver. In spite of his wounds and the fact that they were infected, Tomé survived and made a full recovery. As he was in the hospital, though, his family, all the survivors from Sete, learned that it was the Pirahãs who had attacked them and that no Pirahã wanted them to remain on the Maici. Even Armando's Apurinã brother, Aprígio, who lived downriver at Terra Preta (Black Earth), was forced to leave, with his Diarroi wife and their two sons.

After more than fifty years, the Pirahãs were expelling the Apurinãs from the Maici. It was a terrible shock. The Apurinãs left to face a life of indentured servitude as they went to Brazilian settlements on the Marmelos River, downriver a day's canoe trip from the mouth of the Maici. They were allowed to stay only if they would work all day, every day, without pay for the Brazilians whose land they had been relocated to. Tomé swore revenge on the Pirahãs and sent threats via river traders. His family persuaded him not to try. The Pirahãs were waiting for him and would surely have killed him had he returned to the Maici. He knew this too. No one can come onto the Pirahãs' land without their knowing. At the same time, the Pirahãs feared Tomé. They knew that he was as familiar with the Maici and its forest as they were. And they had no doubt that he would be a formidable foe.

The broken band of residents of Sete and Aprígio knew that they could no longer call the beautiful, nurturing Maici their home. Within two years, most of the Apurinãs were dead, except for Tomé, his wife, Aprígio's son (and Tomé's cousin) Roque, and Otávio's wife, Rai-munda. Otávio stayed only a short time off the Maici with his Apurinã wife and family. He eventually returned alone to live with his people again, as all the Pirahãs desired. Armando died, perhaps of poison. No one knew exactly how he had died, only that it had been sudden. His wife and daughter poisoned themselves. Several years later, Aprígio also died.

The Apurinã experience illustrates the dark side of Pirahã culture. While the Pirahãs are very tolerant and peaceful to one another, they can be violent in keeping others out of their land. It also shows us once again that tolerance toward a group of outsiders and coexistence with them does not mean long-term acceptance. The Apurinãs had believed that a lifetime among another people could overcome the differences in culture and society that separated them from this other people. They learned the deadly lesson that these barriers are nearly impossible to overcome, in spite of appearances over time—just as residents of the former Yugoslavia, Rwanda, and many other places have learned in the course of history.

But there is another lesson to take away from this story. It concerns the fate of Túkaaga himself. Just a few months after murdering Joaquim and attempting to murder Tomé, Túkaaga was living alone, away from all other Pirahã villages. A month or so after his isolation, he was dead in mysterious circumstances (meaning that the Pirahãs by and large did not want to talk about it—some said he died of a "cold," which is possible). I think he may have been killed by fellow Pirahãs. All the Pirahãs felt eventually endangered by what Túkaaga had done, after police came to investigate Joaquim's death. And the Pirahãs had heard rumblings that nearby settlers were considering a punitive attack against them. Initially, the Pirahãs told me that they were not afraid, though it was obvious to me that they were, in spite of their bravado.

They realized as they talked more about the reaction against them for Joaquim's murder that in fact many Pirahãs could die. This may be why Túkaaga was ostracized. Ostracization is an extreme form of punishment in the Amazon, where social cooperation is necessary for protection, for help in hunting and gathering food, and so on.

We already know that the Pirahãs do not need to have a chief or laws or regulations to exercise control over their members. Survival and ostracism are all they need. Túkaaga learned a hard lesson. His two helpers were never punished, so far as I can tell. Both are friends of mine, though I never ask about Túkaaga or the death of Joaquim anymore.

The most common challenges the Pirahãs face are disease and incursions into their land by people from other parts of the world—especially divers, fishermen, and hunters from a variety of countries, including Brazil. Japanese sport fishermen and Brazilian commercial fishing boats on the Marmelos have been a frequent sight, the visitors paying the Pirahãs in sugarcane rum, cloth, manioc meal, and even relatively expensive trade items, like canoes, to help them locate fish, through a caboclo intermediary. They also suffer ill effects from trade with caboclos, who usually only give them sugarcane rum in exchange for food and jungle products. Rather than cause offense and risk a dangerous encounter with any of these outsiders, the Pirahãs will often give them all the food that they have to placate them.

The solutions that the Pirahãs needed outside help with most were demarcation of their land, to prevent the incursions, and medicines against the diseases. Keren and I helped them with the latter regularly. But I was sensing a stronger responsibility to help them with the former too. The need for a reservation became more obvious as we traveled in by river to their village, learning more about the caboclo culture that enveloped the Pirahãs. Although we flew to the Pirahãs on our first family visit, which was cut short by malaria, on our next trip we went by boat to the Maici.

We intended to stay longer this time, most of the year, and boat travel was cheaper than plane travel for getting in the bulk of our supplies. I had a more personal reason to prefer boat travel—to avoid airsickness. We arrived at the docks in Porto Velho for our first long family visit with our goods packed in fifty-five-gallon metal barrels, fuel containers, wooden crates, suitcases, duffel bags, and cardboard boxes. Dockworkers came running to "help." But I had learned from others that if they touched just one bag they extorted large sums. So I shooed them all away and carried all the cargo alone, down a very steep mud bank, across a foot-wide, bouncy gangplank, onto the leaking *recreio*. All of these supplies would need to be transported multiple times, across lengthy stretches of muddy, flooded paths and the fresh tracks of big jungle animals (once with the animal, a puma, still visible).

Looking back now, I wonder if we were aware of the possible impact of all those goods on the Pirahãs. I think we must have assumed that this huge quantity of supplies, to meet the needs of a California family for a year, would not bother the Pirahãs. We never considered living any other way at this point in our careers. Luckily for us and for the Pirahãs, I think we turned out to be right, but not because of any insight or carefully reasoned conclusions on our part. The Pirahãs never showed much interest in our things, never tried to steal them (except food), and never asked for them. They always seemed to think of our things as not related to them in any significant way.

In any case, river travel became our preferred way of getting to the village over the next couple of years. We could take more supplies, thus extending our stays, and we also were able to stop at small settlements along the way and get to know the Brazilians who lived near the Pirahãs. Many of these people went regularly to the Pirahãs to trade with them.

As I got to know these people, I learned one thing that disturbed me: many of them were interested in the Pirahãs' land. Often they asked why the Pirahãs should be given this prime hunting and fishing ground. *"Mas, Seu Daniel, porque aqueles bichinhos têm direito à toda aquela terra bonita e os civilizados não?"* (But, Mr. Daniel, why do those little creatures have rights to all the beautiful land but civilized people do not?) This kind of talk worried me because I could easily imagine some of these folks moving onto the Pirahãs' land and trying to take bits or even large sections away from them. I knew I should help the Pirahãs get a legally recognized reservation, but I wasn't sure how to go about it.

By now, my family and I had been in Brazil for many years. After I finished my Ph.D. we decided to spend a year in the United States so that I could do postdoctoral work at the center of my linguistic world, the Department of Linguistics and Philosophy at the Massachusetts Institute of Technology, in Cambridge, Massachusetts—the department of Noam Chomsky, whose theory of grammar had become so influential in my professional life.

After we had been at MIT for five months, however, I received word via Dr. Waud Kracke, an anthropologist at the University of Illinois, Chicago Circle, that the Brazilian National Indian Foundation (FUNAI) wanted me to join them on an expedition to identify the boundaries of an officially recognized reservation for the Pirahãs. I agreed to this enthusiastically.

I would need to travel all night from Boston to Rio de Janeiro and then do another seven hours of puddle-hopping flying to Porto Velho. The FUNAI had invited me to help them determine the extent of land to be reserved for the Pirahãs. The FUNAI representative who invited me was known to me simply as Xará (shaRA). He held a senior position in the FUNAI. Xará had spent a couple of years traveling around the lands of the Pirahãs, the Mundurucus, and the Parintintins, and he wanted to see to it that they all had fully legal reservations to maintain their traditional way of life. He was of medium height and build, handsome, with a full black beard and long hair, traveling with his pretty blond Brazilian companion, Ana. Simultaneously serious and laid-back, always dressed casually, they reminded me of a couple of concerned hippies. But they spent their time trying to help guarantee that the Indians of Brazil could carry on their way of life by at least keeping the land of their ancestors.

Xará and I had become friends during his visits to the Pirahã village of Posto Novo, where I worked from 1977 to 1985. We had talked at length about the Pirahãs' need for a reservation. Xará had renewed his career within the FUNAI and had risen to a place where he had the authority to organize an expedition to identify a reservation for the Pirahãs and Parintintins (the first step in a three-stage process of demarcating Indian land). He sent an inquiry to Waud, who studied Parintintin culture, and me to see if we could go to Brazil to help as interpreters, since we were then the only outsiders known who spoke these languages. The FUNAI, Xará said, could pay for our expenses within Brazil, but we would have to cover our international travel.

Waud then called me and suggested that Cultural Survival, an organization founded by the late Harvard anthropologist David Mayberry-Lewis for the preservation of traditional ways of life for endangered groups, might be willing to pay my way down. Mayberry-Lewis responded to my request immediately and assured me that Cultural Survival would be delighted to purchase my ticket to Brazil for such an important mission.

I had been trying since 1979, to no avail, to get the relevant officials interested in protecting the Pirahãs' land from the growing threat of incursion from the outside. I had appealed to four separate FUNAI directors in Porto Velho (the brothers Delcio and Amaury Vieira, who served in succession; Apoena Meirelles, who actually visited me in the village to discuss the possibility; and a director I only knew by the name of Benamor), practically begging for the establishment of a reservation. Amaury sent a FUNAI employee in for two weeks in the early eighties to get a feel for the place, but then he was replaced. Benamor simply told me, "No one wants to live out there with those Pirahãs and their language. It sounds like they are crying all the time."

I was excited to have the opportunity to travel the entire length of the Maici River, something I had never done, and to visit *all* the villages of the Pirahãs. There was so much I wanted to see and learn, including whether all Pirahã villages looked the same as the villages I had already seen and whether all Pirahãs spoke the same dialect and would understand my form of their language. During my first several years among the Pirahãs, I had spent almost all my time at Posto Novo, which lies at the river's mouth. I had yet to travel to the other Pirahã villages because they were more remote and difficult and expensive to get to.

The FUNAI had invited me to come on this trip to serve as an interpreter. I was to translate their stories and answers for a FUNAI anthropologist who was interested in their traditional patterns and areas of land use. His job in turn was to interview all known Pirahãs along the Maici about the land and to then chart out what lands they used now and what parts they might claim as theirs traditionally.

After hours of travel, I arrived at Humaitá. I had to find a boat to take me to the Maici, so I caught a cab and asked the driver to take me the two miles to the banks of the Madeira. I could have walked there, but by this time the temperature was nearing one hundred degrees and

I was hot and tired. Dozens of wooden-hulled, mostly unpainted and rickety-looking boats were at the dock. Not knowing anyone and being uncertain whether the FUNAI would actually reimburse me for the boat rental, I just asked who was available, hoping to get the cheapest ride possible. I approached two brothers who owned a precarious-looking wooden tub about twenty-five feet long. One was under the stern, as boat owners on the Amazon system often are, trying to fix a leak. The other brother was staring lazily from his hammock at me as I approached the banks, clapping my hands in the Brazilian equivalent of knocking where there are no doors.

"*Olá*" (Hello), I called out above the noise of boat motors, shouting boat mechanics, and children running around the bank playing and yelling.

"*Olá*," he replied impassively.

"I wonder if you would be able to rent your boat to take me to the Maici River. The FUNAI will pay you when we arrive at the Maici."

"But if the FUNAI is not there?" the fellow in the hammock quizzed me skeptically.

"Then I will pay you myself," I promised him.

I didn't know this man, but he said, "OK, we'll take you."

"Great. Let me have lunch and then we'll leave."

"Fine," he responded.

I ran upstream along the bank and stopped at one of the dozen or so eating houses.

"*Quero um prato feito, por favor*" (I want a made plate, please), I announced to the heavyset woman behind the wide plank that served as the bar. A made plate is most commonly a large heaping plate of meat, beans, rice, and spaghetti, covered in yellow, Grape Nuts–consistency manioc meal.

"*Você quer carne ou peixe ou frango?*" (Do you want meat, fish, or chicken?), the woman asked.

"*Todos*" (All of them), I answered hungrily.

In less than ten minutes a steaming hot plate of oily food was put in front of me with a plastic bottle at the side full of *tucupi*, a yellow sauce made from cooked manioc juice with chili peppers. I ate the entire plate in about five minutes, washed it down with a liter of ice-cold Brazilian lager, Brahma, and paid about three U.S. dollars for it all.

"*Obrigado*," I said perfunctorily as I headed out the door to the dock.

"*Pronto?*" (Ready?) the boat owner asked.

His brother was now out of the water and fueling the engine.

"Yes, let's go," I answered.

I walked up the narrow plank and tossed my two small bags on board. I took out my hammock and hung it in the main (very small) cabin. Then I went onto the prow.

"How long will it take us to get there?" I asked, uselessly—it would take what it would take and there was no other boat.

"If we go all night, we will be there by noon tomorrow."

It was now about 3 p.m. The engine cranked over and came to life, *putt-putt*ing loudly.

"*Embora!*" (Away!) came the shout.

As we began to pick up speed, heading down the mighty Madeira, the still, hot air gave way to a refreshing breeze off the water. The effects of my trip, the meal, the beer, and relief to be under way made me suddenly sleepy again. I went to my hammock. The warmth, the breeze, and the comfort of the hammock had a predictable effect on me—I slept most of the voyage, except for a few minutes of lucidity here and there and a breakfast of hard crackers, sweet black coffee, canned butter, and some milk. During one three-hour period coming up the

Marmelos River, I watched the beautiful dark waters go lazily beneath us, thinking again of how fortunate I was to be able to experience this dream world. The high banks of the Marmelos, formed of sandy earth, strongly contrasted with the thick mud banks of the Madeira.

We arrived nearly twenty-four hours later, true to the owner's prediction. I awoke from a final doze to the sounds of animated talk from some Pirahãs on shore. No mistaking the Pirahãs when they were excited—they were loud and full of laughter and exclamations. My hammock was swinging gently as the boat slowed and pulled up next to another boat near the river path to a Pirahã village at the mouth of the Maici River. The other boat, already moored, was larger. I had expected perhaps two FUNAI employees to be waiting for me, but standing on deck staring at me were representatives of two Brazilian government agencies, an anthropologist and a cartographer from the FUNAI, and a specialist in land claims from INCRA (National Institute for Colonization and Agrarian Reform).

As soon as I appeared on the deck of the small vessel, the Pirahãs started shouting and calling my name. The brothers who had taken me there asked if they would be safe. "As long as you're with me," I joked (but they believed me).

"Hey, Dan. Where is Keren?" the Pirahãs asked.

"The boat she was on sank and sat on the bottom of the Maici. She drowned, I'm afraid."

For about half a second the Pirahãs all gawked at me. Then they broke out in laughter. All the Brazilians watching this exchange stared in amazement.

"At first when we were ordered to wait at the mouth of the Maici for an American linguist, I was upset," the FUNAI anthropologist, Levinho, admitted to me. "Why should Brazilians wait for a gringo to interpret for them in Brazil? But now I understand. We have been here for three days and haven't been able to understand or communicate one thing to them."

We interviewed Pirahãs at each village about their concept of the land they were on, how they used it, if they thought of individual Pirahãs as owners of the land, and so on. Levinho asked the questions and I interpreted. From there we traveled slowly up the Maici, stopping at each Pirahã settlement we encountered. We took Kóhoibiíihíai as

our guide, because his Portuguese was the closest to functional, in
order to avoid missing hidden settlements just out of sight from the
river. For each of the settlements of Pirahã (ranging from a single
nuclear family to several families in size), the boat would pass the village going upriver, then turn with its engine off to approach with the
current, and I would stand on the bow, yelling at the village in the
Pirahã language, "It is Dan with some non-Pirahã friends. We have
come to talk to you." Then Kóhoi would add that no one meant any
harm, that we had fishhooks to give away, and otherwise put people at
ease. As Pirahãs I had never met stepped onto the boat, some of the
men would speak with me excitedly. The women and children just
stared at me from the bank or from their huts as I climbed the bank to
the village.

After a week with the FUNAI team delineating the Pirahãs' reservation, my job as interpreter was done. We had reached the Transamazon
Highway, which I saw now for the first time. Since there were no Pirahã
villages above the highway, FUNAI gave me a choice: remain with the
boat for another two weeks while they descended the Maici slowly and
then the Madeira to Manaus, or hitchhike back to Porto Velho on the
Transamazon. I chose to hitchhike, so the boat let me off at the bridge
over the Maici, a small wooden structure that looked totally inadequate
to support the weight of the heavy trucks that regularly rolled over it
full of logs or minerals, from the mining company Mineração Taboca,
some two hundred miles to the east.

   We had learned many things during this trip. The FUNAI cartographer learned on our fifth day that the Brazilian government's map of
the area, produced by aerial photography, was wrong. Over coffee one
morning he said that we would not make the next village for two or
more days at our current speed. This worried us because we were running low on food and fuel. I turned and asked Kóhoi if the next village
was close or far. He said that the next village was Toitoi's and that we
would be there by noon. I relayed this to the FUNAI cartographer. He
said, "Well, I'm not going to argue with a Pirahã about his own river,
but if he's right, the army's map is wrong." About noon we pulled up to
Toitoi's village. The cartographer looked at the map carefully. Then he

realized that the central section of his map, representing the Maici between Kóhoi's village and Toitoi's village, had been inadvertently duplicated by the person who made the map for the army. This was a very important lesson for the Brazilian government.

For the Pirahãs and for me the results were even better. The Pirahãs now had an officially identified reservation. The long bureaucratic process of getting a reservation approved for them could now begin. Levinho and I talked for hours and hours about Pirahã culture. He was fascinated by the absence of creation myths. He tried very hard to get some from the Pirahãs, but could not. He was also fascinated by the absence of oral history and oral literature. Levinho was probably the first person ever to get me to think about how unusual this is. His enthusiasm was contagious. Eventually a friend of his, Marco Antonio Gonçalves, a Ph.D. student in anthropology from Rio, came to study Pirahã culture.

I met, and got to know the name of, nearly every living Pirahã. They were fascinated by me. They had heard of the white man who spoke their language, but most of them had never seen me. The children and women in particular stood openmouthed as I addressed them in Pirahã. At every village, I was invited to come back with my family and live among them. This was an attractive possibility, because I noticed that the Pirahãs farther upriver that I was now meeting made virtually no effort to throw pidgin Portuguese into their conversations. The Pirahãs downriver often knew Portuguese verbs, and when they spoke Pirahã with me, they tried to use these verbs, in an effort to help, no doubt. But their use of even a little Portuguese adversely affected my ability to learn natural Pirahã. I could see that by moving to a village upriver I would encounter much less Portuguese "static."

So this trip seemed to be positive for everyone involved: the Pirahãs, the Brazilian government, science, and me.

10 Caboclos: Vignettes of Amazonian Brazilian Life

Caboclos are by and large descendants of Amazonian indigenous peoples who now speak only Portuguese, are integrated into the regional economy, and consider themselves Brazilians rather than members of a tribe. The Pirahãs call caboclos *xaoói-gíi* (authentic foreigners; the suffix *-gíi* means "authentic" or "real"). Americans and other foreigners, including Brazilians from the city, are simply *xaoói*. The Pirahãs relate better to the caboclos because they see them more often and because they and the caboclos share the same environment and many of the same skills of hunting, fishing, canoeing, and knowledge of the jungle.

Caboclo culture has impinged on the Pirahãs almost daily for more than two hundred years. It is a macho culture, not unlike the cowboy culture I was raised in. But it has another side, an aspect of stoicism, almost fatalism, that is hard to find in most U.S. subcultures.

The Pirahãs' knowledge of the outside world is almost exclusively gained from their contact with caboclos. Americans and caboclos have very different values. And the Pirahãs see these differences, usually favoring the caboclo view because it is more like their own.

For example, Americans and caboclos see the human body differently. Caboclos are more uniformly judgmental about laziness and being overweight than Americans. In general, caboclos believe that working hard is a sign of health, good character, and stewardship of God's blessings. If you are healthy enough to work, God must be watching out for you. Fat means corruption to most caboclos. Overweight people are lazy idlers who take more than they need for themselves. Hence, even among fairly well-off caboclos (and there are a few), there is a strong work ethic. It is common to find caboclos who never need to work again clearing their own fields, swinging a machete, or going into the jungle to search for products with their employees. These values are to some degree shared by the Pirahãs—leanness, toughness, knowledge of the jungle, hunting, fishing, and self-reliance.

To understand the Pirahãs' view of outsiders and where I fit in, I realized that I would need to understand caboclos. But since I was not going to build a house and live among caboclos, my knowledge of them would have to come from occasional personal contact. And the most common contact with caboclo culture occurred during river travel.

One trip in particular stands out. I was taking a dentist and my cousin, who was trained to check vision and fit glasses, to visit the Pirahãs, to offer dental assistance and (free) eyeglasses. At the dock in Porto Velho, I saw a boat that I hadn't noticed before. It was a large, newish-looking vessel with a sign that announced trips to Manaus and Manicoré, the latter a small town near the mouth of the Madeira. These boats were nearly the only means of long-distance transport known by the caboclo population of the Amazon River system.

I descended the riverbank, steep during this dry-season month of July, and walked the narrow plank onto the boat. I asked for the *dono* (owner).

A bare-chested, bald man about forty-five years old, five feet ten, approached and declared, "*Eu sou o dono*" (I am the owner).

Like all men working the Amazonian system, he was strong, and his skin was weather-hardened and tan. Like most donos, his body showed that he enjoyed easy access to food and drink. He was wearing white but soiled bermuda shorts and flip-flops—the ubiquitous footware of the Amazon.

"When are you leaving for Manaus?" I queried.

"*A gente vai sair lá pelas cinco horas da tarde*" (We are going to leave about 5 p.m.), he answered politely and confidently.

On our way to town, I highlighted the pleasures of traveling by *recreio* on the Madeira River for my traveling companions.

"You guys are gonna love this! The breeze from the movement of the boat, the birds and wildlife, the jungle, one of the biggest rivers in the world, and Brazilian cooking!"

About 3:30 p.m., thanks to my prodding, we got to the boat and all of us crossed the plank, enthusiastic and joking. We did notice that several trucks were still being unloaded into "our" boat, but assumed that this work would be done soon and that we'd be under way as promised by five o'clock. After hanging our hammocks, we bought some ice-cold fresh coconuts, with straws in openings in their tops to drink their sweet liquid. Refreshed and relaxed, we talked about the upcoming trip, watching the stevedores toil in the waning sun, under their burdens of boxes, butane bottles, and bananas (tons of them) on their way to market in Manaus. We expected them to finish soon, because it was now after five. There did seem to be a lot of trucks, though—too many I thought to be unloaded in an hour, but that was OK. Being an hour or so late is common in the Amazon. Six o'clock came and went. I went to the dono and asked when he expected to leave.

"*Daqui a pouco*" (Shortly), came the jovial reply.

I informed my traveling companions. The dono said he would supply a free dinner to all of us. That was a good deal, I thought, because on these trips there was generally no dinner served the first night. Then I noticed something curious: no more passengers had come on the boat in all of this time, except for one lean, muscular, and quite drunk fellow, wearing a cowboy hat over his face as he snored in his hammock.

After dinner, cargo from a number of trucks was still being loaded below the decks and on the lower deck of the boat. It was almost comical. How much could this boat carry? It already had about twice as much as I would have imagined possible. Seven o'clock came, then eight. At 9:30 I asked what the hell was going on.

"Oh, sorry. We cannot leave tonight; I'm still waiting for more shipments," replied the dono matter-of-factly.

There was no other boat leaving. We had no car to return to the SIL center. The mission had already picked up the *kombi* (Volkswagen minibus) we had rented. We had to make the best of it. Bugs were out, especially mosquitoes. We got in our hammocks and spent a predictably unpleasant night. I remembered then, too late, that Brazilians who travel the rivers avoid boats they don't know. Since this boat was new to the Porto Velho–Manaus route, people were avoiding it until they had a chance to know whether it was reliable, safe, inexpensive, served good food, and so on. Or so I figured.

When morning finally came, I noticed that other passengers had come on board—as though everyone except us gringos knew that the boat would only leave in the morning. So much for my vast experience. About 10 a.m., after a breakfast of syrupy-sweet, extremely strong coffee, hard crackers, and canned butter (I really like it), we were finally off. My small group went to the top deck and enjoyed the breeze, talking comfortably two decks above the boat's loud motor. We were under way! All of us eventually settled into our hammocks to read and relax in the shade and breeze.

At about 4 p.m., though, the boat came to a sudden stop. The other passengers informed me that we had run aground on a sandbar—again the crew's inexperience was showing. For the next twenty-four hours the captain worked to get us off the sandbar. After hours of trying to move us with a combination of the boat's own engines and his outboard motorboat, he sped off in the late afternoon. At about 3 a.m. he returned with two other larger boats, though both were considerably smaller than our boat. My traveling companions woke me up.

"Dan, we're in danger!"

They motioned me to follow them. I went to the first deck and looked through an opening in the floor to see the dono and the captain trying to fix the steering. Water was coming in slowly where they were working (because they had loosened gaskets). "We're going to sink, Dan," my friends exclaimed.

"We *are* sunk," I responded. "We're sitting on a damned sandbar. We cannot sink further."

The new passengers that had boarded after us were all poor. Anyone with any money, unless they were going to visit the Pirahãs, would have either flown to Manaus or not made the trip at all. Though tourist brochures touted this kind of trip as a pleasure cruise, one glance at any *recreio* was enough to put the lie to this claim. These were almost all precarious-looking vessels, worn and abused. The poor used them for lack of other options. Passengers were wearing flip-flops, with a few pairs of cowboy boots and Nike and Reebok footwear scattered here and there. Most women wore tight shorts and halter tops, a few jeans and blouses. Many of the men wore long pants, though most wore shorts; some were bare-chested, but others wore T-shirts with political slogans, polo shirts, or brightly patterned short-sleeved shirts. They all looked fit and tan and spoke animatedly to one another. Brazilians are talkative and always fun on such voyages, the pleasure of the trip and freedom from their routines combining to raise their awareness, humor, and the enjoyment of interaction with strangers, even unusual-looking gringos.

We chatted with some of the passengers, though the fellow from the night before wearing a cowboy hat was beginning to annoy me. He was still drunk. He was about fifty, but very fit. He kept trying to speak Spanish with me (many Brazilians know that Americans are much more likely to understand Spanish than Portuguese). Even though I answered him in fluent Portuguese and told him that I had made this trip many times before, he kept poking me in the chest aggressively and telling me things like "This boat goes to Manicoré; you have to sleep in hammocks on this boat; everyone here speaks Portuguese," and other trivialities. I would try to walk away but he kept following me about. This continued for several hours—extremely irritating. People noticing strangers and harrassing them is a growing phenomenon in northern Brazil.

An experience that reveals to some degree the essence of being cabo-clo happened during a visit long ago on the Marmelos. I was traveling down the river in the rain with my family. We were leaving the Pirahã village after several months. Our trip would take us first to the Auxili-adora to board the *recreio* to Porto Velho, where we would catch a plane to São Paulo so that I could resume my doctoral studies at UNICAMP. This route, which we had taken to evacuate Keren and Shannon when they were stricken with malaria, had now become part of our yearly routine and we had come to enjoy it. People who had seemed strange in that first emergency trip with Keren now were acquaintances whose friendship we cherished.

As we approached the settlement of Pau Queimado, I saw a woman on the shore beckoning to us to stop. I didn't really want to stop because of the rain, but I knew that Amazonenses (Brazilians from the state of Amazonas) don't bother you unless there is a serious need. So I turned toward her; within a couple of minutes, the motor was off and we were paddling into shore.

"What is it?" I asked.

"My dad is very sick. Please come look at him."

We tied the boat to the shore. The same steep bank was between us and the houses that had been there when I was so desperately looking for help and feeling lost. Now it was our turn to be of service. Keren got our medicine kit, and with our kids trailing behind, we started up to the house.

The house was dark inside, the walls a combination of boards and poles from jungle trees. The roof was palm thatch, like most roofs in the area. The floor was wood, with large spaces between the boards, large enough to allow various reptiles and bugs to slither or crawl into the room. Indeed, the ubiquitous Amazonian cockroaches were to be seen in several dark places in the corners, large beetles over three inches long—the kind that spurted out white gunk if you stepped on them.

Unusually, since almost all caboclos in the Amazon sleep in hammocks, there was a homemade double bed in the corner with a mosquito net suspended above it, to be lowered at night. The bed was made of boards and palm wood poles, with a simple foam-rubber mattress on top, stained with years of droppings and drippings of substances I was not curious about. On the bed was the old man that everyone knew as Seu Alfredo (Mr. Alfred).

Alfredo was a master canoe maker, and his sons had learned the craft from him. Everyone in the area came to him for canoes. He made large *canoas* with a solid base of itauba wood and sides of four-by-one-inch boards, caulked like larger boats. And he made *cascos* (shells)—dugout canoes of solid itauba. No one made canoes like him. The Pirahãs liked him and said that he never tried to take their women, an unusual trait for a caboclo in the area, according to the Pirahãs.

Arlo Heinrichs had persuaded Alfredo to become a Christian, and he had lived his life since that time, more than twenty years, as a proponent of that faith. He was known throughout the area as a man who could be trusted, a kind man who visited the sick, sang hymns, and befriended everyone.

I had watched him on occasion pull up to a bank near a settlement in the early morning and get out of his canoe, with his ukelele in his hand. He would come up the bank and begin strumming a hymn, then singing and smiling to people as they went about their work in the center of the settlement—women carrying clothes to the river to wash, men getting their hunting gear together. Everyone smiled and stopped what they were doing to hear Alfredo sing, in a high-pitched voice, more enthusiastic than lovely, of how he was not afraid of tomorrow because he knew Jesus today. After singing for a while, he would visit with the sick and wander about the village, telling jokes and talking about how Jesus had changed his life. A one-man missionary organization.

It is a rare thing for a caboclo to be trusted among other caboclos, but Alfredo was both trusted and respected. He was the only man I ever knew in that area that no one voiced any suspicions of.

I approached him on his sickbed now and asked, "Are you ill?"

"Yes, I am very sick. Come closer. I can't see you," he whispered in a raspy voice.

As I drew nearer I could see that his arms were thin and his face grimaced with pain, and he was shivering.

"*Ah, é Seu Daniel!*" (Oh, it is Mr. Daniel!) he acknowledged.

A smell of diarrhea and vomit was in the air.

"Are you in pain? Would you like me to take you to the hospital in Porto Velho?"

I was one of Alfredo's admirers. He had always been so supportive of me, the white Protestant missionary, and never treated me as though he distrusted me.

"No, I am dying. I told my daughter that there was no need to call you. I will be dead soon."

As I looked at Alfredo's dark eyes, and saw his wizened, dark body, weakened by disease, immobile in the bed he had made for himself, I could feel a lump growing in my throat. Keren had tears in her eyes. The children were still at the doorway, staring.

"But let me help you, Alfredo. Surely the doctors in Porto Velho have medicines that can help you."

"No, Daniel," he replied. "One knows when one is dying. But there is no reason to be sad. I am happy to end this pain in death. And I can tell you that I am not afraid of death. I know that I am going to be with Jesus. And I am grateful that I had a long life and a very good life. I am surrounded by my children and my grandchildren. They all love me. They are all here for me. I am so thankful for my life and my family."

In his pain and his sickness and in spite of everyone's grief, Alfredo brought comfort and communicated a maturity and a fearlessness in the face of death that I had never seen before and have never seen since. I held his right hand. His daughter was rubbing his forehead with a moist cloth and crying. She thanked us for coming. Alfredo thanked us for coming.

"C'mon, kids," I said. "Let's go."

"What is it, Daddy? Is he dying?" Shannon asked.

Kristene and Caleb looked into the room, then at me.

"He is sure that he is dying, yes," I answered, barely keeping back the tears. "People here seem to know when death is near. But I hope you were all paying attention to Alfredo. He is unafraid. He has faith in Jesus. He knows he is going to heaven. That is how I want to die."

I felt as though I had been in the presence of a saint.

We turned down the family's offer of coffee and cookies, saying that we needed to get to the Auxiliadora and see some people before the *recreio* came to pick us up. As I started our motor and pointed the boat downriver, I began to think again, as I often did, about the character of these caboclos. I had learned from hardship that wherever you see a house along the Amazon or its tributaries, you had a haven. That family, one you had never met in your life, would come to your aid in time of need. They would let you stay with them. They would feed you. If need be they would paddle you out to the nearest help. They would give you their last possessions.

That is a code of the Amazon. You help the person in need today, because you may be the person in need tomorrow. I have never witnessed a clearer example of the golden rule.

One thing, however, I have never completely understood about caboclos is their racism against Indians. They say to me frequently, "Daniel, we are Indians who learned how to work. We are not lazy. No one gives us anything. We do not like the Indians because they beg and they always get more help than we do."

Interestingly, the caboclos themselves call Indians caboclos. Caboclos rarely refer to themselves seriously as caboclos. They refer to themselves as *ribeirinhos* (people who live at the river's edge) or, more commonly and simply, Brazilians.

This caboclo attitude toward Indians needs to be taken into account if you are looking for uncontacted or little-contacted Indians in the area. Often the caboclos are the only ones who actually know if there are Indians in the region. But you would never ask a caboclo, "Are there Indians around here who still speak their language?" If you wanted to find this out, the best way to ask, at least in certain regions of the Amazon, would be: *"Tem caboclos por aqui que sabem cortar a giria?"* (Are there caboclos here who know how to "cut" the slang?) The reason for this otherwise strange circumlocution is easy enough to discover if you talk to a caboclo long enough: they do not think of the Indians' speech as a real language, nor do they believe that the various Indian languages are in fact all that different from one another.

Caboclos believe that they are poor, and they will go to great lengths, even risking their lives, to improve their financial lot. Like most people in the Western economy, they want to get ahead. They feel their poverty desperately. The Pirahãs, on the other hand, though they have less materially than the caboclos, do not have a concept of "poor" and they are satisfied with their material lives. Caboclo interest in money was never more evident to me than during the gold rush days in Porto Velho, in the early 1980s. In those years, gold was discovered in the Madeira River and its tributaries. This was a boom time for the cities along the Madeira, especially Porto Velho. Many caboclos turned their industry to gold prospecting and became rich, at least for a little while. Prospecting was incredibly dangerous work and extremely hard. Caboclos with no training in diving at all volunteered to wear diving helmets and descend without lights, in the pitch black, fifty feet of muddy, fast-moving water, to the bottom of the Madeira, with anacondas, caimans, and stingrays, there to hold large vacuum hoses and move them slowly over the riverbed.

The barge above them supplied their air. Other caboclos on top worked at the filtering system that combined mercury and gravity to separate the gold from the dirt, rocks, and other debris being vacuumed up. Mercury pollution of the Madeira became a serious problem.

If the diver was sending up gold, they pulled on his air hose as a signal to remain where he was. This was extremely dangerous. If caboclos at a neighboring barge saw that the barge next to them was bringing up gold but theirs wasn't, things could get homicidal. More than one barge crew was killed by their neighbors. Then the encroachers would simply cut the air hose of the diver and send their own diver down to finish him off, if he was not dead already.

My friend Juarez, the son of Godofredo Monteiro, became a diver. He told me that the first time he descended, blood came out of his ears because of the pressure. "But you have to stick with it if you want to get rich," he advised me.

He did make some money. Eventually he brought up enough gold to pay off his father's debts, buy a house in town, and set himself up with an ice-cream stand and a keyboard for his budding singing career in the nearby town of Humaitá. Eventually the gold petered out, but the contributions that it made to the economy of Amazonas were only possible because of the industry of the caboclos and other poor Brazilians. The wealthy owned the barges but the poor mined the gold.

In addition to their hard work, this gold rush revealed more than once to me that caboclos have a hilarious sense of humor. During the gold rush, I saw a caboclo walking down the streets of Porto Velho in new clothes, with strings of money tied behind his back.

"What is that money there for?" I asked him.

"*Filho de Deus*" (Son of God), he began his response (a common Amazonian vocative expression—intended to be ironic). "I have spent my entire life chasing money. Now that I have found gold, money can chase me for a while."

Another example of caboclo humor comes from a night along the banks of the Madeira in the city of Humaitá. It was early evening, about 7:30, still *passear* time, when it is customary to stroll with your spouse, boyfriend, or girlfriend, and visit friends. It was warm and humid, but not uncomfortable, like a pleasant sauna. Some people gathered in the little plaza. The plaza pavement was of cracked gray concrete, surrounded by low whitewashed walls topped with slick red clay tiles that people could sit on. There were couples dressed in spotless, freshly laundered clothes, often white pants or shorts and bright-colored tops hanging attractively on their hard brown bodies. They were sitting around the plaza eating ice cream, popcorn, and sandwiches. Bugs of all sorts, including mosquitoes, gnats, wasps, and rhinoceros beetles, were flying into lights wherever they could find them. Two-wheeled carts stood at strategic points around the plaza, like New York hot-dog

stands, with electric lights and coals burning brightly in hibachis next to the carts, grilling kebabs. The carts carried the makings for sandwiches called *x-baguncas* (cheese messes—the Portuguese letter *x* is pronounced "shees," which is identical to the Brazilians' pronunciation of the English word *cheese*). At one end of the plaza an older woman sold sandwiches, while her grandson played with a plastic truck on the concrete pavement of the plaza, close by. At the other end of the plaza was the father. Both carts were doing brisk business. Their sandwiches were very good—ham, mashed potatoes, peas, mayonnaise, frankfurters, and cheese, all at once.

The little boy asked his grandmother something. She said no. He ran across to his father and cried, "Dad, Grandma says I can't have a Coca-Cola."

The little boy was very angry with his grandmother.

His dad looked at him and after a moment of silence offered a solution: "Let's go kill her, then," he said, with apparent sincerity.

The little boy looked at his father, puzzled. Then he responded emotionally, "No, Dad. We can't kill her. She's my grandma."

"You don't want to kill her?"

"No! That's Grandma!"

"OK, well, then I have to work."

"OK."

And the little boy ran back to his grandma. I could see the dad chuckling to himself.

The most influential aspect of caboclo life on the Pirahãs is their beliefs about the supernatural, conveyed in broken sentences and words borrowed from the *Lingua Geral* (the "general tongue" spoken throughout the Amazon during the early history of Brazil). The Pirahãs talk frequently about caboclo beliefs and ask me about them.

These beliefs are an amalgam of Catholic teachings, Tupi and other indigenous folktales and myths, and macumba—an African-Brazilian form of spiritism like voodoo. They believe in the *curupira,* a jungle elf (some say beautiful woman) who leads people into the center of the jungle because its feet point backward and the lost soul thinks it is leaving the jungle. They believe that the pink Amazonian river dolphin turns into a man at night and seduces young virgins.

I remember Godofredo telling me about this dolphin's transmogrification. He related an elaborate story of how the dolphin, transformed into a pale-skinned man, but still with his enormous and elongated penis, had impregnated an unfortunate girl near the Auxiliadora. After telling me the story, he asked, "Do you believe this, Daniel?"

"Well, I am sure that many people do," I answered.

"I do believe it," he said, trying to pressure me with my respect for our friendship to believe him.

Godofredo had two daughters when I met him, Sônia and Regina. Sônia was about my daughter Shannon's age and Regina was roughly Kristene's age. When Sônia was twelve years old, during a period when my family and I lived in the state of São Paulo while I was studying for my doctorate at UNICAMP, she and a girlfriend of hers from the Auxiliadora died suddenly with terrible abdominal cramps. From the description we received later by mail (Godo dictated a letter and had a friend take it by boat to Humaitá to mail it), which included vomiting up fecal material and an inability to defecate, we thought it sounded like intestinal blockage, though it could have been botulism or any number of other things.

Godo's diagnosis was typical of people of the region: "*Ela mixturou as frutas*" (She mixed her fruits). Caboclos, unlike the Pirahãs, are very superstitious about what they eat—mixing certain foods, they believe, can lead to a quick and painful death. For example, one must never drink milk while eating acidic fruits like mangoes.

Once we visited Godofredo when his son, Juarez, was recovering from a near-death case of falciparum malaria. Godo had watched Juarez writhe for days on the floor in fever, pain, and nauseated agony, yet had made no effort to get medical help for him.

"Why didn't you take him to the doctor in town?" I asked, somewhat perturbed. "I can still take him to the doctor if you like. I will pay all the expenses."

"Look, Mr. Daniel. Everyone dies when it is their time to die. That is why one doctor dies in the arms of another. Isn't that true? Doctors don't control death," came the sagacious caboclo reply.

A couple of years later, when Juarez was nearing his seventeenth birthday, I wanted to provide him with an opportunity to better himself financially. I sat down with Godo during a trip through the Auxiliadora to the Pirahãs.

"Godo, we both know that Juarez is a very smart young man. I have seen that he likes to work on record players and radios. I think that with good training, tools, and some financial help, he could start a shop and make good money. I have a friend in Porto Velho, an American radio technician named Ricardo, and he has agreed to teach Juarez his trade, to let him board with him and his wife, and then to supply him with tools when Juarez is done training. I am willing to pay for all of this. What do you think, Godo? I would like to take Juarez with me when I leave the village."

Godo put me off temporarily. "Let me think about this, Daniel. When you leave for Porto Velho, I will give you my answer."

A few weeks later, during a visit by Godo to the Pirahãs to trade for Brazil nuts, I boarded his boat to visit with him and drink some coffee.

"Daniel, I have thought a lot about your offer," Godo began. "I cannot accept it. You see, I need my son to work with me. I am too poor to hire help. But if he leaves and learns all these new things, I am sure that he will stay in the city and never come back here. He will stay and make money in Porto Velho or Humaitá and not help his father."

"But Godo," I pleaded, uncontrollably meddling in his family affairs because I was shocked at this selfishness, "you are ruining Juarez's future just for your own interests."

I was really upset. I noticed that Juarez and his stepmother, Cesária, were looking askance at us from the back of the boat, their heads down.

"Maybe I am ruining his future. Or maybe I am not. Only God knows, Daniel. But I know that I need Juarez here with me, now."

In complete exasperation, I gulped down the rest of my *cafezinho* (a small cup of strong black coffee) and excused myself to go back up the bank of the Maici to my house. I knew that Godo's attitude was typical of most caboclos. Children were for the economic help of the parents. People didn't waste their primary assets, their children. They were yours to do with what you wanted, and you wanted them to help you financially.

Years later Godo asked if he could still accept my offer. Juarez was in his midtwenties by this time. "No, Godo. Ricardo no longer lives in Porto Velho, so I don't know anyone there now who could train him."

Ultimately, Juarez's story became a tragedy, common enough among the caboclos. As I was completing the first version of this chapter, I learned that he had been killed in a motorcycle accident on the Transamazon Highway. I have nearly been killed more than once riding my motorcycle down the Transamazon. I thought long sad thoughts about Juarez and the miserable end of the promising young life whose potential was never realized.

Summing up caboclo culture fails to do justice to their rich system of beliefs and way of life. Ultimately, the caboclos had come to play as much a role in my life as the Pirahãs, as I immersed myself more deeply into the world of the Amazon. Like the Pirahãs, they have been among my dearest friends and my most exasperating acquaintances.

But I couldn't conclude even this cursory survey of them without mentioning their readiness to fight. Caboclos live by a code similar to that of John Bernard Books, John Wayne's final movie character, in *The Shootist*: "I won't be wronged, I won't be insulted, and I won't be laid a hand on. I don't do these things to other people and I expect the same from them." Amazonians will help you if you ask. They will give you their last food if you need it. But they are severely sensitive to slights or any sign that you think you are superior to them.

Sometimes just my white skin and foreignness offends this sensitivity. This is because many Brazilians have come to believe that Americans are racist and feel superior to all other peoples. Sometimes those offended by my mere presence feel it incumbent upon them to try to intimidate me for their friends to see.

Many times I have been asked, "*O que é você?*" (What are you?) or "What are you doing in Brazil?" or "What are you trying to steal from our country?"

The balance between showing toughness and using common sense is a vital one to acquire when traveling in the Amazon. The Pirahãs have learned this lesson. And so have the caboclos. Neither will back down if the odds are even. But both will avoid a fight if the odds are obviously against them. It took me some time to learn the lesson for myself, after committing mistakes that could have been very costly.

Once when my family was living with the tribe, an enormous boat, of a size normally seen on the Madeira, the Amazon, or the Rio Negro, three decks high and one hundred feet long, came up the Maici to our village. It was high water, so the boat seemed to be parked right in front of our house at the river's edge. The river was only a foot or so from the top of the bank then, though it is more than forty feet below the top in the dry season. The boat was so close and the river so high that the crew could peer into my house. The crew was large, perhaps as many as thirty-five men. I could see that they were staring at Keren and my daughters, now just past puberty. I reacted instinctively and boarded the boat, a thirty-year-old gringo, five feet nine and 155 pounds.

"What are you doing on Indian land?" I demanded of the owner, a huge man named Romano.

"We are looking for hardwoods," he replied coolly.

I looked around. One man on the crew had a white fleshy orb in the socket where I expected to see his eye. Another had a scar from his forehead to his throat, clearly from a knife. Another had a scar across his belly. I noticed that all of them were built better than I was, with rippling, well-defined muscles exuding power. But as an indignant father and husband, I ordered them off the Pirahãs' land.

"Who are you to tell us to leave?" Romano asked. "An American ordering Brazilians off Brazilian land?"

"The FUNAI *delegado* in Porto Velho, Apoena Meirelles, told me to make sure that no one came on this land without his permission," I responded truthfully but naively, simply not grasping how offensive this could be to a native-born Brazilian. I also did not realize that the FUNAI was largely irrelevant to caboclos, even though I could not function without the foundation's permission and support. This happened early on in my career, before I knew better.

I was ready to act. I didn't know what I would do if this turned out badly, though. I had no plan. But to my relief, after a silence during which the crew continued to stare at my house and Romano just looked at me, he suddenly ordered his men to start the boat and prepare to leave. He offered me coffee and we drank it, syrupy sweet espresso. He said goodbye politely and they pulled out. Another lesson I have learned: mean-looking people can in fact be nice.

Caboclos, like the Pirahãs, are isolated even from other Brazilians, something that the Pirahãs notice when other Brazilians or foreigners come onto their land. This was made clear to me years ago by caboclo reactions to members of the Projeto Rondon. This project was a government-sponsored initiative to aid the health of the poor of Northern Brazil and increase the social awareness of privileged Southern Brazilians by bringing teams of college students from the South to the more remote and primitive areas of Brazil for short visits to provide dental and medical care. Once when I arrived at the Auxiliadora, where Godofredo and Césaria still lived, some men called to me as I was passing the shade tree that they sat under. They were sipping iced-cold Antarctica beer, dressed in shorts with flip-flops, and shirtless.

"*Seu Daniel, como é que vai? Sabe rapaz, na semana passada tinha um grupo de estrangeiros do seu pais aqui. Falavam português enrolado que nem você!*" (Mr. Daniel, how is it going? Last week there was a group of foreigners here from your country. They spoke Portuguese poorly just like you!)

"A group from *my* country?" I asked, surprised that any group of Americans would ever travel to the Auxiliadora. "Where were they from?"

"They were here with the Projeto Rondon. They were all from São Paulo."

I walked away amused that to the caboclos there was little difference between a gringo from the United States and a Brazilian from São Paulo.

Part Two LANGUAGE

Caboclos, travel, and other experiences of the Amazon were ultimately just means to an end. My experiences in the region were
ordered around my struggle to figure out the grammar of
Pirahã. As I made progress, excruciatingly slowly, I realized that this
language was unusual—profoundly so. Initially I recognized this as I
analyzed the way it organized its sounds into words. I based my conclusions about its uniqueness on field research with Tzeltales in southern
Mexico, training with Comanche and Cherokee speakers in Oklahoma,
helping missionaries analyze other Amazonian languages, and wide
reading.

I usually did my serious work on the language in the loft of our tribal
house. It was built parallel to the river's edge to catch breezes. Our
house had a storeroom and a ceiling made of ax-hewn boards over our
sleeping areas (to prevent crawling, hopping, and slithering life from
falling on us while we slept and also to make those rooms a bit cooler).

The triangular space created between my thatched roof and board
ceiling was open on both sides, and there was enough room for me to
put a table and a couple of chairs up there for my linguistics work. I
referred to this space as my study. It was extremely hot in this relatively
closed space, and there were snakes, frogs, tarantulas, and other critters
in the thatch, but it gave a small bit of privacy from the village, so that
my language teachers and I would have fewer distractions. Access to
this space was by a homemade ladder nailed onto the living room wall
just below my desk.

When I worked in my study, I was so hot that my T-shirt clung to me
and my hair stuck to the sides of my head. But I learned to ignore that.
It was the animal life that continued to keep me alert and wary.

From time to time I would have to stop working while small frogs jumped out of the thatch in panic with snakes slithering behind them. None of the snakes were very large, but some were venomous. They lived in the thatch, which was apparently a great hunting ground. I learned to keep a hardwood club at my feet or on the chair next to me. When I heard the thatch above my head rustle, I would scoot back my chair, pick up my club, and wait. First a frightened frog would jump out. I tried to kill them too. (I wanted all life out of the thatch.) But they were too fast and small. Then I knew that whatever had frightened the frog would not be long behind, so I would wait. Several times a snake would poke its head out. Since I was waiting, the slithery pest was almost always a goner. *Wham!* The club would bang the snake's head against the thatch and support poles. I would toss the snake out into the jungle and go back to work.

I lived and breathed the Pirahã language while I was in the village. But my initial optimism about analyzing their language faded as I began to grasp just how difficult it was.

We have all seen Hollywood movies in which some explorer or scientist learns a tribal language fluently in just a short period of time. These seemed silly to me now as I struggled to learn more about this language and express myself in it. There were no textbooks. There was no one who could translate Pirahã sentences into Portuguese, except in the simplest paraphrases. Even after six months, I wasn't sure that I understood anything my teachers were saying to me. It got very discouraging at times. But I saw that three- and four-year-old Pirahã children learned the language and I dared to believe that I might eventually speak as well as a three-year-old.

Although linguistics was my intellectual pursuit among the Pirahãs, I never lost sight of the fact that I was being paid by churches and individual Christians to translate the Bible into the Pirahã language. However, in order to do this I needed a thorough understanding of the structure of the language. The two goals were at least compatible at this stage.

Pirahã has one of the smallest sets of speech sounds or phonemes in the world, with only three vowels (*i, a, o*) and just eight consonants (*p, t, k, s, h, b, g*, and the glottal stop *x*) for men and three vowels (*i, a, o*) and seven consonants (*p, t, k, h, b, g*, and *x*) for women (they use *h* both

where men use *h* and also where men use *s*). Women have fewer consonants than men. This is not unheard of, but it is unusual.

The term *glottal stop* will not mean much to many readers since it is
a sound that is lacking from the phonemes of most European languages, including English. But it is important in Pirahã. In English we
occasionally make the glottal stop in interjections, such as *uh-uh* (no).
Whereas a consonant like *t* stops the flow of air coming out of the
mouth just behind the teeth and a *k* cuts off the air with the back of the
tongue raised against the palate, a glottal stop is produced by closing
the vocal folds tightly and cutting off the flow of air before it gets into
the upper portion of the throat (the pharynx).

To appreciate how small Pirahã's list of sounds is, consider that English has approximately forty phonemes, depending on the dialect. And
English's inventory is by no means unusually large. Hmong of Vietnam
has over eighty. At the other extreme, only Rotokas (New Guinea) and
Hawaiian vie with Pirahã for smallness of phonemic inventory—both
have eleven phonemes, the same number as Pirahã men.

Some have asked whether a language can communicate complicated
information with only eleven phonemes. A computer scientist knows,
however, that computers can communicate anything we program them
to do, and that they do this with only two "letters"—1 and 0, which can
be thought of as phonemes. Morse code also has only two "letters," long
and short.

And that is all any language needs. In fact, a language could get by
with a single phoneme. In such a language words might look like *a, aa,
aaa, aaaa,* and so on. It's not surprising that there is no language
known with only one or two sounds, since the smaller the phonemic
inventory, the longer words have to be to provide enough information
for speakers to distinguish one word from another (otherwise they
would sound too much alike) and the harder it becomes for our brains
to tell words apart (words that are too long would require too much
memory to distinguish, among other problems). So if there were a
human language like the binary language of computers, humans would
need computerlike brains to use and recognize the very long words that
would be necessary. Imagine trying to tell a word of fifty consecutive *a*'s
apart from a word of fifty-one *a*'s.

There is therefore a tension between learning a large number of phonemes to keep words a more manageable size, versus learning fewer phonemes while letting words "grow" a bit. Some languages can be complicated in both ways. German has both long words and a large set of phonemes, for example.

A couple of English examples can help us see how we use phonemes to distinguish words. In the words *pin* versus *bin,* for most speakers the only way to distinguish which word means a small pointed fastener and which is a container is that one has the phoneme *p* and the other has *b;* otherwise the words are identical. This means that *p* and *b* are meaningfully separate sounds in English, unlike the two types of *p* in *pin* and *spin.*

In the latter words, the *p* of *pin* is aspirated, meaning that a puff of air is emitted with its pronunciation, whereas the *p* of *spin* is not aspirated. (You can see this by holding a piece of notebook paper about three inches from your mouth when pronouncing these words in a normal voice. The paper will bend forward with the "wind" of aspiration from the first word, but not the second.) For this reason, in our alphabet we distinguish between *p* and *b,* a meaningful distinction, but not between the two *p* sounds of *pin* and *spin,* since we can recognize such words with or without aspiration. (Audrey Hepburn, influenced by her native Dutch, tended not to aspirate consonants and most people hardly noticed.)

This distinction between some sounds according to their position in the syllable is important for linguists but is not meaningful in English—any English speaker will understand *pin* and *spin* whether or not the *p*'s in the words are aspirated.

In *sheet* versus *shit,* the difference in sound for a native speaker of English is found in the tenseness of the tongue in producing the vowels. However, since the second word uses a vowel not found in Romance languages, like Spanish or Portuguese, speakers from these languages can have embarrassing moments trying to distinguish such words, since the two sounds are separate phonemes in English but not in Spanish or Portuguese.

For an inventory the size of Pirahã's, words need not be quite so long as we might expect, however, because of two additional tools: context and the tones I mentioned earlier.

Context helps to distinguish meanings in all languages. Consider the

English homonyms *to* versus *two*. If I ask you, "How many did you say?" and you respond *tu* (spelled phonetically), we know that only *two* and not *to* could be meant in this context. In fact most potential ambiguities are avoided by context.

I sat one day with Kóxoí at the table under my thatched roof in order to learn more about the sound structure of Pirahã words. Keren appeared with a cup of coffee. She gestured at Kóxoí to see if he would also like a cup. Kóxoí smiled and said, "*Tí píai,*" which I immediately guessed to mean "Me too."

To check this out, I organized a few elicitation sentences to confirm my hunch, acting out and saying, "Kóxoí drinks coffee, Dan *píai,*" "Kóxoí drinks coffee, me *píai,*" and so on.

I recorded examples and isolated the phrases for *me too, you too, her too,* and so on. Then I asked Kóxoí to repeat them to me so that I could verify their pronunciation.

What he gave me was surprising and confusing.

He repeated, "*Tí píai.*"

I repeated.

He said, "Right, *kí píai.*"

"What did you say?" I asked with frustration and surprise. Why was he changing the pronunciation? Was there a more simple expression than I had thought?

"*Kí kíai,*" he repeated.

Now I was beginning to question my own sanity. Three different pronunciations in three repetitions. I was sure that the *k* sound, the *t* sound, and the *p* sound were meaningful units of speech—phonemes—of Pirahã. Phonemes are not supposed to be interchangeable! Change Tim to Kim to Pim in English, for example, and you don't just get alternative pronunciations, you get separate words.

"*Kí kíai?*" I asked.

"That's right, *pí píai*" came the exasperating answer.

In other repetitions, Kóxoí then gave additional pronunciations (again, the *x* represents the glottal stop of Pirahã): "*xí píai,*" "*xí xíai.*"

I wondered whether Kóxoí's pronunciation was just "sloppy" compared to other Pirahãs or whether some deeper principle of the language was being illustrated by this variation. It might be that this word was changing meaning in ways that I wasn't perceiving. Or it could just have been an example of "free variation"—a nonmeaningful difference in pronunciation, as in my Southern Californian alternative pronunciations of *economics* as "*ee*conomics" and "*eh*conomics," with no intended differences in meaning. I eventually concluded that it was indeed free variation.

I observed several other examples of this variation from many speakers. Some people gave me many pronunciations for a single word, like *xapapaí, kapapaí, papapaí, xaxaxaí,* and *kakakaí* for the English word *head.* Or *xísiihoái, kísiihoái, písiihoái, píhiihoái,* and *kíhiihoái* for *liquid fuel* (kerosene, gasoline, butane, etc.).

I saw that Pirahã allows an astonishing range of variation among consonants. This surprised me, especially in a language with so few phonemes. But at the same time I discovered that Pirahã makes such extensive use of tone, accent, and the weight of its syllables that the language can be whistled, hummed, yelled, or sung.

For example, the sentence *Káixihí xaoxaagá, gáihí* (There is a paca there) has a musical form. It is this musical form that is whistled or hummed or sung.

The vertical lines in the example indicate word boundaries. The notes between the lines are the musical representation of one word. The caret (∧) under a note indicates that the syllable is louder than other syllables in the same word. A whole note (hollow oval) represents the longest syllable type in the language (consonant + vowel + vowel) and a quarter note (black oval) represents the shortest syllable in the language (consonant + vowel). The other notes and length dots represent syllables of other lengths—Pirahã has five syllable lengths. The relative height of the notes, that is, the syllables, indicates the tone. A higher note is a syllable with high tone. A lower note is a syllable with low tone. A connecting line between two notes, a musical "tie," indicates that there is a movement from a low tone to a high tone or a high tone to a low tone, with no pause between the two end points. In the musical representation of *káixihí,* the first group of notes has a falling tone, followed by a short low tone, with a preceding break in the whistle (where the glottal stop would have been in *káixihí*), followed by another short break (where the *h* would be) and a short high tone, and so on. The word, without consonants or vowels, is stressed (volume-adjusted) according to syllable weight. Thus, the syllable boundaries are clearly present in whistle, humming, and yelling channels, all of which figure in this musical representation even though the phonemes themselves are missing.

There is no staff in my music analogy because Pirahã tones do not have precise pitches like musical notes (middle C on a piano keyboard produces sound waves of 256 hertz), but are relative. A high tone in Pirahã or any other tone language is not a specific number of hertz, but is simply made with greater frequency of vibrations in the vocal cords than a low tone.

I began to feel that there was a connection between the small number of phonemes and the presence of these "channels of discourse." I hypothesized that these channels were the key to understanding both the small number of consonants and vowels in Pirahã and the astonishing variation among the consonants. Since all these channels rely crucially on the fact that Pirahã words can be represented musically, we should try to understand a bit of what that musicality derives from.

First there are the tones. Each vowel in every word has either a high tone or a low tone, in a way similar to Chinese and other tone languages.

Linguistic tones evolve from a ubiquitous property of the world's languages, *pitch*, the relative frequency of vibration of the vocal cords. All languages use pitch to distinguish meanings. In English, for example, a rising pitch at the end of a sentence generally indicates a question, whereas falling pitch indicates a statement.

John is coming. (Statement, with falling pitch.)

John is coming? (Question, with rising pitch.)

In English punctuation, a period is used to mark falling pitch, while the question mark indicates rising pitch. When pitch is used to distinguish the meanings of sentences in this way, it is called *intonation*. There are many variations of intonation possible. To see just a glimpse of complexity in English's use of pitch and stress, consider one of my favorite examples, known among linguists as "stress clash override." When uttered alone, the word *thirteen* has higher pitch on the last syllable— "thirTEEN." And the word *women* has higher pitch on the first syllable, "WOmen." But put the two words together and what do you get? You don't get "thirTEEN WOmen," you get "THIRteen WOmen." Why? Because English, like several other languages, doesn't like two high-pitched, or accented, syllables next to each other. It prefers to have an alternating pattern—ACCENTED nonaccented ACCENTED nonaccented, and so on. So speakers of English change the accent on words like *thirteen* when they precede and modify other words, in order to get the result of alternating accents while at the same time maintaining the accent on the main word of the phrase, in this case the noun *women* in the noun phrase *THIRteen WOmen*. And no English-speaking child ever had to be taught this pattern of accents! They just do it. Figuring out how this is possible is one of the puzzles that make linguistics fun.

All languages, whether spoken in the deserts of Australia, the streets of Los Angeles, or the jungles of Brazil, use intonation. But many languages use pitch in another way as well. Although English uses pitch to change meaning in sentences, it does not use pitch to change the meanings of words, with some exceptions that can help us to understand what goes on in a tonal language like Pirahã or Chinese.

Consider what differentiates pairs of nouns and verbs like *CONtract* (noun) versus *conTRACT* (verb), *PERmit* (noun) versus *perMIT* (verb), and *CONstruct* (noun) versus *conSTRUCT* (verb). In these pairs, the noun has higher pitch on the first syllable, while the verb has higher pitch on the second syllable.

But while English uses pitch to distinguish meanings of only a few pairs of words, in tone languages, every syllable or vowel or word bears a distinctive pitch, called a *tone*.

I first learned this distinction, as I learned many things about the language, by committing an egregious error. Kóhoi and I were working on some terms that I thought might be needed for Bible translation, among other things.

I asked him, "When you like someone very much, what do you call him?"

"*Bagiái*," Kóhoi responded.

I tried putting the word to use right away. "You are my *bágiái*," I said, smiling.

"No!" he responded, laughing.

"What," I asked, "you don't like me?"

"I do like you," he said, giggling a bit. "I like you. You are my *bagiái.*" But there are *bágiái* and we don't like them," he clarified.

To help me get what he was saying, Kóhoi whistled the words for me, slowly. Then for the first time I heard the difference! The word for *friend* is *bagiái,* with a single high tone on the last *a:* "ba-gi-Ai." But the word for *enemy* has two high tones, one on each *a:* "bA-gi-Ai." That little difference is what separates friend from enemy in the Pirahã language. The words are related to the Pirahãs because *bagiái* (friend) means literally "to be touching"—someone you touch affectionately—and *bágiái* (enemy) means "to cause to come together." Culturally, though, *bágiái* has an idiomatic meaning—an enemy is someone who causes things that are not his own to come together. Idioms like this rely on more than the literal meaning of the words, which can in fact be irrelevant, like the English expression *kick the bucket,* which means "to die," completely disconnected from the literal meaning of the individual words of the phrase.

Clearly, I had to write the tones as part of the language. So I adopted a fairly common linguistic convention and used the acute accent to mark the high tone. When there is no mark above a vowel, the vowel has a low tone.

Here is another set of Pirahã words, each one distinguished from the others by the relative pitch of the vowels:

xaoói (aoOI)	"skin"
xaoói (aoOi)	"foreigner"
xáoói (AoOi)	"ear"
xaóoí (aOoI)	"Brazil nut shell"

Because Pirahã uses pitch so widely, it has communication channel options that most European languages lack. I call these channels of discourse, following the pioneering work of sociolinguist Dell Hymes. There are five such channels in Pirahã, each having a unique cultural function. These are whistle speech, hum speech, musical speech, yell speech, and normal speech—that is, speech using consonants and vowels.

To know the Pirahãs, one has to know about these channels and their functions. I had heard of these before going to the Pirahãs. And I knew that other languages had similar modes of expression (such as the drum languages found in Africa or the whistle speech of the Canary Islands). But when I heard an example in Pirahã for the first time, it was quite a novel experience for me.

This happened one afternoon after I had set out some old *National Geographic* magazines for the Pirahãs to thumb through. They love pictures of animals and peoples, whether from the Amazon or other parts of the world. Xiooitaóhoagí (i-owi-taO-hoa-gI) sat on the floor, looking through the magazine, with her baby suckling at her breast. Her legs straight out in front of her, dress pulled down to her knees, in the normal Pirahã manner, she was humming rhythmically to the child on her lap as he nursed energetically. I watched for a bit before I realized that what she was humming was a description of the whale and Eskimos whose pictures she was examining. The boy would look away from her breast to the picture from time to time, and she would point and hum louder.

Like all true communication channels, hum speech can "say" anything that can be said with consonants and vowels. But also like the other channels, it has a specific set of functions. Hum speech is used to disguise either what one is saying or one's identity. It does this because even for a native Pirahã who is not paying close attention, it is hard to follow. And hum speech is conducted at very low volume. So it is also used for privacy, like our whispering. (The Pirahãs don't whisper, they hum instead. I wondered about this for a while until German linguist Manfred Krifka reminded me of the obvious reason for it. In whispering, the vocal cords are unable to produce different tones, so Pirahã speech would be rendered unintelligible.) Hum speech is also used to talk when one's mouth is full. Finally, it is frequently used by mothers when talking to their children.

Yell speech is the use of the vowel *a* or, occasionally, the original vowels of the words being spoken and one of the two consonants *k* or *x* (glottal stop), to yell the musical form of the speech, that is, its tone, syllables, and stress. Yell speech is commonly used on rainy days when the rain and thunder are loud. It is used to communicate with Pirahã at long distances. It is as loud as a yell, but without consonants. It can occasionally be in falsetto.

Koobio lives at Xagiopai, a seven-day canoe trip upriver from Posto Novo. One rainy day when I was there visiting, Koobio was across the river at his father Toitoi's house. His wife, Xiáisoxái, was back at Koobio's, about to cross to Toitoi's side of the river. Koobio began yelling in this fashion.

"*Ká, Kadakakáa, kaákaá.*"

In normal Pirahã speech this would be "*Kó Xiáisoxái. Baósaí*" (Hey Xiáisoxái. Cloth).

Surprisingly, though the rain muffled most sounds, this speech carried impressively. Shortly thereafter we heard Xiáisoxái yell back, "OK, I'll bring your shirt when I come."

And then there is musical speech, one of the two communication channels that the Pirahãs have special names for. They refer to musical speech as "jaw going" or "jaw leaving." It is produced by exaggerating the relative pitch differences between high tone and low tone and changing the rhythm of words and phrases to produce something like a melody. This channel has perhaps the most interesting array of functions in the language. It is used to communicate important new information. It is used to communicate with spirits (and often it is used by the *kaodíbógi*, or spirits, themselves). But it is mainly used when the people are dancing. Interestingly, though I have no explanation for this fact, when I ask Pirahã to repeat something in musical speech, women produce it less self-consciously than do the men.

Whistle speech, which the Pirahãs refer to as talking with a "sour mouth" or a "puckered mouth"—the same description they use of the mouth when sucking a lemon—is used only by men. For some reason, this restriction to men is true of most other languages with whistle speech. It is used to communicate while hunting and in aggressive play between boys.

My first intense contact with whistle speech came one day when the Pirahãs had given me permission to go hunting with them. After we'd been walking for about an hour, they decided that they weren't seeing any game because I, with my clunking canteens and machete and congenital clumsiness, was making too much noise.

"You stay here and we will be back for you later," Xaikáibaí said gently but firmly.

I watched the men leave me. I was standing by a large tree. I had no idea where I was or when they would come back. The jungle was dark from the shade of the climax forest trees. There were mosquitoes buzzing around me. I took out my machete in case an animal came prowling around. I wondered if the Pirahãs would ever be back to get me. (If they hadn't returned, my skeleton would likely be there now.)

As I tried to make the best of my solitary confinement, I heard the men whistling to one another. They were saying, "I'll go over there; you go that way," and other such hunting talk. But clearly they were communicating. It was fascinating because it sounded so different from anything I had heard before. The whistles carried long and clear in the jungle. I could immediately see the importance and usefulness of this channel, which I guessed would also be much less likely to scare away game than the lower frequencies of the men's normal voices.

These channels show how culture can influence language. If I didn't know about the channels of discourse, I would not know the culturally appropriate way to communicate the different types of information that each of these channels is used for. A complete description of Pirahã culture has to include a discussion of how one communicates spiritual information, intimate information, and so on. The function of the channels is cultural. That is, the linguistic facts, the small number of phonemes and the amount of free variation between consonants that almost drove me crazy at the beginning of my work can't be explained without the cultural information.

Simply put, Pirahã may have so few sounds because it doesn't need any more. The importance it places on these different channels makes consonants and vowels less important for the Pirahãs than they are for English, French, Navajo, Hausa, Vietnamese, and other languages. This challenges modern theories of language because these don't expect culture to enter into the sound structure.

Some have suggested an alternative to my account above, namely, that the small number of consonants and vowels is what facilitates the channels just discussed. This would turn my explanation on its head and would mean that it is the language that affects the culture, rather than the culture that affects language in this case. But there are many languages with different channels, such as whistle speech, but which have very large numbers of consonants and vowels. Two such languages are Lalana Chinantec of southern Mexico, and Yoruba of West Africa. One reason that these two languages can have both large numbers of consonants and vowels and whistle speech is that consonants and vowels seem to be more frequently used (but much more research is needed on this type of comparison from a variety of languages before we can make such assertions with much confidence) and thus have a higher communicative burden placed upon them than the consonants and vowels of Piraha. Also, they seem to use fewer prosodic channels (so they do not have channels such as hum speech and yell speech along-side whistle speech) than Piraha and use them less frequently. There is a lot of research to be done in understanding the relationship between culture and sound systems, so I doubt if my explanations are remotely complete at this point. But the explanations I am proposing are not only promising; they address a set of phenomena that Chomskyan linguistics, for example, ignores altogether.

In 1984 I published my first journal article on Piraha sound structure, a "squib" in the journal *Linguistic Inquiry*. It made, I thought, a small point and corrected a theoretical error common in the literature about the nature of stress systems and the theory of syllable structure. When the article appeared, I was a visiting scholar at Massachusetts Institute of Technology, with an office across the hall from Chomsky's, and I was supported by grants from the National Science Foundation and the American Council of Learned Societies. I thought I had "arrived" as a scholar.

After the article appeared, I received unexpectedly emotional letters (this was before e-mail). Ellen Kaisse, a professor at the University of Washington, sent a postcard to say that the article hit her like a "bomb" and that she had postponed the planned content of her lectures to discuss Piraha's sound structure with her students.

Several other linguists wrote letters. A couple told me I clearly didn't know what I was talking about—no sound system could work that way. A couple were encouraging. Since this was my first article in an international forum, I was unprepared for the reactions. I guess I figured that no one would read this little piece and that it would simply adorn my curriculum vitae.

By 1995, after I had published extensively on Pirahã phonology, Pirahã had become well known and figured in a number of theoretical controversies about the nature of sound structure. At the heart of these controversies about sounds is the conflict between deduction and induction. Linguistic theorists believed that they had successfully established parameters within which the sound systems of human languages could vary—no variation would occur outside of these parameters. These parameters, in turn, had been *deduced* from more general theoretical axioms and were considered elegant and almost necessarily true. Yet inductive work on Pirahã revealed a system beyond these boundaries, if my work was correct.

The controversy attracted the attention of the person who was to become the most important visitor I ever hosted in Brazil, Professor Peter Ladefoged of the University of California at Los Angeles. Peter had a large grant from the National Science Foundation to document the sounds of small, endangered languages around the world. He had asked if he could come to the Pirahãs with me to hear for himself the stress system that I had described in my publications.

I was already in Brazil and drove to the airport at Pôrto Velho to meet Peter's plane. On the drive I felt as if I was about to be audited by the Internal Revenue Service. I had made controversial claims about the sound structure of Pirahã, and now the world's leading phonetician was coming to check these claims. I had done my best, I had been honest, and I was confident that I was right. But I was still nervous.

Peter, who died in 2006, was a tall, patrician-looking man. He had a deep voice, shaped by the dialect of upper-class English known as Received Pronunciation, or RP, English—the Queen's English. He had been a consultant for *My Fair Lady,* the film that helped determine my choice to become a linguist after I watched it at the Egyptian Theater in Hollywood the year it was released, 1962. It is Peter's voice that emerges from the gramophones in Henry Higgins's (Rex Harrison's) office and Peter's handwriting in the little notebooks that Higgins keeps and shows in an early scene in front of London's Covent Gardens to Eliza Doolittle (Audrey Hepburn).

After collecting his luggage, Peter emerged from the baggage claim area and waved. I went over to him and told him how pleased I was that he had come, trying to hide the tension in my voice.

"I'm skeptical of the claims you have made about Pirahã's sound system" were the first words out of his mouth. "Bruce and Donca are also skeptical and have asked me to check this out carefully," Peter added, referring to two well-known colleagues of his at UCLA. Over the days we spent in the village, Peter made high-quality recordings of Pirahã that ultimately supported my published analyses and contributed to the impact that the Pirahã language has had in theories and research on sound structure.

But the experiments occasionally required a lot of patience from the Pirahãs. To measure things well, we had to set up a solar-powered phonetics lab. The Pirahãs had to wear headsets with microphones two inches from their mouths, and, occasionally, to tolerate tubes up their noses to measure supraglottalic pressure (airflow above the vocal cords). They took it good-naturedly and sat still for all of these experiments, surprisingly enough. Once again, science was indebted to them.

The recordings that we made were archived at the phonetics laboratory at UCLA and have been used by other researchers, such as Matthew Gordon of the University of California at Santa Barbara, to further develop theories of human speech sound structure. Because of such work, any researcher can access Pirahã sound data and not only check my analysis, but use Pirahã data, as did Gordon, to deepen our understanding of similar phenomena from a variety of other languages.

Fieldwork demands constant attention to details. And it can be hard in the jungle to continue to pay close attention day after day to anything, whether language or any other important part of life. Each day requires disciplined routine.

During the rainy season, there are frequent all-night downpours. I learned that it took only a couple of hours for a heavy rain to sink my boat. My motor was bolted onto the stern and it weighed about 150 pounds, so I could not remove it at the end of each day and put it on dry land. The motor stayed on the boat. But when it rained, the weight of the motor pulled the boat down just enough so that all the rainwater rushed aft. In an Amazonian rainstorm, it doesn't take long for enough water to accumulate there to push the stern under the water and sink the boat—even though my boat could hold one ton of cargo.

So when I heard rain arrive about midnight, I knew that if it was a strong, hard rain, I would have to get up about 3 a.m. and walk in the downpour to my boat to bail the water out of the stern. This was paying attention to detail, part of the disciplined routine I tried to follow. But it was so *hard* to get out of a warm, comfortable hammock at 3 a.m. and go out into a driving rain, worrying about snakes and other animals, including Piraha dogs, and walk through the village down to my boat. I knew I had to and I always did—except for one time.

It was pouring rain, but when I woke up I just couldn't get myself to walk down to where my boat was moored, even though it was only about a hundred feet away. I told myself that the rain wasn't that bad and that my boat would, after all, hold more than a thousand pounds of water before sinking.

As usual, about 5 a.m., I got up to begin planning my day. I noticed a smell of gasoline. Deep down I think that I knew something was wrong, but I didn't want to admit this to myself. So I went about business as usual and was making my coffee when Xioitaóhoagí yelled out, "Hey Dan! Come see your boat!" I ran out of the house and down the path to the river. There was gasoline floating on the surface of the water. I saw the nylon rope that moored my boat stretched tight—in a nearly vertical line into the water. I walked to the edge and looked down. At the end of the rope, in some thirty feet of water, I could see my boat, sunroof still up.

I was one hundred miles by water from the Transamazon Highway. My boat was my only way out. I had no idea whether I could get it out of the water, whether I could get it running again, or what I would do if I couldn't get it working. A group of Pirahã men and women came running to help. I got some twelve-foot-long ironwood two-by-four boards that were left over from constructing my house and I thought of a plan.

Several of us tugged on the boat until we moved it up a few feet to a submerged ledge on the bank. Then, with straining and red faces, we worked it into a still shallower area where it was only a few feet below the surface. I gave men two-by-fours and explained that we needed to use these as levers to work it bit by bit up the bank. After a couple of hours, we worked it up until the rims of the boat were just above the surface of the water. At that moment, without any prompting from me, women jumped in with gourds and started bailing out the water. We finally got about two-thirds of the water out of it. I tied its bow and stern to the shore and inserted a siphon hose into the built-in gas tank. I was able to drain out most of the water that had entered the tank. Since water is heavier than gasoline, I got the milky water-gas mixture out until pure gasoline began to exit the hose. I had about one-fourth of my gasoline left. Maybe it would be enough to get me to the road. But the pressing problem was to see if the motor would run. If not, I wouldn't need the gasoline anyway.

The first step was to remove both carburetors and dismantle them, drying them out and coating the inside with rubbing alcohol. Then I removed and dried the spark plugs. Next I took a syringe and injected three cubic centimeters of alcohol into each of the motor's cylinders. Finally, I pulled to start the motor. It started up on the third pull. Alcohol in the cylinders, though a bit of a risk for explosion, can really spark

the gasoline. I took off and quickly got up to full speed, careful to stay within sight of the village, in case the motor died. Once the motor was warmed up I knew it would dry out the remaining water. I was pretty proud of myself.

Except that then I remembered that if I had simply gotten up for about fifteen minutes of light work during the night, none of this would have been necessary. Details. I read biographies of explorers and realized that success depended on hard work, planning, and attention to details. This attention to details would be a challenge as I began the study of Pirahã words, a far more demanding task than cleaning out a couple of Johnson carburetors.

And the analysis of the language was more important, even though not as urgent at the time, than fixing my boat. Pirahã's importance for our understanding of human language ranges far beyond its sounds. It is in the grammar that the more profound challenges to most modern theories of the nature, origin, and use of human language lie. I was now coming to realize that Pirahã grammar was a particularly hard nut to crack for Chomsky's hypothesis that specific grammatical principles are innate, as well as for much of his theory's account of how the components of grammar work and fit together. Since the stakes in our conclusions about this issue are so high for our understanding of human language and the human mind, it is important that we work through all of this carefully.

The place to begin, at least following linguistic tradition in discussing the grammar of a language, is with the words. Sentences are built from words and stories are built from sentences. So linguistic studies tend to follow this order in discussions of grammars of different languages.

One of the first word groups I was interested in recording, because of its usefulness and because of what I expected to be its simplicity, was the set of words for body parts: hand, arm, eye, foot, butt, and so forth.

As usual, I was working with Kóhoibiíihíai.

"What is this?" I asked, pointing at my nose.

"*Xitaooí.*"

"*Xitaooí,*" I repeated, perfectly I thought.

"*Xaió, xitaopaí,*" he said.

Aargh, I thought. What is that *-paí* business doing at the end of the word?

So, naively, I asked, "Why are there two words for nose?"

"There is one word, *xitaopaí,*" came the exasperating answer.

"Just *xitaopaí*?"

"Right, *xitaooí,*" he said.

It took a long time to figure this out, but the *-paí* at the end of a body-part word (and it can occur on all of those, but on no other words in the language except body-part words) means something like "my own." So *xitaooí* means just "nose" but *xitaopaí* means "my own nose." The Pirahãs could no more tell me that than the average English speaker could tell me what *to* means in *I want to go.* Why isn't it just *I want go*? Linguists have to figure this kind of thing out for themselves.

Aside from this, Pirahã nouns are for the most part very simple. They have no other prefixes or suffixes, they do not have plural or singular forms, and they don't have any tricky features, like irregular forms and so on.

The lack of grammatical number in Pirahã is unique among the world's languages, according to British linguist Greville Corbett's book-length survey of grammatical number in the world's languages, though now-extinct languages or earlier stages of spoken languages appear to have lacked number too. Thus there is no distinction between *dog* and *dogs, man* and *men*, and so on. It's as though every Pirahã word were like the English words *fish* and *sheep* in having no plural.

So a sentence like *Hiaitíihí hi kaoáíbogi bai -aagá* is vague in various ways. It could mean "The Pirahãs are afraid of evil spirits," or "A Pirahã is afraid of an evil spirit," or "The Pirahãs are afraid of an evil spirit," or "A Pirahã is afraid of evil spirits."

This unique lack of grammatical number could follow from the immediacy of experience principle in the same way that the lack of counting did. Number entails a violation of immediacy of experience in many of its uses—as a category it generalizes beyond the immediate, establishing larger generalizations.

Although Pirahã nouns are simple, Pirahã verbs are much more complicated. Each verb can have as many as sixteen suffixes—that is, up to sixteen suffixes in a row. Not all suffixes are always required, however. Since a suffix can be present or absent, this gives us two possibilities for each of the sixteen suffixes—2^{16}, or 65,536, possible forms for any Pirahã verb. The number is not this large in reality because some of the meanings of different suffixes are incompatible and could not both appear simultaneously. But the number is still many times larger than in any European language. English only has in the neighborhood of five forms for any verb—*sing, sang, sung, sings, singing*. Spanish, Portuguese, and some other Romance languages have forty or fifty forms for each verb.

Perhaps the most interesting suffixes, however (though these are not unique to Pirahã), are what linguists call evidentials, elements that represent the speaker's evaluation of his or her knowledge of what he or she is saying. There are three of these in Pirahã: hearsay, observation, and deduction.

To see what these do, let's use an English example. If I ask you, "Did Joe go fishing?" you could answer, "Yes, at least I heard that he did," or "Yes, I know because I saw him leave," or "Yes, at least I suppose he did because his boat is gone." The difference between English and Pirahã is that what English does with a sentence, Pirahã does with a verbal suffix.

The placement of all the various suffixes on the basic verb is a feature of grammar. There are sixteen of these suffixes. Meaning plays at least a partial role in how they are placed. So, for example, the evidentials are at the very end because they represent a judgment about the entire event being described.

The role of a verb in a sentence is crucial. So word structure is important to sentence structure. The meaning of each verb determines most of what needs to be in a simple sentence. Think about the English verb *die*. The meaning of this verb is what makes the sentence *John died Bill* sound bad. "To die" is something that happens to a single individual. If you know what *to die* means in English, you know that there are too many nouns in *John died Bill*, because dying is not something that you do to someone else. But we can say that "John *caused* Bill to die" or, more simply, "John killed Bill," by adding to the meaning of *die* the meaning of *cause*. Thus John becomes responsible for someone else's dying in the *kill* or *cause to die* sentence (both include the semantics of *cause to die*), so that *John died Bill* is ungrammatical but *John killed Bill* is fine. Changing the meaning structure, either by following the English options of adding other words, such as *cause to*, or selecting a related but nonidentical form, such as *kill*, alters the meaning of the entire sentence. As we study the role of verbs in sentence formation further, we see that most of the syntax of a sentence is little more than a projection of the meaning of the verb (some linguistic theories make this an explicit part of their theoretical apparatus).

Although I initially embedded my discussions of Pirahã grammar in Chomsky's generative grammar, it became clearer and clearer over the years that this theory really had little enlightening to say about the Pirahã language, especially when culture seemed to play a role in the grammar.

According to Chomsky's theory, what sets humans apart from all other terrestrial forms of life is the ability to use grammar. It is not the ability to communicate, since Chomsky recognizes that many other species communicate.

Certainly we have to know how to form sentences and compute the meanings of sentences that we hear or speak—some grammatical knowledge is thus vital for human speech. But since humans are not the only creatures that communicate, grammar cannot be crucial to communication per se. To live is to communicate. All living things, plants and animals and bacteria, communicate.

What makes the give-and-take of information within and across species possible? That is, what makes communication possible? There is a two-word answer: meaning and form. This is essentially what the great Swiss linguist, Ferdinand de Saussure, underscored with his concept of the linguistic sign—linguistic units are composites of form and meaning.

A bee communicates the meaning that food is near by the form of dancing. An ant communicates the meaning that a picnic is under way (though it might not use that term) by secreting chemicals, the form of ant communication. A dog communicates lack of aggression by specific forms—wagging its tail, barking, licking, and so on. And humans communicate meanings by the forms of making sounds or gestures.

But form is not all there is to human communication. Surely human communication differs from that of other species by more than a larger set of sounds, gestures, or words. There must be more to human communication than that. We are able to discuss much more complex matters and a much wider range of subjects than any other species. How do we do that? Two ways. The first and most obvious way is that we are smarter than other species. Human brains are the highest cognitive accomplishment of nature on this planet, so far as we know. The expression of this greater complexity of human thinking and communication requires tools that go beyond the tools available to other species. Linguists vary as to what they think these tools are, though there is wide consensus about several of them. My own vote for the most important tool goes for what the late linguist Charles Hockett labeled "duality of patterning." There are different ways to conceive of this. But basically humans organize their sounds into patterns and then organize these sound patterns into grammatical patterns of words and sentences. This layered organization of human speech is what enables us to communicate so much more than any other species, given our larger, but still finite, brains.

We can illustrate the organization of sounds looking at an example similar (but not identical) to one we have already seen, using the simple words *pin, pan, bin,* and *spin. Pin* is formed by the sequence *p + i + n.* Think of each of these three positions of letters as "slots" and the letters themselves (*p, i, n*) as "fillers." The slots represent the horizontal, or linear, organization of the word from left to right on the page or first to last as spoken sounds emerge from the mouth. The fillers are the vertical organization of the word. If we add a unit to the linear organization, we get a longer word, such as *spin*, by adding *s* to the front of *pin*. If we change things around in the vertical organization, we get different words of the same size, like *pan* from *pin*, when we substitute an *a* for the *i* in *pin*, and so on.

This is more complex than it might seem, though, because not just any filler or extension of a word is possible. We can add an *s* to *pin* to get *spin*, for example, but we cannot add a *t*, to get *tpin*. We can replace *i* with *e* to get *pen*, but we cannot place an *s* there to get *psn*, at least not if we want to form English words. This sound-based organization of the language is referred to as phonology. The physical nature of the individual sounds used in the organization is, roughly, phonetics. This is the first part of duality—the organization of sounds into words.

I should add immediately, however, that humans are resourceful, and that if for some reason they are unable to, or choose not to, use speech sounds, another channel of communication, sign language, is available. In sign languages the forms corresponding to sounds in spoken language are gestures or signs. Linguists have discovered that although the physical nature of gestures is obviously different from the physical nature of sounds, the organization of these elements into words and larger units, such as phrases and sentences, follows similar principles. Thus we can have a conception of phonology that includes both gestures and sounds.

Whether we use gestures or sounds, we need more than just words to have a grammar. Since grammar is essential to human communication, speakers of all human languages organize words into larger units— phrases, sentences, stories, conversations, and so forth. This form of compositionality is called grammar by some and syntax by others. No other creature has anything remotely like duality of patterning or compositionality. Yet *all* humans have this.

The Pirahãs certainly do. So consider the Pirahã sentence *Kóhoi kabatií kohóaipí* (Kóhoi eats the tapir). The Pirahãs put the object before the verb, a pattern we find in many languages, so *kabatií* means "tapir" and *kohóaipí* means "eat." This shows us that Pirahã organizes its phonemes into words and its words into sentences. So the Pirahã language has duality of patterning and compositionality. It is hard to imagine a human language without these.

The most crucial component of language to my way of thinking, though, is meaning. Meaning is the gyroscope of grammar. I like this gyroscope metaphor because it expresses the belief of a large number of linguists, including me, that a slight difference in meaning, like the slight motion of a gyroscope, can lead to a large difference in the attitude of the rocket or the form of the sentence.

In other words, language is about meaning. We begin with a meaning and we encase it in grammar. All of grammar is guided by meaning. But what is meaning? That question has bothered thinkers for millennia. At the risk of biting off much more than I can chew, here's my sketch of the core parts.

Philosophers and linguists talk about meaning in terms of its two parts, sense and reference. Reference is the use of language by the speaker and the hearer to agree on a specific object that they are talking about. So when two people in conversation use, say, the nouns *boy, Bill, you,* these words refer to entities in the real world. We know the boy or the person named Bill or who "you" is when we talk (or there will be severe miscommunication until both the hearer and the speaker agree on who or what they are referring to).

On the other hand, there are nouns that do not refer to anything. When I say that "John rode the unicorn," it is pretty clear that *unicorn* doesn't refer to anything in the real world. Likewise, if I say that "I will keep tabs on you," *tabs* doesn't actually refer to any object in this expression—it is part of an idiom. And there are things other than nouns that refer to things; for example, in *I had built a house, had built* includes a reference to a point of past completion. In *The house is yellow, yellow* refers to a particular color quality. There is disagreement on what it means to refer to things (some linguists deny that verbs and adjectives can refer) or how important this property is for defining parts of speech.

The other basic component of meaning is sense. We can understand sense as having two subparts. First, it includes the way that speakers think about entities, actions, and qualities—all those things we use in our speech. (What do I have in mind when I say "big," for example, in *big butterfly,* versus *big loss* or *big elephant*?) Second, sense is about the relations between words and the ways that they are used.

Think of what *break* means in examples like *John broke his arm, John* broke the ice in the frigid conversation, John broke the sentence down for me, or John broke into the house, for example. The only way that we can know what break means is to know how it is used. And using a word means selecting a particular context, a set of background assumptions shared by the speaker and the hearer, including how particular words should be used, and the other words that the word in question is used with.

That is meaning in a nutshell: the way a word or a sentence is used, the way it relates to other words and sentences, and what speakers agree that a word or a sentence points to in the world. And the Pirahãs, like all humans, mean things when they speak. But that doesn't mean that we all use the same meanings. Like all humans, what Pirahãs mean when they talk is severely circumscribed by their values and beliefs.

We learn, therefore, when we study words from any language, that we must understand each word at various levels simultaneously. We must understand a word's cultural relevance and use. We must understand its sound structure. And we must understand how the word is used in context, in specific sentences and stories. Most linguists agree on these three levels of understanding the word. But Pirahã has also taught us something else. It has taught us that not only can the meaning of individual words be the result of culture, such as the closely related words for friend and enemy, but that the very sounds of the words, whether they are whistled, hummed, and so on, can themselves be determined by culture—and this latter lesson, which is abundantly illustrated in other languages, has not been discussed much in the linguistic literature. Pirahã gives us an extremely clear example for future linguistic investigations.

n *Mrs. Doubtfire,* the Robin Williams character phones the Sally Field character and says, in reference to an ad, "I . . . am . . . job?" Besides being funny in the context of the film, both the movie characters and the audience know immediately that what the speaker *means* is "I want the job you have advertised."

How does the audience know this? It isn't in the words or the way they are put together in a sentence, not completely anyway. The relevant meaning that someone wants a job comes rather from the context, in a movie or in life, and the culture in which the sentence is spoken. That is, grammar is a component of communication but it is not all there is to communication. In the *Mrs. Doubtfire* example, the grammar is almost all wrong and yet the correct meaning is still communicated.

When we learn to convey meaning in another language, our first step, like Robin Williams's, is not grammar but culture. To appreciate how culture can affect language (even effect it on occasion), think about the process of learning another language.

What does this task entail? If you learn to pronounce French vowels perfectly and come to completely understand and control the meaning of every French word, can you rightly claim to speak French? Would pronunciation and knowledge of words be enough to tell you the appropriate sentence to use in a particular social setting? Would this knowledge suffice to read Voltaire in the original like a French intellectual? The answer to these questions is no. Language is not only more than the sum of its parts (words and sounds and sentences)—it is by itself insufficient for full communication and understanding without knowledge of an enveloping culture.

Culture guides us all in the meanings that we perceive in the world around us, and language is part of the world around us. An American is not likely to talk about the behavior of the Amazonian bush dog (*Speothos venaticus*)—these dogs are unknown to most Americans. This is an obvious way in which culture and experience restrict our "universe of discourse," the things that we talk about. But there are often less obvious, more interesting ways in which culture affects our language. In the content of our stories, culture plays the major role in comprehension.

For example, comparing Pirahãs with Americans, Americans usually talk about seeing ghosts only in fiction. This is not because most Americans have not heard of ghosts, but because they do not believe in them. And even among those Americans who claim to believe in ghosts, very few claim to have actually seen a ghost. This is fairly recent in the history of English. In the colonial days, Americans talked often about supernatural events that they had witnessed—as transcripts of witch trials reveal. Culture affects the way that we talk in some instances. Most of us agree on this.

Like Americans, Pirahãs restrict their conversation to conform to their cultural experiences and values.

One of these values is the nonimportation of outside subject matter for conversations. The Pirahãs, for example, will not discuss how to build a house out of bricks, because Pirahãs do not build brick houses. They might well describe a brick house that they have seen, in response to a question from an outsider or to a question from another Pirahã just after their arrival back from the city. But after that a brick house wouldn't arise spontaneously in their conversation.

By and large, Pirahãs do not import foreign thoughts, philosophies, or technology. They do enjoy using labor-saving devices, such as mechanized manioc grinders and small outboard motors for their canoes, but they see these things as elements "gathered" from outsiders, with outsiders responsible for the fuel, care, and replacement required. They have rejected in the past any device that would require change in their knowledge or their practices. If such devices cannot simply be appended to Pirahãs' traditional ways of doing things, they are rejected.

For example, a motor may be used if it attaches easily to a canoe and helps the Pirahãs continue traditional activities, because the Pirahãs have seen motors used by caboclos. And Pirahãs consider the caboclo culture to be a subset of their own; caboclos are just another part of the world around them. A fishing pole, on the other hand, would not be used because it requires a way of fishing that the Pirahãs do not observe either among themselves or among caboclos. Pirahã verbs for fishing mean literally "to spear fish" and "to pull out fish by hand." There is no word for pulling out fish with a pole. They are not interested in skills demonstrated only by Americans. Americans are not part of their normal environment. They have gotten to know only six Americans, all missionaries, and a smattering of very short-term visitors, in the past fifty years. You might hear Pirahãs talk about how to install a motor that was given to them, for example: "The foreigner said to attach the propeller after the motor is seated in the canoe." But you won't hear them talk about how to use a rod and reel, even though Americans have given them these devices and shown them how to use them.

To talk about things that have no place in their own culture, such as other gods, Western ideas of germs, and so on, would require the Pirahãs to adopt a change in life and thought. So they avoid such talk. There are some apparent exceptions. For example, the Pirahãs do talk occasionally about caboclo beliefs—but these beliefs have long been part of their own environment, since caboclos talk to them about their beliefs frequently. Such beliefs have become subjects of conversation after centuries of contact, gradually becoming part of the Pirahãs' environment.

In this sense, the Pirahãs' discourse is more esoteric than exoteric, more directed to topics that do not challenge Pirahãs' views. Of course, all peoples are like this to some degree. It is the extent to which this is enforced among the Pirahãs that makes them stand out from, say, Western societies, in which discussion of new ideas and foreign ways is also not generally highly valued.*

---

*The concept of esoteric communication comes from work by Carol Thurston and by George Grace and Alison Wray. Its relevance to the analysis of Pirahã was first suggested in research by Jeanette Sakel and Eugenie Stapert, of the University of Manchester, England. Esoteric communication is communication that is used within, and partially defines, a well-defined group. Esoteric communication facilitates understanding because hearers are likely to anticipate what speakers are going to say in different situations. The language is not limited to old or predictable information, but that is the default. In fact, in Pirahã there is a special channel, as we have seen, musical

There is no one single example that illustrates esoteric versus exoteric communication. Rather, esoteric communication is a product of narrow ranges of culturally acceptable ways of talking and topics for talking. The information conveyed is new, but not novel, in the sense that it fits general expectations. One American can say on the radio, "The Martians are landing down the street," and other Americans can react in shock to this entirely new threat.

But not only can Americans say that the Martians are coming, they do say all sorts of things like that, every day. The Pirahãs could say that the Martians are coming, if they had seen any, but they won't unless they do. Pirahãs talk about fishing, hunting, other Pirahãs, spirits they have seen, and so on—about experiences that they live daily. This is not because they are not creative but because this is a cultural value. It is a very conservative culture.

What does grammar entail ultimately, beyond culture, general human intelligence, and meaning? How much grammar does one need? A big part of grammar, once again, is projecting the meaning of a verb onto a sentence. On the other hand, forming sentences is more complicated than just filling in the meaning of the sentence's verb. One of the additional devices that many grammars call upon is modification.

Modification narrows the meaning of a word or a phrase. It complicates the meaning and the form by adding words and meanings that are not required by the verb. So I can say, "John gave the book to the boy," or "John gave the book to the *fat* boy," or "*Yesterday,* John gave the book to the boy," or "John gave the book to the boy *in the club.*"

The italicized portions of the sentences are not required by the

speech, that is used for new information. This might explain the relative richness of both prosody and phonemes in musical speech—new information might require a slower rate of information and greater perceptibility in an esoteric group in the sense intended here. The linguist Tom Givon refers to a concept similar to esoteric communication in his phrase *society of intimates.* By this felicitous expression, Givon refers to small groups of people who speak together frequently and form a culture group together. Such groups share a greater amount of implicit information than other groups, even other groups who speak the same language.

meaning of the verb. They only limit further the meaning of what is being talked about. This is modification in its briefest essence.

Another aspect of language that can affect grammar is what Chomsky often calls displacement, uttering a sentence that is grammatical, but where the words are not in their expected order—they are instead in different places in the sentence for pragmatic effect, that is, to alter the relationship between new and old information or important versus background or less important information in a story.

If we look at a couple of English sentences we can get an idea about displacement and its functions. If I say "John saw Bill," I use the order that we expect as speakers of English. The subject, *John,* comes first, followed by the verb, then the direct object, *Bill.* If I say, though, that "Bill was seen by John," the verb *see* is lacking a direct object. *Bill* is the subject in this sentence, and the former subject, *John,* is the object of the preposition *by.* The contrast between the first, active-voice sentence and the second, passive-voice sentence is related, according to most studies, to the function of the two sentences in English stories. For example, we might use the passive voice when Bill is the topic of our story and the active voice when John is the topic.

Another example of displacement is found in the different moods of a sentence, such as declarative, interrogative, and imperative. If I say, "The man is in the room," the order is again what we expect for this kind of sentence. But if I make this a question, the verb, *is,* is displaced to the beginning of the sentence, as in "Is the man in the room?" In this type of question, the verb precedes the subject, whereas the verb normally follows the subject. Or we can make this into a different type of question, one that asks for more information, and say, "Where is the man?" In this type of question, both the verb and the thing being questioned precede the subject—they are displaced from their normal positions.

Most of Chomsky's research career has been concerned with understanding how constituents of the sentence can be displaced in this way. He has never been interested in why they are displaced (except to say that it is for "pragmatic reasons" or some such), only in the mechanics of how the displacement works.

But in esoteric societies of intimates like the Pirahãs' society, displacement can be rare or nonexistent. There is none or nearly none in

Pirahã. The story and the context communicate the sorts of things that displacement handles in English. And many other languages are the same.

One possibility, a possibility explored at length in Chomsky's theory, is that when we don't hear displacement it is still there, at an abstract level of grammar that Chomsky calls "logical form," and that the grammar of such a language is no different from English's, except that you can hear the displacement in English but not, say, in Pirahã. But we might legitmately criticize Chomsky's theory on this score for being more baroque than is necessary. If there is a way to understand sentences without displacement at any level, abstract or otherwise, then perhaps grammar is less important than we imagined.

And in fact there are many theories that can accept languages like Pirahã, languages without displacement and with very little modification, at face value, with no need for "logical form" and other such abstractions.

I suggest that we get on with our discussion of Pirahã without the assumption of abstract levels and without an inflated sense of the importance of grammar in language and cognition and see how far this gets us.

Maybe we don't need much grammar after all in an esoteric culture. If this were true, then we would have a way of better understanding the relative simplicity of Pirahã grammar. If my cultural suggestions are plausible, then there is nothing primitive about the Pirahãs cognitive abilities. There is nothing bizarre about them or their language. Rather, their language and grammar perfectly fit their esoteric culture. And if this is on the right track, we have begun to see the need for a novel and fresh approach to the understanding of human grammar.

In this approach grammar would neither be as necessary nor as autonomous as Chomsky has claimed for more than forty years. To take one example, Robert Van Valin of the University of Düsseldorf has developed an alternative to Chomsky's theory in which the latter's meaning-independent grammar plays a much-reduced role in the overall understanding of human language and in which grammar is driven largely by meaning. He calls his theory "Role and Reference Grammar." There is a natural place in Van Valin's theory for using culture to explain aspects of grammar. So, although this has not yet been developed, the theory might provide a comfortable home for the ideas I am proposing here.

Van Valin is not the only one to develop a well-articulated alternative to universal grammar. William Croft of the University of New Mexico has developed a theory in which it is claimed that all the commonalities among human languages are really commonalities of human cognition across our species and require nothing so baroque as a Chomskyan universal grammar. Croft refers to his theory as "Radical Construction Grammar."

A study of Pirahã supports these alternative approaches even while it suggests that they are not quite complete. As we examine more languages like Pirahã, we should be able to develop a stronger theory, based on the foundation of these important pioneering works. Such a theory might provide a more likely source for human grammar than the universal grammar of Chomsky (which Pinker calls "the language instinct"). The universal grammar/language instinct hypothesis simply has nothing of interest to tell us about how culture and grammar interact, which now seems to be vital to any complete understanding of language.

O ne of the most interesting conversations I've had about food
was with a Pirahã. It occurred when I ate a salad in the village
for the first time.

Rice, beans, fish, and wild game, smothered under copious amounts
of Tabasco sauce, can keep one's culinary drive satisfied up to a point.
But if you like the crunch of fresh lettuce, then after a few months you
might begin to dream about eating a salad.

The missionary plane visited us every eight weeks in the jungle to
bring mail and supplies. It was our only contact with the world outside
the Pirahãs. On one trip, I sent out a note to a fellow missionary and
asked if he would do me the tremendous favor of sending some salad
makings on the next flight. Two months later, our salad arrived.

That evening I sat down to my first taste of lettuce, tomatoes, and
cabbage in six months. Xahóápati walked up to watch me eat. He
looked bemused.

"Why are you eating leaves?" he asked. "Don't you have any meat?"

The Pirahãs are very particular about foods, and they believe, as we
do to some degree, that the foods you eat determine the person you
become.

"Yes, I have a lot of canned meat," I assured him. "But I like these
leaves! I have not had any for many moons."

My Pirahã friend looked at me, then at the leaves, then back at me.
"Pirahãs don't eat leaves," he informed me. "This is why you don't
speak our language well. We Pirahãs speak our language well and we
don't eat leaves."

He walked away, apparently thinking that he had just given me the
key to learning his language. But I found the correlation between lettuce eating and Pirahã speaking unfathomable. What on earth did he

mean? A connection between what I ate and the language that I spoke? How ridiculous. The words continued to nag me, however, as though Xahóápati's remarks had something useful in them, if only I could put my finger on it.

Then I noticed another bemusing fact. The Pirahãs would converse with me and then turn to one another, in my presence, to talk about me, as though I was not even there.

"Say, Dan, could you give me some matches?" Xipoógi asked me one day with others present.

"OK, sure."

"OK, he is giving us two matches. Now I am going to ask for cloth."

Why would they talk about me in front of my face like this, as though I could not understand them? I had just demonstrated that I *could* understand them by answering the question about the matches. What was I missing?

Their language, in their view, emerges from their lives as Pirahãs and from their relationships to other Pirahãs. If I could utter appropriate responses to their questions, this was no more evidence that I spoke their language than a recorded message is to me evidence that my telephone is a native speaker of English. I was like one of the bright macaws or parrots so abundant along the Maici. My "speaking" was just some cute trick to some of them. It was not really *speaking*.

Although I am claiming neither that the Pirahãs have nor that they do not have a theory of the relationship between language and culture, their questions and actions did serve as a catalyst to get me thinking about this relationship.

Like most unusual things I observed or heard among the Pirahãs, I realized ultimately that Xahóápati was telling me more than I had realized: that to speak their language is to live their culture. A few linguists today, in the tradition of early-twentieth-century pioneers Edward Sapir and Franz Boas, also believe that culture impinges on grammar and language in nontrivial ways. But my reasons are different from most of even this minority. My difficulty in successfully translating the Bible owed largely to the fact that Pirahã society and language are interconnected in ways that make even the understanding of grammar, a subcomponent of language, impossible without studying the language and culture simultaneously. And I believe that this is true for all languages and societies. Language is the product of synergism between values of a society, communication theory, biology, physiology, physics (of the inherent limitations of our brains as well as our phonetics), and human thought. I believe this is also true of the engine of language, grammar.

Both modern linguistics and the bulk of the philosophy of language have chosen to separate language from culture in their quests to understand human communication. But by this move they fail to come to grips with language as a "natural phenomenon," to use the words of philosopher John Searle. Many linguists and philosophers since the 1950s have characterized language almost exclusively in terms of mathematical logic. It is almost as if the fact that language has meaning and is spoken by human beings is irrelevant to the enterprise of understanding it.

Language is perhaps our greatest accomplishment as a species. Once a people have established a language, they have a series of agreements on how to label, characterize, and categorize the world around them, as Searle has also pointed out. These agreements then serve as the foundation for all other agreements in the society. Rousseau's social contract is not the first contractual foundation of human society, therefore, at least not as he thought of it. Language is. Language, on the other hand, is not the only source of societal values. Tradition and biology play a strong, nonlinguistic role as well. Many values of society are transmitted without language.

Biologists such as E. O. Wilson have shown that some of our values arise from our biology as primates and biological entities. Our need for companionship, our need for food, clothing, shelter, and so on are significantly related to our biology.

Other values arise from personal or family or cultural traditions. As an example, take the propensity to be a couch potato. Some people enjoy lying on the couch, eating greasy food, and watching TV, especially the food channel. This is unhealthy. Still, some enjoy it. Why? Well, *some* of this is biological. Apparently, our taste buds love the sensation and taste of fatty foods (such as Fritos and bean dip), our bodies like to conserve energy (the appeal of a soft sofa), and our minds like sensory stimulation (men chasing a ball, women prancing in bikinis, large desert vistas, or the latest creation from Emeril Lagasse).

But the explanation for such unsalubrious behavior is not exclusively biological. After all, not everyone is a couch potato. So why do some people satisfy their biological propensities one way while others satisfy their urges in different, perhaps even healthy, ways? This type of behavior is not learned via language. Rather, it is acquired by example in individual families or other groups.

The couch potato life is just one of many examples of learning cultural values without language. Specific values like this, along with the directly biological values (like shelter, clothing, food, and health), act together to produce an integrated whole of language and culture, by means of which we interpret and talk about the world. We often think that our values and ways of talking about our values are completely "natural," but they are not. They are partially an accident of our birth into a particular culture and society.

The Pirahãs frequently allow their dogs to eat off their bowls or plates while they themselves are still eating. Some people get squeamish about this, but others think it is fine. Eating with dogs is not something I would normally do. I feed my dog snacks by hand and sometimes, when I forget, I then eat without washing my hands. But that is as close as I get. I know some people who let their dogs lick their plates clean, under the assumption that the dishwasher will sterilize it all. But I wouldn't allow my dog to sit by me and share my plate.

I don't want to share my plate with my dog because I believe in germs, which I think can make me ill. On the other hand, I have no direct evidence for germs. I am not sure I would know how to go about proving to anyone that germs exist or what their properties are. But I believe in them just the same, because the knowledge of germs and their connection to disease is a product of my culture. (Whether germs from dogs might ever make a human sick, I do not know. But my culturally inspired fear of germs makes the prospect of eating with dogs unappealing nonetheless.)

Like many other peoples around the world, the Pirahãs do not believe in germs. Therefore, they have no aversion to letting their dogs eat off the same plate at the same time. Their dogs are their allies in the fight for survival in the jungle and they love their dogs. So, without a belief in germs, the Pirahãs do not find it remotely repugnant to share a plate of food with their dogs.

Linguists know these things, of course. So do anthropologists, psychologists, philosophers, and many others. Thus far, therefore, what I have said about cultural values and language is not intended to be new. But I missed the significance of much of this until the salad conversation with Xahóápati.

As we now know, the Pirahãs highly value direct experience and observation. In the sense of this concept, the Pirahãs are like people from Missouri, the "show me" state. However, the Pirahãs not only would agree that "seeing is believing," but that "believing is seeing." If you want to tell the Pirahãs something, they are going to want to know how you came by your knowledge. And especially they will want to know if you have direct evidence for your assertion.

Since for the Pirahãs spirits and dreams are immediate experiences, they often talk about them. Talk of the spiritual for the Pirahãs is not talk of fiction but talk of real events. For the principle of immediacy of experience to have an explanatory role in Pirahã spiritual life, the only crucial condition is that they believe that they see the spirits that they talk about. And this condition is easily met.

The following is a short recounting of a dream originally recorded by Steve Sheldon. There is nothing particularly special about this. The

Pirahãs attach no mystical significance to their dreams. They are experiences like all others, though these may involve experiences in places other than the Maici or the lower "boundary," or *bigí*.

Casimiro Dreams
Informant: Kaboibagi
Recorded and transcribed by Steve Sheldon

Synopsis: This is a text about a dream that the speaker in the story had. He is dreaming about a Brazilian woman who used to live near the village, a very large woman.

1. *Ti xaogií xaipipaábahoagaíhiai kai.*
   I dreamed about his wife.

2. *Ti xaí xaogií xaixaagá apipaábahoagaí.*
   I then the Brazilian woman dreamed.

3. *Xao gáxaiaiao xapipaába xao hi gía xabaáti.*
   She spoke in the dream. You will stay with the Brazilian man.

4. *Gíxa hi xaoabikoí.*
   You will stay with him.

5. *Ti xaigía xao xogígió ai hi xahápita.*
   With respect to me therefore the big Brazilian woman disappeared.

6. *Xaipipaá kagahaoogí poogíhiai.*
   Next, I dreamed about papayas and bananas.

The lack of transition between the first five lines and the sixth line could be curious if we approached this dream as a simple story. But it is just a recounting of what the speaker did. It is not that the Pirahãs confuse dreaming with daily activities. But they classify the two roughly the same: just types of experiences that we have and witness. They exemplify the immediacy of experience principle.

Now culture and language are intertwined for every society and people in multiple ways. The fact that culture can affect grammar, for example, is not incompatible with the idea that grammar can affect culture too. In fact, separating out the different kinds of relations between culture and grammar is a useful research priority for linguistics and anthropology generally.

The effects of grammar on culture are varied. Sometimes they can be as obvious as your right hand, as I discovered on one of the innumerable days I spent working with Kóhoi at the desk.

"OK. This hand is the one that Americans call the 'left hand.' Brazilians call it *mão esquerda*. What do the Pirahãs call it?"

"Hand."

"Yes, I know that it is a hand. But how do you say *left* hand?"

"Your hand."

"No, look. Here is your left hand. Here is your right hand. Here is my left hand. Here is my right hand. How do you say *that*?"

"This is my hand. That is your hand. This is my other hand. That is your other hand."

Asking informants to tell me how they distinguished one hand from another in their language was clearly not working. I just could not for the life of me understand why it was so hard to get the names for left hand and right hand.

I decided I needed a cookie. I took a break and my language teacher and I had some instant coffee and cookies. I planned to ask Kóhoi to work with me on this again. If he couldn't help this second time around, I'd need to come up with a very different plan.

How am I ever going to translate the Bible into Pirahã, I thought, if I can't even figure out terms as simple as *left hand* and *right hand*? Aargh. I was exasperated. At least Kóhoi agreed to work with me more on this. So I went through my routine again.

"*Mão esquerda*."

He answered, "The hand is upriver."

What on earth is going on? I thought, completely frustrated. So now he is making fun of me?

I pointed to his right hand.

"The hand is downriver."

I give up, I decided. I moved onto something else. But for days I felt utterly incompetent as a linguist.

A week later, I went hunting with a group of men. We came to a fork in the path about two miles from the village. Kaaxaóoi yelled from near the back of our line, "Hey Kóhoi, go upriver."

Kóhoi turned right. Kaaxaóoi didn't say turn right, but he turned right. As we walked further, our orientation changed.

Another person spoke to Kóhoi, still in the lead. "Turn upriver!" This time he turned left, not right, in response to the same command to turn upriver.

During the rest of our hunt, I noticed that directions were given either in terms of the river (upriver, downriver, to the river) or the jungle (into the jungle). The Pirahãs knew where the river was (I couldn't tell—I was thoroughly disoriented). They all seemed to orient themselves to their geography rather than to their bodies, as we do when we use *left hand* and *right hand* for directions.

I didn't understand this. I had never found the words for *left hand* and *right hand*. The discovery of the Pirahãs' use of the river in giving directions did explain, however, why when the Pirahãs visited towns with me, one of their first questions was "Where is the river?" They needed to know how to orient themselves in the world!

Only years later did I read the fascinating research coming from the Max Planck Institute for Psycholinguistics in Nijmegen, the Netherlands, under the direction of Dr. Stephen C. Levinson. In studies from different cultures and languages, Levinson's team discovered two broad divisions in the ways cultures and languages give local directions. Many cultures are like American and European cultures and orient themselves in relative terms, dependent on body orientation, such as left and right. This is called by some endocentric orientation. Others, like the Pirahãs, orient themselves to objects external to their body, what some refer to as exocentric orientation.

Clearly the Pirahã way of giving directions is very different from the average American's. But even in English we can use an "absolute" directional system similar to the Pirahãs'. For example, we might naturally say, "The United States is north of Mexico." Or we might say, "When you get to the stop sign, turn west." Compass-based directions are similar to the river-based directions of the Pirahãs in that they are anchored in the world external to the speaker. But in English and many other languages, unlike in Pirahã, there is also a system of directions oriented to our bodies. So we say things like "turn left," "go straight ahead," "turn right," and so on, with terms that are based on body orientation.

This system can be useful, but it requires that the hearer know where the speaker is and how her body is oriented before the hearer can follow the speaker's directions. This is harder than it sounds in many cases. Imagine a speaker facing you. Then her left is your right, her straight ahead is your straight behind, and so on. Or imagine a speaker on the phone or otherwise out of sight, where the orientation of her body is unknown. This "relative," body-oriented system of directionals can work in some situations, but it is inherently imprecise and sometimes confusing.

So English has both an externally anchored, efficient system of directionals and a body-oriented, occasionally confusing system. It is largely facts of history and English-speaking cultures that are responsible for the persistence of the dual systems. The Pirahãs lack a body-oriented system and only have the nonambiguous, externally anchored system (true, the Pirahãs have the advantage of always being close to the river, with respect to which they orient themselves). So the Pirahãs need to think more explicitly and consistently about their location in the world than we do. This in turn means that the Pirahãs' language forces them to think differently about the world.

The implication of this finding is that language and culture are not cognitively isolated from each other. At the same time, we must guard against drawing unwarranted conclusions from this. We wouldn't want to conclude, for example, that Brazilians and Mexicans think that Coca-Cola is female, just because they assign it to the feminine gender in their grammar. Nor would we want to say that the Pirahãs are unable to perform counting-related tasks, such as tallying on their fingers or toes, because they lack number words. This could be a misapplication of the idea that language shapes thought.

This idea has always been controversial. It is known by various names—linguistic determinism, linguistic relativity, the Whorf hypothesis, and the Sapir-Whorf hypothesis, among others, although the hypothesis is mainly associated with Benjamin Lee Whorf these days, because he was one of the first linguists to write extensively about specific examples of language shaping thought.

But Sapir also continues to be associated with the idea that language can affect culture profoundly. Sapir was a founder of American linguistics. He was also a student, along with Ruth Benedict, Margaret Mead, and other American anthropologists, of Franz Boas, a physicist-turned-anthropologist at Columbia University, considered by some to be the father of American anthropology. Sapir's conclusions and proposals on the language-culture-cognition interface were based on his vast field experience, studies of languages of North America, their structures, their cultures, their histories, and the relationship between their cultures and their languages. A famous paper of Sapir's claims:

> *Human beings do not live in the objective world alone, nor alone in the world of social activity as ordinarily understood, but are very much at the mercy of the particular language which has become the medium of expression for their society. It is quite an illusion to imagine that one adjusts to reality essentially without the use of language and that language is merely an incidental means of solving specific problems of communication or reflection. . . . No two languages are ever sufficiently similar to be considered as representing the same social reality. The worlds in which different societies live are distinct worlds, not merely the same worlds with different labels attached. (From Sapir's* The Status of Linguistics as a Science *[1929], p. 209)*

According to Sapir, our language affects how we perceive things. In his view, what we see and hear in our day-to-day existence results from the way that we talk about the world. This would certainly help us understand how it is that when walking with the Pirahãs in the jungle, I might say I saw a branch move and they might say that they saw a spirit move the branch. Sapir even goes so far as to claim that our view of the world is constructed by our languages, and that there is no "real world" that we can actually perceive without the filter of language telling us what we are seeing and what it means.

If Sapir and Whorf are correct, the implications for philosophy, linguistics, anthropology, and psychology, among other fields of study, are vast. Whorf went so far as to claim that Western science is largely the result of the grammatical limitations of Western languages.

Could Kant's a priori categories of morality be an artifact of the distribution of nouns and verbs in the grammar of German? Could Einstein's theory of relativity? Unlikely though such hypotheses seem, they are raised by Whorf's suggestions.

For linguistics and anthropology, the Sapir-Whorf hypothesis suggests research questions for investigating how our languages cause us to think differently about the world.

The Sapir-Whorf view implies a symbiosis between language and thought. In the extreme version of this view (linguistic determinism), which virtually no one accepts, thought cannot escape the bounds of language. Speaking a particular language can give our thinking an immutable advantage or disadvantage, depending on the task and language involved.

A more widely accepted version is that while we can think "out of the language box," we normally do not because we don't even perceive how language affects the way we think. This version is even observed in practice among people who might explicitly reject the Sapir-Whorf hypothesis.

As an example of how intelligent people can be "conflicted" about the idea that the way we talk can affect the way we think, consider the views of members of the Linguistic Society of America. The LSA has strict guidelines against sexist language. This means that at least some members of the LSA think that the way we speak affects the way we think in ways identical or at least related to a mild form of the Sapir-Whorf hypothesis.

However, other LSA members reject almost every version of this hypothesis. What fascinates me is that both of these groups agree that the LSA should promote the use of gender-neutral language. One member, for example, might simultaneously give a paper against the hypothesis of linguistic relativity while being very careful to use only *they* or forms like *s/he* in his or her paper, as opposed to lapsing into use of *he* for both genders, as in "If anyone wants this job, *they* can have it" versus "If anyone wants this job, *he* can have it."

This is not happening simply because gender-neutral language is more polite than gender-specific language. The pressure to change English in this way arose because people believe that the way we talk, whether offense is consciously intended or whether or not politeness is at stake, affects the way we think about others.

I have seen a sufficient number of psycholinguistic studies and have heard enough anecdotal evidence of the effects of language on thought to conclude that this weaker version of the Sapir-Whorf hypothesis is not an unreasonable idea.

At the same time, I don't think the hypothesis does the work that some people have wanted it to do. In explaining the lack of counting in Pirahã, for example, it seems unhelpful. If the Sapir-Whorf hypothesis were taken as explaining the Pirahãs' lack of counting (they don't count because they lack number words), several facts would be left unexplained.

For example, many other groups around the world have had very impoverished numeral systems, but they have had counting and have borrowed numerals from surrounding languages as socioeconomic pressure builds to be able to use numbers in trade. The Warlpiri of Australia are an example. And the Pirahãs have been engaged in trade with Brazilians for more than two centuries. Yet they have not borrowed any numerals to facilitate their trade. Under a Whorfian account of Pirahã counting, there is little reason to borrow words to express concepts that become useful, because concepts couldn't become useful without the words to begin with. That account would predict, wrongly, that without the words there cannot be the concept. In fact, this strong Whorfian account is incompatible with science, because science is largely about discovering concepts for which we previously had no words!

The Sapir-Whorf hypothesis fails to offer any unified account of the range of unusual facts about Pirahã culture and language, such as the absence of color words, quantifiers, or numerals, the simple kinship system, and so on.

Our quest for an account of the interaction of Pirahã language and culture needs to be placed in the context of the intellectual territory to be traversed. We need to map out some of the different relationships between grammar, cognition, and culture that have been proposed over the years. I summarize the leading ideas in the table opposite:

Cognition, Grammar, Culture Connections

Constraint Relationship	Representative Theory
1. *cognition* → *grammar*	Chomsky's universal grammar
2. *grammar* → *cognition*	Linguistic relativity (Whorf)
3. *cognition* → *culture*	Brent Berlin and Paul Kay's work on color terms
4. *grammar* → *culture*	Greg Urban's work on discourse-centered culture
5. *culture* → *cognition*	Long-term effects on thinking of cultural restrictions on certain behaviors
6. *culture* → *grammar*	Ethnogrammar; individual forms structured by culture

We all know that any attempt to understand how culture, cognition, and grammar interact and affect one another must avoid simplistic solutions to the understanding of what shapes the "human experience." At the same time, it is useful and necessary to begin with some idealization or deliberate simplification by which we can focus our attention on salient points of connection among these three domains while ignoring others momentarily. This is a useful way to come to grips with such complex material.

The first row in the table above expresses the case in which cognition, by which I loosely mean either the cerebral or mental structures necessary for thought or thought itself, exercises control over grammar. Noam Chomsky has focused exclusively on the effects of cognition, in this sense, on grammar for several decades, proposing the idea of a universal grammar as his idea of how cognition limits human grammar.

Universal grammar (UG) claims that there is in effect just one grammar for all the world's languages, with variation allowed by a relatively small number of "principles and parameters." The experience of growing up in one environment and hearing a particular language spoken will flip switches that call forth this or that grammatical property in the child's emerging grammar. So suppose that you are born in Brazil and grow up hearing Portuguese. According to the UG line of reasoning, as a child you adopt a parameter called the "null-subject" parameter, the fact that sentences do not have to have overtly expressed subjects. So in Portuguese the equivalent of *Saw me yesterday* is grammatical, whereas in English it is ungrammatical. And Portuguese will have more information in its verbs about the nature of the subject (at least person and number) than in English. And so on. This has been easily the most influential of all the research traditions looking into the relationship between grammar and cognition.

Row two of the table symbolizes the Sapir-Whorf research tradition, which looks at the grammar-cognition interface from the perspective of how grammar, that is, the way our languages are structured, might affect the way we think.

For the third row, the names that come to mind are Brent Berlin and Paul Kay, both emeritus professors of the University of California at Berkeley. Their work purports to show that all cultures' classification of colors follows restrictions imposed by the human brain's physical constraints for recognizing tints, hues, and relative brilliance of colors. This cerebral-cognitive limitation imposes constraints on the classification of colors in all cultures.

Row four represents the perspective of linguistic anthropologists like Greg Urban of the University of Pennsylvania. Urban's work makes the case that language can affect culture in interesting and subtle ways. One of the examples he discusses concerns the effect of passive (such as *John was seen by Bill*) versus active (*Bill saw John*) grammatical constructions on the concept of the hero in different societies.

Urban claims that in some languages the proportion of passive clauses may be much higher in natural oral or written discourse than active clauses, while in other languages active sentences may occur much more frequently. He further makes a case that when passives are the more natural and most frequent type of construction, heroes discussed in discourses will be perceived more naturally as having things done to them rather than initiating actions. These heroes will be perceived as having more passive personalities than the heroes of languages where active sentences predominate.

In the case of a language without passive constructions, we would encounter sentences like *The man killed the jaguar* and *The jaguar killed the man*, but not *The man was killed by the jaguar*. When an action is performed, the one doing the action is central to the telling of the story.

On the other hand, in a language that favors passive constructions the one doing the action is less central to the story. For example, if we compare closely the active versus passive contrasts of examples like *The man killed the jaguar* and *The jaguar was killed by the man* (or, even more likely in a passive construction, *The jaguar was killed*) occurring time and time again in stories, we would soon realize that in the passive, the role of "the man" is reduced in centrality. What becomes central is the object of the action, here "the jaguar," and not the subject or doer of the action. Such contrasts can work hand in hand with the culture to produce either heroes that are central to the telling of stories or stories in which doers of action are not so crucial, not so central, and, hence, not so heroic.

Since Pirahã lacks passive constructions, its principal characters in stories, like the panther story, are active initiators of actions and much more heroic than their counterparts in languages that favor passives. (I will not give an example of the latter, since I am only offering a simple summary of Urban's theory. In fact, I think examples of languages like this might be more complicated than this theory suspects.) In any case, this underscores how crucial it is to study language and culture together, rather than in isolation. Like my own work—though from the opposite direction—this goes against the traditions of both modern linguistics and much of modern anthropology.

Row five represents the research that investigates how culture can affect cognition. The Pirahã case is a good example. Pirahã's lack of counting is a result of cultural constraints, as we discussed earlier. But this cultural by-product has cognitive effects—Pirahã adults find it nearly impossible to learn to count after a lifetime spent in a number-less environment.

Finally, the last row in the table represents the research that others, including me, are doing on local and global effects of cultural values on sentence formation, word structure, and sound structure. This is controversial work too and also goes against much received knowledge in linguistics. It is what the immediacy of experience principle, for example, is trying to get at.

Theories affect our perceptions. They are part of the cultural information that constrains the way we see the world around us. There are many examples of culture-perception connections that don't involve science but which illustrate my point, such as the time I mistook an anaconda for a floating log. My culture told me to look for logs when traveling by boat (universally good advice!). And it gave me information on what floating logs look like in a river. But it didn't have anything to tell me about what very large anacondas look like swimming toward you.

We were traveling out of the village in our own motorboat, all the way to Humaitá to catch the bus to Pôrto Velho. Keren had made tuna sandwiches with homemade bread and we had Kool-Aid to drink. As I piloted the boat down the Maici and then the Marmelos, everyone was relaxed. Shannon was reading the Brazilian comic book *Monica* while the others dozed or watched the scenery go by.

We came to my favorite part of the entire trip, the *encontro das aguas*, where the dark green water of the Marmelos meets the chocolate-milk-colored water of the Madeira. I shouted for everyone to look and we all watched as the two colors of water ran for a bit side by side, then we saw swirls of muddy water in the green water, then finally the green water was absorbed, about five hundred yards past the mouth.

I then turned my attention upriver, as we skirted the island that sits at the mouth of the Marmelos, motoring toward the Auxiliadora, where we would spend the night. The Madeira River is so named for the trees that are washed from its muddy banks and float down it toward the Amazon. There are huge trunks and branches in the river, especially dangerous when they float invisibly just beneath the surface. About two hundred yards upriver I saw a log floating in the fast current. It was twisted. When I first began to travel the Amazon system, I expected to see new things in this new world, so I mistook every log in the river for a snake, because the water makes wood seem to undulate. This log seemed to undulate as well, though by now I knew enough not to mistake it for a snake. And I also knew that snakes were not as big as logs. This one, as I watched it more closely, was perhaps forty feet long and three feet thick.

I shifted to look at two macaws flying and squawking overhead. Then I looked back at the log. It was closer to us now. Strange, I thought, the log is floating toward the bank, perpendicular to the current.

Then as it got closer, I saw that it really was undulating. Suddenly it came straight toward my end of the boat. This was no log. This was the largest anaconda I had ever seen. Its head was larger than mine. Its body was much thicker than mine and over thirty feet long. It opened its mouth wide and swam toward me. I swerved sharply, throwing my family to the side hard, and I managed to hit the snake with the propeller of my 15-horsepower outboard motor as it dove under the boat. *Thud.* A solid hit. I thought I had hit it in the head, but I wasn't sure.

The snake disappeared. Then a second later the entire snake's body stood up out of the water, towering above the boat, but receding behind us as we pressed forward, at about ten miles per hour. I looked at the entire length of the snake's whitish underbelly as it fell backward with a loud, large splash into the Madeira River.

I didn't know anacondas could to that, I thought. That damned thing could have jumped in the boat with us!

I was just staring. Shannon looked up now from her comic and said "Wow!"

This experience of mistaken perception taught me what psychologists have long known: perception is learned. We perceive the world, both as theoreticians and as citizens of the universe, according to our experiences and expectations, not always, perhaps even never, according to how the world actually is.

As I became more fluent in Pirahã, I began to harbor a suspicion that the people were keeping their speech simple for my sake. When they spoke to me, the sentences seemed short, with only one verb each. So I decided that it would be worth listening more carefully to how they spoke to one another, rather than basing my conclusions on how they spoke to me. My best opportunity, I knew, would come from Báígipóhoái, Xahoábisi's wife. Each morning she talked loudly, beginning around five o'clock, sitting up in her hut in the dark, with Xahoábisi getting the fire going strong, only a few feet from my bedroom. She spoke to the entire village about what she had dreamed. She asked people by name what they were going to do that day. She told men leaving in canoes what kind of fish to catch, where the best places to fish were, how foreigners could be best avoided, and on and on. She was the village crier and gossip rolled into one. She was enjoyable to listen to. There was a certain artistry to her discourse, with her deep voice, the range of intonation in her talk (from very low to very high and back down again), the stylistically different way she pronounced her words—as if breath were going into her lungs and mouth rather than coming out. If ever there was a speaker that was speaking Pirahã for Pirahãs and not for me, the linguist, Báígi was it. Important for me, as I recorded then transcribed her sentences, they were structured identically to the sentences spoken to me by Kóhoi and other teachers—just one verb each.

This was especially challenging, since in my analysis of Pirahã grammar, I tried hard to collect examples where one phrase or sentence occurred inside another, as any linguist would, since such structures are supposed to reveal the grammar better than the simple sentences I was collecting. I began by looking for sentences like *The man who caught the fish is in the house,* where a sentence-like relative clause (*who caught the fish*) occurs within a noun phrase (*The man ...*), which occurs within another sentence (*The man is in the house*). At the time, I believed that relative clauses existed in all languages.

In trying to figure out whether or not Pirahã had relative clauses, I decided to ask Kóhoi one day to tell me if I was "talking pretty" when I said, "The man came into the house. He was tall." These are two simple sentences. In English, though, we would prefer to put the second sentence inside the former, to get a relative clause—"The man who was tall came into the house." When I asked the Pirahã men whether my speech was pretty or not, usually they would say yes, to avoid rudeness. But then, if I had in fact expressed myself poorly, they would repeat the sentence I had mangled back to me in correct Pirahã, without ever telling me I was wrong. I was therefore hoping when I asked this particular question that Kóhoi would utter a corrective sentence and say something like "The man who is tall came into the house." But, no, Kóhoi just said I was speaking pretty and repeated the phrases after me just as I had said them originally, something that the Pirahãs rarely do if the grammar is incorrect.

I experimented with various sentences using several different Pirahã teachers. All would either answer that I was speaking pretty or say "*Xaió!*" (Correct!)

So in a draft section of my Pirahã grammar about relative clauses I wrote that there were none in the language. But then one day Kóhoi was making a fishing arrow and needed a nail for the tip.

He spoke to his son, Paitá: "*Ko Paitá, tapoá xigaboopaáti. Xoogiai hi goo tapoá xoáboi. Xaisigíai*" (Hey Paitá, bring back some nails. Dan bought those very nails. They are the same).

I heard this and it stopped me in my tracks. I realized that these phrases were functioning together like a single sentence with a relative clause and that they could even be translated as such a sentence in English, but that their form was significantly different. They were three separate sentences, not one sentence with another sentence inside of it as in English. This Pirahã construction therefore lacked a relative clause in the sense that linguists usually mean. Crucially, the last sentence, *Xaisigíai* (They are the same), equated the word *nails* from the first two sentences. In English we would say, "Bring back *the nails that Dan bought*" (I have italicized the relative clause portion). I was thus seeing the separate clauses interpreted together even though they were not part of the same sentence. So there was a way of producing something like a relative clause in meaning, even if there were no relative clauses proper.

A sentence to most linguists is the expression in words of a proposition, an unspoken unit of meaning that represents a single thought, such as *I ate, John saw Bill,* or a single state, such as *The ball is red, I have a hammer,* and so on. Most languages not only have simple sentences like these, though, but they also have a way of putting one sentence or one phrase inside of another. This matrioshka-doll characteristic is known as recursion by computer scientists, linguists, psychologists, and philosophers. This issue is currently setting linguistics, philosophy of language, anthropology, and psychology ablaze, in a debate on the potential significance of Pirahã's grammar for the understanding of humans and their languages.

In this respect, the evidence I was collecting was beginning to build support for two ideas I later came to hold about Pirahã sentence structure. The first was that Pirahã sentences lacked recursion. The second idea was that recursion wasn't all that important—apparently, whatever you could say with recursion in one language, you could say without it in another. Linguists have long believed, though not always using the same terminology, that recursion is very important in language. And so I knew that any evidence that Pirahã could bring to bear on the issue would be important.

Chomsky was one of the first to ask how humans could produce so many sentences, an unbounded number, with only finite brains. There must be some tool available to allow us to make, as the common linguistics saying goes, "infinite use of finite means" (though I don't think any linguist could really provide a coherent story of what that expression really means in scientific terms). Chomsky claimed that the fundamental tool that underlies all of this creativity of human language is recursion.

Recursion has traditionally been defined as the ability to put one item inside another of the same type (for the more mathematically inclined, it is a function with a procedure or a subroutine whose implementation references itself). A visual form of recursion occurs when you hold a mirror up to a mirror and see an infinite regress of mirrors in the reflection. And an auditory form of recursion is feedback, the squeal from an amplifier picking up and continuing to amplify its own output over and over.

These are the standard definitions of recursion. In syntax, again, this would translate into putting one unit inside another unit of the same type. Take a phrase like *John's brother's son*, which contains the noun phrases *John, his brother,* and *his son*. And a sentence like *I said that you are ugly* contains the sentence *you are ugly*.

In 2002, in the journal *Science*, Marc Hauser, Noam Chomsky, and Tecumseh Fitch placed a great burden on recursion by labeling it the unique component of human language. They claimed that recursion is

the key to the creativity of language, in that as a grammar possesses this formal device, it can produce an infinite number of sentences of unbounded length.

However, as word has reached the scientific world of my claim that Pirahã lacks recursion in the mathematical, matrioshka-doll sense, a curious thing has happened. The definition of recursion has changed among some followers of Chomsky. In a sense this is an example of something the philosopher Richmond Thomason used to say to people who changed their mind on some subjects: "If at first you don't succeed, redefine success."

The newest definition of recursion to emerge from Chomsky's school makes recursion a form of compositionality. Simply put, it says that you can put parts together to make something new and you can do that endlessly. Under this novel notion of recursion, which is not accepted by any mathematical linguists or computer scientists that I know of, if I can put words together to form a sentence, that is recursion, and if I can put sentences together to form a story, that is recursion.

My own reaction to this is that it errs by conflating reasoning with language. People clearly can put sentences together and then interpret them as a whole story. But this is the same ability crime scene investigators use when they interpret apparently disparate bits of evidence and assemble them into a story of how the crime was committed. This is not language, it is reasoning. Yet the major appeal of Chomskyan theory for most scientists is that it has separated reasoning and language, and in particular that Chomsky has distinguished the structure of stories from the structure of sentences and phrases. He has claimed many times that stories and sentences are put together by very different principles. So failing to draw that distinction in this new notion of recursion is, ironically, inconsistent with Chomsky's own theory but consistent with mine.

If I am right about Pirahã lacking recursion, Chomsky and other researchers have some head scratching to do. They need to suggest how a language without recursion can fit into a theory in which recursion is the crucial component of language.

One answer that Chomsky and others have given to my claim that Pirahã lacks recursion is that recursion is a tool that's made available by the brain, but it doesn't have to be used. But then that's very difficult to reconcile with the idea that it's an essential property of human language, because if recursion doesn't have to appear in one given language, then, in principle, it doesn't have to appear in any language. This places them in the unenviable position of claiming that the unique property of human language does not actually have to be found in any human language.

It is not that hard, really, to tell whether recursion does any work in figuring out the grammar of a specific language. Quite simply, the question is twofold. First, can the grammar you write without recursion handle the language you are studying more simply than a grammar with recursion? Second, what kinds of phrases would you expect to find if the grammar did in fact have recursion? A language without recursion will look different from a language that has recursion. The main way is that it will not have phrases inside other phrases. If you find a phrase within a phrase, the language has recursion, period. If you don't, it might not, though more data will be needed. The first question, then, is whether there are phrases within phrases in Pirahã. The answer is that there are not, following the standard argumentation used in theoretical linguistics to establish this: it lacks the pitch marking, words, or sentence size of a language with recursion.

The grammars of the world's languages employ various markers to indicate that a given structure is recursive, that is, that one phrase is inside another. Such marking is not required, but it is very common. Some of these markers are independent words. In English, we say things like *I said that he was coming*. In this sentence, the phrase *he was coming* is located inside the phrase *I said . . .* ; *He was coming* is the content of what was said. In English, *that* is a frequently used "complementizer" for marking recursion. If we look at the relative clause complex that Kóhoi gave me, we see three independent sentences, interpreted jointly, without a shred of evidence that one sentence is inside another.

Another common marker of recursion is intonation, the use of pitch to mark different meaning and structural relations between sentences and their parts. The verb phrases of main clauses, for example, often get a higher pitch in English than the verb phrases of subordinate clauses. For example, in the most common pronunciation of the sentence *The man that you saw yesterday is here, is here* gets a higher pitch than *saw yesterday*. This is because *saw yesterday* is the subordinate, or embedded verb, phrase and *is here* is the main verb phrase. But Robert Van Valin and I, in a three-year National Science Foundation project dedicated to the study of intonation and its relation to syntax in five Amazonian languages, found no evidence that Pirahã uses intonation as an alternative marker of recursion. Now, Pirahã intonation does group sets of sentences together in paragraphs and stories, but this is not recursion in the grammar proper, at least not according to the entire history of Chomskyan grammar (though many linguists disagree with Chomsky and do place stories in the grammar—I have no quarrel at all with these other schools of linguistics in this sense). It is recursion in reasoning. In fact, many specialists on the role of intonation in human speech believe that it would be naive to try to link intonation directly to the structure of sentences rather than to the meanings of sentences and how they are used in stories. If this is correct, then intonation has nothing conclusive to say about whether a language has recursion or not.

Confusing language and reasoning is something that we have already seen to be a serious mistake. It is easy to confuse the two because reasoning involves many of the cognitive operations that some linguists associate with language, including recursion. Herbert Simon's classic 1962 article, "The Architecture of Complexity," gives a fascinating example of recursion outside of language. Simon's example even shows how recursion can help your business! His example is worth citing in full:

> There once was [sic] two watchmakers, named Hora and Tempus, who manufactured very fine watches. Both of them were highly regarded, and the phones in their workshops rang frequently. New customers were constantly calling them. However, Hora prospered while Tempus became poorer and poorer and finally lost his shop. What was the reason?
>
> The watches the men made consisted of about 1,000 parts each. Tempus had so constructed his that if he had one partially assembled and had to put it down—to answer the phone, say—it immediately fell to pieces and had to be reassembled from the elements. The better the customers liked his watches the more they phoned him and the more difficult it became for him to find enough uninterrupted time to finish a watch.
>
> The watches Hora handled were no less complex than those of Tempus, but he had designed them so that he could put together subassemblies of about ten elements each. Ten of these subassemblies, again, could be put together into a larger subassembly and a system of ten of the latter constituted the whole watch. Hence, when Hora had to put down a partly assembled watch in order to answer the phone, he lost only a small part of his work, and he assembled his watches in only a fraction of the man-hours it took Tempus.

This watchmaking example has nothing to do with language. So by this example, and many others, we know that human reasoning is recursive. In fact we know that many things in the world apart from humans are recursive (even atoms manifest recursivelike hierarchies in their construction from subatomic particles). Familiar Russian matrioshka dolls illustrate another type of recursion, known as nesting, where one doll is placed inside another of the same type, and that pair into another of the same type, and so on.

An important inference from the presence of recursion is this: if a language has recursion then there should be no longest sentence in the language. For example, in English any sentence that someone utters can be made longer. *The cat that ate the rat is well* can be extended to *The cat that ate the rat that ate the cheese is well,* and so on.

Crucially, *none of these diverse types of evidence for recursion is found in Pirahã.* The story about the panther that Kaaboogí told me is typical. No evidence along any of these dimensions is found in that or other Pirahã texts for recursion in the grammar.

Most interesting, perhaps, for illustrating my point against recursion, is a sentence like the following, because there is no obvious way to make it longer in Pirahã: *Xahoapióxio xigihí toioxaagá hi kabatií xogií xi mahaháíhiigí xiboítopí piohoaó, hoíhio* (Another day an old man slowly butchered big tapirs by the side of the water, two of them). Anything else added to this, like the word *brown* in *big brown tapirs,* would render the sentence ungrammatical. Phrases can have a single modifier (phrases that are found in natural stories—I do have some artificial examples where I was able to get some Pirahãs to place more modifiers in the phrase, but they didn't like it and never use more than one in a phrase in natural stories). A second one can occasionally be inserted at the end of the sentence as an afterthought—like the *two of them* at the end of this sentence. If this is correct, then Pirahã is finite and cannot be recursive.

I should rule out one final bit of potential evidence for recursion in Pirahã that has been suggested to me by several linguists. The first linguist to do so was Professor Ian Roberts, the head of linguistics at Cambridge University, during a debate with me on the BBC's radio program *Material World.* He claimed that Pirahã must have recursion if it can add or repeat words or phrases after sentences, because, as he put it, "Iteration is a form of recursion." Logically this is correct. Putting one phrase inside another at the end of a sentence is mathematically identical to repeating elements after a phrase or sentence. If I say, "John says that he is coming," the sentence *that he is coming* is placed inside the sentence *John says . . .* at the end. This is known as "tail recursion." Mathematically or logically this is equivalent to saying, "John runs, he does," where the sentence *he does* is just a sentence repeated after another sentence. Pirahã can, indeed must, have one sentence follow another sentence, as in "*Kóxoí soxóá kahapii. Hi xaoxai hiaba*" (Kóxoí already left. He is not here). But if mere repetition, iteration, of one sentence after another satisfies Hauser, Chomsky, and Fitch's definition of recursion (as some of their followers tell me it would), then it is found in species other than *Homo sapiens*.

Our Rhodesian ridgeback, Bentley, is an emotional soul. Among the things he gets emotional about is other dogs passing our house—he wants to eat them or otherwise harm them. He always barks when they go by. I for one don't think his barks are devoid of content. I think he is communicating with his barks something like "Get the hell out of my yard." But it doesn't matter what exactly he is communicating—he is communicating *something* with his barks. Now sometimes Bentley barks once or twice and then stops. This is because the dog he is barking at has left the lawn. Other times he barks repeatedly, that is, he iterates his barks, and this indicates his rising anger/desire that the dog leave our yard (or whatever it means to him). What does his repeated barking mean? Well, if iteration just is a form of recursion, it means Bentley has recursive barking. But Bentley is not a human. So recursion isn't limited to humans. Or, more sensibly, iteration shouldn't be considered recursion.

Yet the reasons that lead me to claim that Pirahã lacks recursion are not merely negative. Saying that a language lacks recursion makes claims about what the language's grammar will look like. We want to look at those predictions and see how they fare with respect to Pirahã.

The pervasive immediacy of experience principle (IEP) could explain why Pirahã lacks embedded sentences. Consider relative clauses again, as in *The man who is tall is on the path*. This English sentence is composed of two smaller sentences: the main sentence, *The man is on the path*, and the embedded, or subordinate, sentence, *who is tall*. The new information, or what linguists call the assertion, is found in the main sentence, *The man is on the path*. The embedded sentence merely adds some old information shared by the hearer and the speaker—there is a tall man that we both know—and draws attention to a particular man in order to help the hearer know who the man on the path is. This is not an assertion. Embedded sentences rarely, if ever, are used to make assertions. So the IEP predicts that Pirahã will lack embedded sentences because it says that declarative utterances may contain only assertions. Containing an embedded clause would be to contain a nonassertion, in violation of the IEP.

Another example comes from sentences like *The dog's tail's tip is broken.* This is something the Pirahãs would say regularly, since a high proportion of their dogs have damaged tails. One evening I noticed a dog in the village with the end of its tail missing. I said, *"Giopaí xígatoi xaóxio baábikoi,"* which is how I thought I should say, "The dog's tail's tip is malformed." It literally means "Dog tail at the end is bad." The Pirahãs responded, *"Xígatoi xaóxio baábikoi"* (The tip of the tail is bad). I didn't think anything about the omission initially because omissions are common in any language when speakers share information in common—no need to restate that we're talking about a dog; we all knew that already.

But as I investigated further, the only way to get something like *The dog's tail's tip is broken* is *"Giopaí xígatoi baábikoi, xaóxio"* (The dog's tail is bad, on the tip). What I discovered is that no more than one possessor can occur in a given phrase (*dog* is the possessor of *tail*, for example). If there were no recursion in the language, this would make sense. You can get one possessor without recursion by simply having a cultural or linguistic understanding shared by speakers that when two nouns are next to each other, the first one is interpreted as the possessor. But if you have two possessors in the clause, one of them has to be in a phrase that is within another phrase.

Pirahã lacks these structures. It is hard for many linguists to see how culture could be responsible for this. And I agree that the route from a cultural constraint to complex noun phrases can seem a bit circuitous.

Starting with subordinate clauses, the first thing to remember is that according to the IEP, the embedded clause is not allowed because it is not an assertion. The question this raises is how the grammar of Pirahã could eliminate the unwanted embedded clauses in order to obey a cultural taboo.

There are three ways that it could do this. First, the grammar could prohibit the emergence of rules that create recursive structures—rules that are technically expressed like $A \rightarrow AB$. If the grammar does not contain this rule, it cannot place one phrase or sentence immediately inside another phrase or sentence of the same type.

Second, the grammar could fail to have evolved recursion. There is a growing consensus among linguists that grammars without recursion precede grammars with recursion evolutionarily and that even in grammars with recursion, nonrecursive structures are used in most environments.

A final possibility is that Pirahã grammar simply fails to provide for structure in sentences. There would be no recursion because in effect there would be no phrases, only words placed side by side and interpreted as a sentence.

Without syntax, Pirahã's grammar would lack verb phrases, noun phrases, embedded sentences, and so forth. In fact it does seem possible to interpret all Pirahã sentences as beads on a string, with no need for more complex structure of the type that phrase structures would predict. A sentence would be simply the list of words needed to complete the meaning of a verb, plus a minimum of modification, usually no more than one adjectivelike or adverblike modifier per sentence. Pirahã would lack syntax, in my rather extreme view, to guarantee that nonassertions do not appear within declarative sentences, in violation of the IEP. The IEP allows declarative clauses to contain only assertions. Therefore the IEP constrains the grammar of Pirahã.

Take the original relative clause sequence I overheard from Kóhoi: "Hey Paitá, bring back some nails. Dan bought those very nails. They are the same." There are two assertions here, *Dan bought the nails* and *the nails are the same.* But in the English relative *the nails that Dan bought,* there is no assertion. So the immediacy of experience principle is violated.

If my reasoning here is on the right track, what other predictions does it make about Pirahã grammar? Exactly the right ones, it turns out.

It predicts that Pirahã will lack coordination, because this also involves the general property of recursion, something that has been eliminated from the grammar of Pirahã, as we have already discussed, in order to avoid having embedded nonassertions in declarative assertions. Coordinate structures are of course common in English and many other languages. Their recursion is shown in examples like *John and Bill came to town yesterday,* where the noun *John* and the noun *Bill* both occur in the longer noun phrase *John and Bill.* Coordination of verbs and sentences is also ruled out, so Pirahã has no sentences like *Bill ran and Sue watched* or *Sue ran and ate.*

The IEP's restriction against recursion also correctly predicts that Pirahã will lack disjunction, as in *Either Bob or Bill will come, I had some white meat, chicken or pork,* and so on. Pirahã lacks disjunction because it, like coordination, requires putting phrases inside of other phrases—recursion. The Pirahãs would say, for example, rather than "Either Bob or Bill will come," something like "Bob will come. Bill will come. Hmm. I don't know."

These do not exhaust the predictable consequences of the lack of recursion in Pirahã. Other predictions are being tested now by a range of psychologists and anthropologists. This is interesting because the fact that there are testable predictions of the immediacy of experience principle shows that it is not simply a negative statement about what Pirahã lacks, but a positive statement about the nature of Pirahã grammar and how that grammar differs from many well-known grammars.

The statement is positive because Pirahã imposes and enforces a cultural value on its grammar. It is not, again, simply that Pirahã accidentally lacks recursion. It doesn't want it; it doesn't allow it because of a cultural principle.

In addition to the Pirahãs' grammar, the IEP helps to account for the other gaps in the language we have already discussed, such as the absence of number and numerals, the absence of color words, the simplicity of the kinship system, and so on.

The prohibition against abstractions and generalizations of the immediacy of experience principle is a very narrow prohibition. It by no means entails that Pirahã culture prohibits abstract thought. It is also not a prohibition against all abstractions or generalizations in the language. For example, the Pirahãs have words for kinds or categories of things, as all languages do, and these words, usually nouns, are by definition a type of abstraction. How is this seeming contradiction tolerated in Pirahã?

Grammar had once seemed to me too complicated to derive from any general human cognitive properties. It appeared to cry out for a specialized component of the brain, or what some linguists call a language organ or instinct. But such an organ becomes implausible if we can show that it is not needed because there are other forces that can explain language as both ontogenetic and phylogenetic fact.

Like most linguists today, I once believed that culture and language were largely independent. But if I am correct that culture can exercise major effects on grammar, then the theory I committed most of my research career to—the theory that grammar is part of the human genome and that the variations in the grammars of the world's languages are largely insignificant—is dead wrong. There does not have to be a specific genetic capacity for grammar; the biological basis of grammar could also be the basis of gourmet cooking, of mathematical reasoning, and of medical advances. In other words, it could just be human reasoning.

On the evolution of grammar, for example, many researchers have underscored the fact that our ancestors had to talk about things and events, about relative quantities, and about the contents of the minds of fellow members of their species, among other things. If you can't talk about things and what happens to them (events) or what they are like (states), you can't talk about anything. So all languages need verbs and nouns. But I have been convinced by the research of others, as well as my own, that if a language has these, then the basic skeleton of the grammar largely follows. The meanings of verbs require a certain number of nouns, and those nouns plus the verb make simple sentences, ordered in logically restricted ways. Other permutations of this foundational grammar follow from culture, contextual prominence, and modification of nouns and verbs. There are other components to grammar, but not all that many. Put like this, as I began to see things, there really doesn't seem to be much need for grammar proper to be part of the human genome, as it were. Perhaps there is even much less need for grammar as an independent entity than we might have once thought.

Although a language might possess a strong cultural constraint, like the immediacy of experience principle in Pirahã, such constraints cannot override general forces and results of evolution nor the nature of what it means to communicate. Nouns and certain kinds of generalizations are part of our evolutionary heritage and cultural principles cannot override these, even though they do show that culture and grammar are intimately connected.

On the other hand, research is ongoing. The issue of whether Pirahã does or does not have recursion is far from settled. But the evidence being gathered and interpreted by independent researchers is consistent with my conclusions.

One phenomenon that has attracted my attention since the beginning of my reflection on the possible connections between grammar and culture is that theories, regardless of how useful they are in many ways, can impede novel thinking. Our theories are like cultures. Just as there are gaps in Pirahã culture for counting, color words, and so on, some theories can have gaps where other theories might have robust explanatory mechanisms. In this sense both theories and cultures shape our minds' ability to perceive the world, sometimes positively and sometimes not so positively, depending on the goals they set for themselves.

What are the implications for Pirahã grammar if it lacks recursion? First of all, a lack of recursion in its grammar would mean that its grammar is not infinite—there would be an upper limit to the number of sentences generated by it. But this would not mean that the *language* is finite, because recursion is found in Pirahã stories—parts of stories are built up, there are subplots, characters, events, and all sorts of relationships among all of these. This is interesting because it means that the role of grammar in the infinitude of a language is not so important—you can have a nonfinite language with a finite grammar, something Chomsky's recent theory on the importance of recursion can neither accommodate nor elucidate. This would also entail that you could specify the upper size of a particular sentence in that language, though not the upper size of a discourse. That sounds bizarre for a language. Some linguists or cognitive scientists might even leap to the conclusion that an absence of a recursion could render a language deficient in some way. But this would not be correct.

Even if a language's grammar is finite, this doesn't mean that the grammar is not rich or interesting, however. Think of something like chess, which has also got a finite number of moves. This finitude of chess moves doesn't have much practical effect, though. Chess is an enormously productive game that can and has been played for centuries. The fact that chess is finite tells us very little about its richness or its importance. The Pirahã discourse is rich, artistic, and able to express anything that they want to say within their self-imposed parameters.

So if there were a finite grammar, this wouldn't mean that the grammar was spoken by abnormal humans, nor would it mean that it was a poor source of communication. It wouldn't even mean that the language with that grammar was finite. If there were such languages, however, where and under what conditions might we expect to find them?

If you build into the foundation of your theory the constraint that all grammars are nonfinite and that they must therefore be recursive, the absence of recursion will elude you. Your theory will have hindered you, just as my culture's lack of experience with dangerous animals outside of zoos could render me easy caiman prey.

On the other hand, if our theory doesn't require that recursion be a crucial component of language, where does recursion come from? No one can dispute that it is found in most human languages. Nor can anyone seriously doubt that it is found in all human thought. My view is that recursion comes from the brain's general cognitive powers. It is part of how all humans think—even when it is not part of the structures of their languages. Humans have recursion because they are smarter than species without it, though recursion could be a cause or an effect of this greater intelligence—no one knows right now, regardless of what claims are found in the literature.

In fact, as we saw earlier, Herbert Simon claimed almost exactly this in "The Architecture of Complexity." As I noted, in this article he argued that recursive structures are fundamental to information processing and that we use them not just in language, but also in economics and problem solving.

And recursion is crucial in almost all of the stories that we tell. Surprisingly, human discourses have never been the subject of Chomskyan research. But as we just saw, this is a massive oversight, since recursion can be found outside the grammar, tremendously reducing the importance of the grammar in understanding the nature of language and communication. Discourses are purposely ignored by Chomsky as social or at least nonlinguistic constructs. Yet when we examine the stories that the Pirahãs tell, we find recursion, not in individual sentences, but in the fact that ideas are built inside of other ideas—some parts of the story are subordinate to other parts of the story. Such recursion is not part of the syntax proper, but it is part of the way that they tell their stories.

We might propose, following Simon, that recursion is absolutely essential to the human brain, and that it derives from the fact that humans have larger brains or brains with more convolutions than other species. Ultimately, though, it's not even clear that recursion is unique to humans. And it most certainly is not clear that recursion is part of grammar, rather than coming into languages because it is a useful, preexistent cognitive tool.

The crucial application of Simon's proposal for studies of language is that hierarchical structures found in languages that have so long been the focus of Chomskyan research are "emergent" properties, rather than basic properties of language. That is, they appear in languages in response to the interaction of the brain's ability to think recursively and problems or situations in the culture or society that are more efficiently communicated recursively.

If recursion is proposed to be, as Chomsky and many of his followers would have it, the core faculty of the human language capacity, and if recursion is absent in one or more languages, then the Chomskyan proposal is falsified. But if recursion is not the core faculty, then Pirahã suggests that the kind of theory of language we need is not one in which language is an instinct. Instead, we might be better served by looking at syntax, along with the other components of language, as one part of the solution to the problem of communication, that is, the need to communicate appropriately in a specific environment.

I doubt Pirahã is the only language that will challenge our thinking about recursion, human language, and the interaction of culture and grammar. If we look at other groups—groups in New Guinea, Australia, and Africa—we are likely to find similar cases of esoteric communication and societies of intimates that could lead to the lack of recursion. Esoteric communication could very well contribute to our explanation of the some of the more controversial aspects of Pirahã grammar.

The usefulness of the concept of esoteric communication for understanding Pirahã is demonstrated in part in current research by the psychologists Thomas Roeper of the University of Massachusetts and Bart Hollebrandse of the University of Groningen. This research suggests that recursion might be a device that is useful for packing sentences with more information in societies with a higher degree of exoteric communication where more complex information is the rule, such as modern industrialized societies. But in a society like the Pirahãs', the esoteric nature of their communication renders recursion less useful, while the immediacy of experience principle is incompatible with it.

What we need to look for are groups that have been isolated, for various reasons, from larger cultures. The Pirahãs' isolation is due to their very strong sense of superiority to and disdain for other cultures. Far from thinking of themselves as inferior because they lack anything found in other languages and cultures, they consider their way of life the best possible way of life. They're not interested in assimilating other values. So we see little seepage from other cultures or languages into Pirahã. And these are the kinds of culture-language pairings we need to be studying.

One way to describe the creative use of language is that human language, without reference to recursion, is free from control by the environment and is not restricted to merely "practical" functions. The American linguist Charles Hockett called this the "productivity" of language. We can talk about anything, in principle, as the received wisdom goes.

Of course, practically this is false. We cannot talk about just anything. We are ignorant of most things there are to talk about. We do not even know that they exist. Moreover, many things we do or encounter every day, like the faces of people we have seen, directions to a familiar restaurant, and so on, can be very hard to talk about. That is why we find pictures and maps and other visual aids so useful.

Nevertheless, the idea of creativity in language has been rightly influential for nearly four centuries. There is an obvious appeal to the notion that humans are special and that they are, at least in their minds, unfettered by the limitations that beset the rest of the animal kingdom. The French philosopher René Descartes, whom Chomsky popularized among linguists, believed that there is a separate mental, creative essence that distinguishes humans from animals. Hovering over this idea is the concomitant view that man has a spiritual essence alongside his physical structure. This dualism has a "breath of God" smell about it, namely, that human language is profoundly "special," the idea that something animates the physical form of man, the mere dust that houses our consciousness.

Instead of this quasi-religious and somewhat mystical dualism that underlies much of the work of Descartes and, on some readings, Chomsky's work, I would propose a more concrete understanding of language. Language is a by-product of general properties of human cognition, rather than a special universal grammar, in conjunction with the constraints on communication that are common to evolved primates (such as the need for words to appear out of the mouth in a certain order, the need for units like words for things and events, and so on), and the overarching constraints of specific human cultures on the languages that evolve from them. It is clear that the original cultural circumstances can be lost. For example, a Pirahã moving to and adapting to life in Los Angeles would lose many of the cultural constraints of Pirahãs living along the Maici. His or her language might change. But if it didn't, at least initially, this would show us that languages can indeed be separated from cultures.

What I am suggesting here is trying to understand language in a situation as close to the original cultural context as possible. If this is on the right track, one cannot do linguistic field research apart from these cultural contexts—so I could not really hope to understand Pirahã by studying a Pirahã speaker in Los Angeles, or Navajo by studying a Navajo speaker in Tucson. I would need to study a language in its cultural context. I could study a language outside of its cultural context of course, and still discover many interesting things. But fundamental pieces to the puzzle of its grammar would be missing.

16 Crooked Heads and Straight Heads: Perspectives on Language and Truth

The Pirahãs' language and culture began to attract the attention of some Brazilian anthropologists not long after my trip with the FUNAI to map the people's reservation. One new graduate student, a young man from Rio de Janeiro, contacted me to enlist my help in working with the Pirahãs. To aid his efforts in establishing himself among them, I recorded a tape in Pirahã, introducing him to the people, telling them that he wanted to learn their language, and asking them to build him a house. The Pirahãs heard my voice coming out of his tape recorder and assumed that it was like a two-way radio, a device with which they are familiar.

After playing my tape for them and getting started in his investigations, he asked them about the creation of the world. Returning from the village to the city, he visited me one day in São Paulo to show me his results. We sat down to *cafezinhos* to hear the tape.

"You were wrong, Daniel," he blurted out, unable to contain himself any longer, even before we began listening.

I stopped sipping my *cafezinho*. "What do you mean I was wrong?"

"I mean, I found a creation myth," he said with a smile. "You said there weren't any, but I got one. Can you listen to my tape and help me translate the text?"

Part of the reason this student had chosen to do his graduate research on the Pirahãs was that he had heard of my claim that the Pirahãs have no creation myths, that is, no stories about their past—where they come from, how the world was created, and so on.

"OK, let's hear it," I replied, keenly curious.

So we put on the tape. It began with the anthropology student's voice, speaking with a Pirahã man near the tape recorder, in Portuguese. The student did not know more than a few Pirahã words, so was obliged to conduct his interview in Portuguese, even though few Pirahãs spoke more than a few words of Portuguese.

> Student: "Who made the world?"
> Pirahã man: "The world . . ." (repeating only the last two words of the question).
> Student: "How was the world made?"
> Pirahã man: "World made . . ."
> Student: "What was first? First?"
> Longish silence.
> Pirahã voice in the background, quickly repeated by man next to mic: "Bananas!"
> Student: "Then what? Second?"
> Pirahã voice in the background: "Papaya . . ."
> Pirahã man next to mic: "Papaya"—then loudly, switching gears: "Hey, Dan! Are you hearing me? I want matches! I want cloth. My baby is sick. He needs medicine."

The Pirahãs proceeded to talk to me on the tape about the village, who was there, what they wanted, when was I coming back, and so on. The student had thought that this part of the tape, which was clearly fluent and animated, was their creation myth. But the Pirahãs only knew that I could hear them directly on some devices that they had seen, such as phones and radios, so they assumed that communication into any electronic device, like a tape recorder, worked the same way. They were talking to me now, not answering the student's questions. He took the news in apparent good spirits, though with considerable bemusement that he could have been so misguided (we often find what we look for even when it doesn't exist). By then in any case he had realized that he wasn't in fact going to spend enough time with the Pirahãs to learn their language and that this research was going to be a bigger struggle than he had initially supposed.

The problem that my friend faced was that he spoke "crooked head" (Portuguese) and he was trying to communicate with "straight heads." But isn't this really just the problem we all face in communication— getting beyond the constraints of our own conventions of communication and trying to see things from the perspective of another set of conventions? This problem is found in science and in our professional and personal lives, between husbands and wives, parents and children, bosses and employees. We often think we know what our interlocutor is talking about, only to discover when we examine our conversation more closely that we misunderstood a great deal of it.

What do these kinds of misunderstandings tell us about the nature of our minds, our language, and who we are as *Homo sapiens*? To find out, we need to detour briefly to a discussion of the nature of knowledge and humans, for which this faux creation myth story is the catalyst. The purpose of this detour is to set the stage for larger issues that studying the Pirahãs raises for us.

We speak against a backdrop of assumptions that form the tapestry of our culture. When my friend tells me to turn left at the intersection, he doesn't need to add, "Pull up just behind the white line and wait for the stoplight to turn green." He knows that I know this as a member of my culture. Likewise, when a Pirahã father tells his son to shoot a fish in the river, he doesn't have to tell him to to sit motionless in a canoe for hours or to shoot below the fish to compensate for light refraction— sitting still and adjusting for refraction are culturally acquired skills and are known implicitly to the Pirahãs; they don't need to be stated overtly.

For the Pirahãs, like all of us, knowledge is experience interpreted through culture and individual psyches. Knowledge requires eye-witness testimony for the Pirahãs, but they do not subject this testimony to "peer review." If I entered the village to report seeing a bat with a twenty-foot wingspan, most wouldn't immediately believe me. But they might go look for themselves just to check it out. And if I were to report seeing a jaguar turn into a man, they would ask where, when, and how this happened. There is in principle no higher authority than my eyewitness account. This does not mean that one cannot lie. Lying is common among the Pirahãs, frankly, just as in all societies (it has useful evolutionary functions, such as protecting oneself and one's family). Nevertheless, knowledge is the explanation of one's own experiences, the explanation that one considers most useful.

In this sense, the Pirahãs' attitude toward knowledge, truth, and God is similar to the philosophy of pragmatism that emerges from the writings of William James, C. S. Peirce, and others—itself influenced by

North American indigenous peoples' concept of tolerance of physical and cultural differences. The Pirahãs and pragmatism share the idea that the test of knowledge is not whether it is true but whether it is useful. They want to know what they *need* to know in order to act. And the knowledge to act is based mainly on cultural conceptions of useful actions, of which theories are a part. So culture is helpful to us when we are in the locale where the culture developed.

When we're in new territory, though, places of the mind or of the body that our culture hasn't prepared us for, our culture can turn out to be an impediment. As an example of how poorly my culture has prepared me for some environments, I remember a night out walking with a teenage Pirahã, Kaioá. We were walking after dark from his hut to my house, about five hundred yards on a narrow jungle path that passed a shallow swamp. I was talking loudly to Kaioá and guiding myself on the path with my flashlight. Kaioá was slightly behind me, with no flashlight. Suddenly he interrupted the flow of my verbiage and said softly, "Look at the caiman up ahead!"

I directed the beam of my flashlight up the path. I did not see a thing.

"Turn off that lightninglike thing in your hand," Kaioá suggested, "and look in the dark."

I followed his instructions. Now I really saw absolutely nothing.

"What are you talking about?" I asked, beginning to feel that he was having me on. "There's nothing up ahead."

"No! Look!" Kaioá giggled. My inability to see beyond my nose is a source of constant merriment among the Pirahãs. "See those two bloodlike eyes up there?"

I strained my own eyes and then, sure enough, I could just make out two red dots about a hundred feet up ahead. Kaioá said that these were the eyes of a small caiman. He picked up a heavy stick from the dark jungle floor and ran ahead of me. After a couple of seconds I could hear the stick pounding something but I couldn't see anything. Shortly thereafter, Kaioá came back toward me laughing and carrying by the tail a three-foot caiman, beaten unconscious but not yet dead. The small caiman had apparently come out of the swamp to hunt frogs and snakes in the surrounding brush. It was hardly life-threatening. Still, though, it could have bitten off a toe or severely mauled my bare leg, if I had just kept up my chatter and careless walking.

Urban folks like me look for cars, bicycles, and pedestrians in the path, not prehistoric reptiles. I didn't know what to look for when walking briskly down a jungle trail. This had been another lesson about cognition and culture, though I didn't quite recognize that at the time. We all perceive the world the way our cultures have taught us. If our culture-constrained perceptions hinder us, however, then for the particular environment in which they do so, our cultures obscure our perceptions of the world and put us at a disadvantage.

Another day I was swimming with my language teacher, Kóhoibiíi-híai, in the river just in front of my house. We were talking and cooling off, completely relaxed, when some women came to the river just a bit down from us. They had a dead monkey that had just been singed in the fire, its fur burned off and its skin blackened. Its paws and feet had already been removed for the children to snack on. Laying the charred primate on the riverbank, one woman proceeded to slice it open from the crotch to the chest and unceremoniously began to pull its guts out with her hands. When finished gutting it, she chopped off the arms and legs and washed all the blood into the river. She then tossed the gray pile of intestines into the water and started back up the riverbank. I noticed shortly thereafter that the water was beginning to froth.

"What's that?" I ask Kóhoi.

"*Baixoó*" (Piranhas), he answered. "They like to eat blood and guts."

I was concerned. I would have to swim close by that frothing water to get out of the river. And what if the piranhas started looking for food near me, white meat, for example?

"Won't they try to eat us?" I asked.

"No. Just the monkey guts," Kóhoi answered as he splashed contentedly beside me. He shortly announced that he was leaving the water.

"Me too!" I said, staying as close to him as I was able, glad when I stepped up onto the riverbank.

My Southern California culture had prepared me to have an image of piranhas, albeit not a particularly accurate one. But it had not prepared me to recognize them by their signs in the wild. And it had not prepared me to be calm around them, and calmness in the face of jungle life can mean the difference between life and death.

Just as urban, literate societies fail to prepare their members for jungle life, the Pirahãs' jungle-based culture doesn't prepare them well for the demands of urban life. The Pirahãs are unable to perceive some things that even children from Western culture perceive well. For one thing, Pirahãs cannot make out two-dimensional objects, as in drawings and photographs, very well. They often hold pictures sideways or upside down, and ask me what it is that they are supposed to be seeing. They are getting better nowadays, as they have been exposed to many photos, but still this is not easy for them.

Recently a team from MIT and Stanford carried out experiments on Pirahã perception of two-dimensional representations. These experiments involved recognition of both clear photos and photos degraded in various ways. The team later reported its findings:

> While the Pirahã were able to interpret the untransformed photos perfectly, they had difficulty in interpreting the transformed images, even when they were side-by-side with the source photo (a result strikingly different from the pattern shown by control studies with American participants). While preliminary, this study provides suggestive evidence for difficulty (or inexperience with) visual abstraction. . . .

Culture is thus important even in something apparently so universal and simple as reading photographs. How important might it be in more general tasks? I gave some examples earlier of culture's importance in general tasks in my own experience. But there are also plenty of examples of its importance in general tasks for the Pirahãs.

In 1979, while Keren was recuperating from malaria, I brought two Pirahã men to Pôrto Velho to teach me more of their language, since I couldn't be in the village. They only owned a single pair of gym shorts each and were self-conscious in the midst of city-dwelling Brazilians. In the jungle, the Brazilians the Pirahãs saw were mainly river traders, who usually wore only gym shorts and flip-flops, at least while working. But in the city, dress was much more elaborate—especially the brightly colored dresses and blouses of the Brazilian women.

Going to town with me, Xipoógi and Xahoábisi asked me lots of questions about these women. Then they asked me if I could buy them shoes, long pants, and collared shirts so they could fit in at least a little bit better in town. So we walked up Pôrto Velho's main street, Sete de

Setembro, shopping for clothes. We chatted as we walked. The men asked me lots of questions about cars ("Who made those houses? They go fast!"), buildings ("Who made those? Brazilians sure do know how to build houses!"), pavement ("What is this hard black ground?"), and Brazilians in general ("Where do they hunt their food?" "Who makes the goods we are seeing?").

Passersby stared at these barefoot, bare-chested Indians. The Pirahãs stared back. Xipoógi and Xahoábisi thought the clean, nice-smelling, and colorfully dressed Brazilian women were gorgeous. They wondered if these women might have sex with them. I replied that I seriously doubted it because they didn't know the Pirahãs.

We went into a store and a lovely brown-skinned young woman with bracelets and long black hair, tight clothes, sandals, and a sweet smile came to wait on us, smelling lightly of pleasing perfume. The Pirahãs smiled.

With her help we found pants, shoes, and shirts for the men. Like all Pirahã men, they were about five feet two, weighed 110 pounds, and wore pants with twenty-eight-inch waists. The salesgirl had lots of questions for the Pirahãs, which I duly translated. The men asked her a few questions too. They put on their new outfits and we left to buy them toothbrushes, deodorant, combs, and aftershave—things they had heard about and which they considered vital for city living. Their muscular, slim bodies and dark complexions looked very attractive in Western clothes.

I thought that this was all going pretty well. No problem with bringing Pirahãs to the city after all. I wondered what I had been concerned about. True, I did find curious the Pirahãs' insistence on walking single file through town, just as they did through the jungle.

As we strolled down the city's sidewalks, Xipoógi walked behind me, with Xahoábisi behind him. I slowed down to let them catch up. They slowed down too. I slowed down more. Ditto. I stopped. They stopped. They simply would not walk beside me, not even when I asked them to. This makes sense on a narrow jungle path. There isn't room, unless you double the back-wearying work of clearing a path in the jungle by making a path wide enough for two to walk side by side. And it would be unsafe to do this anyway. People walking abreast make a bigger target for predators and offer each other less protection against snakes and other dangers. In the city, though, walking abreast, while spatially inefficient, allows the walkers to converse more easily and to be perceived as a group. I smiled about our walking arrangement and waited at the stoplight for the signal to walk across the street, Pôrto Velho's busiest.

I said to Xipoógi and Xahoábisi as I led the way, "Follow me. We're going to that store there," pointing toward a grocery store across the street.

Three-quarters of the way across the street, I looked back and Xipoógi and Xahoábisi were frozen in fear, looking at the cars that stood perpendicular to them on the road, waiting at the stoplight, revving their motors. I started back toward them but the light changed. The cars started moving forward and honking vigorously at the two Pirahã men, now quite visibly frightened. They were clearly on the verge of panicking and running through the traffic, unable to predict the movements of the cars, so different from any wild animals they had ever encountered. I got to them and took their hands, leading them back to my side of the street. We made it to the sidewalk.

"Those things scare us," they exclaimed, still not over their tension.

"They scare me too," I agreed.

"They are worse than jaguars," Xipoógi concluded.

The debate raging around Pirahã, again, is whether it forces us to rethink major theories about language or culture. Chomsky, founder of the most famous and influential of modern theories of language, says that languages with the properties I have described for Pirahã do not exist—that Pirahã is pretty much like any other language. But to understand why his own theory leads him to this state of denial, we need to know more about that theory.

Chomsky's view is that he is trying to discover the "true theory of universal grammar," where the latter is proposed to be a language-specific component of our biological endowment. It isn't clear what Chomsky means by the "true theory," but I assume that he means the one that completely matches reality (it is hard to know what most scientists and philosophers mean when they use the word *true,* so this problem is hardly unique to Chomsky). This is worth thinking about more carefully. At one level universal grammar seems to be almost a necessary concept—after all, neither plants, rocks, nor dogs talk—only humans do. We all agree there is something about human biology that underlies language. In this sense, Chomsky is trivially right. But the real question is how specific this endowment is to language (as opposed to, say, the proposal that our capacity for language just follows from general cognitive properties) and how much whatever this biological endowment is determines the final form of the grammar of any specific human language. And a related question, one that might initially seem tangential, is how we as scientists come by the knowledge to test our hypotheses.

There are two typical research locales in science—the laboratory and the field. The so-called hard sciences, such as physics and chemistry, as well as most of the social sciences, are done in climate-controlled, comfortable rooms, furnished with the equipment the researcher needs for his or her work. As pursued in wealthy countries like the United States, Germany, England, or France, science is done by a privileged few for society as a whole. At least on paper, its sponsors expect results to benefit the larger society in which the science is supported and takes place. Young scientists work under the security umbrella of an established leader in their field. In linguistics, Chomsky is a Daniel Boone figure, and the majority of linguists are settlers on his land.

Linguistics has changed over the decades. It was at one time more like the "field sciences," those branches of inquiry such as geology, anthropology, and biology, wherein learning entails leaving the laboratory for the rough world of fieldwork. Of course, many linguists continue to do field research on languages around the world.

But the explosive growth of linguistics after the advent of Chomsky in the 1950s has altered the ethos of the discipline in profound ways. Chomsky's attraction for many linguists, including me, is the elegance of his theory, not field research. The lemmas and axioms first given in his breakthrough work, *The Logical Structure of Linguistic Theory*, written while he was in his twenties, and the subsequent books such as *Syntactic Structures, Aspects of the Theory of Syntax, Lectures on Government and Binding*, and *The Minimalist Program*, convinced generations of linguists that Chomsky's theory was likely to lead to significant results. Like many others, I read all of these books cover to cover. I have taught graduate courses on most of them.

The culture of Chomskyan linguistics also spread because his department at MIT attracted some of the best students in the world. This new linguistics culture brought enormous changes in linguistics methodology as well as goals, another defining feature of the Chomsky group. Prior to Chomsky, to be an American linguist almost obligatorily entailed one or two years of living among a minority language community and writing a grammar of their language. This was nearly a rite of passage in North American linguistics. But since Chomsky himself did no field research and apparently had learned more interesting things about language than any fieldworker, many students and incoming professors working under the influence of Chomsky's assumptions understandably believed that the best way to do research might be to work deductively rather than inductively—from the institution rather than from the village, starting with an elegant theory and predetermining where facts best fit.

Here is my understanding of these ideas. An inductive approach to the study of language would be to allow each language to "speak for itself." We might do this by cataloging the observations of the language made by the field researcher and then working out a narrative of just what the elements of that language are (its words, phrases, sentences, texts, or however the field researcher cares to label them—whatever he or she finds most useful in discussing this particular language) and then how these elements fit together (such as, how do speakers of this language form sentences or paragraphs or whatever units they do form, and how do they use these to construct conversations, stories, and other forms of sociolinguistic interaction).

A deductive approach, on the other hand, begins with theories—prelabeled boxes—and fits aspects of language into them. New boxes can be made, but this is frowned upon. Much of the debate in deductive theories is about the aspects and borders of the boxes. The cultural values that have gotten a grip on linguistics partially as a result of Chomsky's deductive approach to language study should not be ignored. These include at least the following: field research is unnecessary to be a good linguist; it can be as important to study one's native language as it is to study previously unstudied languages in the field; grammar is a formal system independent of culture.

In the twenty-first century our knowledge of the form and meaning of parts of language is claimed by some to far exceed prior knowledge. This follows from the concept of scientific progress and the notion that we build "precept upon precept" upon the knowledge of our predecessors, in what Mortimer Adler, in his introduction to the *Great Books of the Western World,* refers to as the "great conversation" of life.

But there is a competing concept that many scientists believe in simultaneously: the notion of the scientific revolution. As developed in the work of the philosopher Thomas Kuhn, this is the idea that scientific theories can paint themselves into a corner and that scientists will then be trapped unless someone blasts a hole in the building and proclaims freedom to do science outside the confines of the previous approach. This blasting takes place as recalcitrant facts begin to accumulate, facts that a particular theory can only handle with a lot of patchwork and tearing and straining—what Kuhn calls "auxiliary hypotheses." Pirahã presents numerous recalcitrant facts, as do languages like it—and I have no doubt that more will be discovered. These facts require a good hole in the wall leading to a new theoretical edifice. This is what Pirahã says to me about the prevailing theory.

Our attempts to study other human beings can be as culturally influenced as my attempt to get the Pirahãs to walk side by side with me in the city. And culture not only affects the scientist-observer, but the subject under study as well. To understand theories about human languages requires us to consider the influence of culture on theory construction as well as the role of culture in shaping the object under study.

This is a controversial point. In one well-known book, Steven Pinker's *The Language Instinct,* little importance is attributed to culture in shaping human grammar. True, Pinker allows that culture bears significant responsibility for the things we talk about (so Americans of a certain age may compare Marlon Brando and Elvis Presley for relative sexiness or star power, or the influence of Google on research in modern American society; the Pirahãs, on the other hand, are more likely to talk about encounters with jungle spirits or the best way to catch bass). And cultures also determine vocabularies. In Scotland we encounter the word *haggis.* The ingredients of haggis are (usually) sheep's "pluck" (heart, liver, and lungs), minced with onion, oatmeal, spices, suet, and salt, mixed with stock, and traditionally boiled in the animal's stomach for approximately three hours. I like it. But it isn't for everyone. And it is only a traditional dish in Scotland. We are not surprised that the Scots have a word for this traditional part of their culture.

Another example is the Brazilian word *jeito* (ZHAY-tu), which literally means "to lie" or "to rest" and refers to a Brazilian concept of themselves as having a special knack or skill for solving problems. It is common to hear Brazilians say, for example, "*Nos brasileiros somos muito jeitosos*" (We Brazilians are good at *jeitos*). This skillfulness and the talking about it among Brazilians is a cultural value. It is neatly expressed as a single word by the members of Brazilian culture—the culture in which talking about the concept is so important. It is therefore another example of culture and language working hand in hand.

And, of course, the Pirahãs have words like *kaoáíbógi* (fast mouth) for a kind of spirit unique to them.

But there is no role attributed to or even allowed for culture in shaping the grammar proper in most linguistic theories. This is why it is important to study languages like Pirahã, in which culture appears to shape grammar in ways that few theorists imagine possible.

We can begin to appreciate Pirahã's relevance to our understanding of the nature of human language by considering one of Chomsky's main concerns, the explanation of similarities among languages.

When we look at the world's languages, we see many similarities; so many and so recurring in fact are these similarities that we know that they cannot be merely coincidental. We are obliged as scientists in the tradition of Western culture to offer an explanation for these.

Chomsky has urged us to place the explanatory locus for these similarities in genetics, and this is a reasonable place to look for explanations. After all, it is our common genome that unites *Homo sapiens* into a single species and produces other similarities among us, including many of our needs, desires, common experiences, and emotions.

So Pygmies and Dutchmen may look very different, but their similarities far outweigh their differences, because they, like all humans, come from the same genetic base. Without an understanding of evolution and genetic explanations, the nature of our species would elude us. So it is worth thinking about some of the similarities across languages that genetics might explain.

First, it could explain why languages all have similar parts of speech (verbs, nouns, prepositions, conjunctions, etc.). It may turn out that not all languages have each of the entire set of possible parts of speech, but what any one language does have, so far as we have seen, is like the categories of other languages.

Or it might explain why languages have similar psycholinguistic constraints on the processing of sentences (which is why in any language a perfectly grammatical sentence with the structure of *Oysters oysters eat eat oysters* can be hard to understand). The problem with this example is that it has "center-embedding"—a clause (the relative clause *oysters eat*) stuck in the middle of another clause (the main clause *Oysters eat oysters*). We can make the example easier to understand by inserting a marker to show us where the embedded clause begins, as in the much-easier-on-the-ears *Oysters that oysters eat eat oysters.*

And languages share similar constraints on meaning. For example, there is no verb in any language we know of that requires more than three nouns to complete its meaning (some theories say no more than four nouns). A language can allow verbs to appear with no nouns, or just nouns that do not refer to anything, a sort of placeholder noun. An example is the *it* of *It rains.* Or there can be verbs that appear with only one noun, as in *John runs;* or with two nouns, as in *Bill kissed Mary;* or even with three nouns, as in *Peter put the book on the shelf.* But not more. *John gave Bill the book Susan* is not possible. To say something with four or more nouns we need multiple verbs, multiple sentences, or prepositions, as in *John gave the book to Bill for Susan.**

Before the current theory that grammar originates in a part of the brain dedicated to it, there was a short period in which purely behavioral approaches to language studies were dominant, as in the work of B. F. Skinner.

But while behaviorism did indeed seem to fall short as an explanation for how we learn languages and the similarities among languages, because it has no place for cognition, theories based on universal gram-

---

*English imperative sentences, to be sure, usually appear without a subject, as in *Run!* But linguists agree that there is an *understood* subject here, since the subject of an imperative is always *you.* When I say "Run!" I don't mean that just anyone should run, but that *you* should run.

mar are not faring much better. There are various reasons for this. First, in the intervening years, excellent new research ideas have emerged which rely neither on Skinner's extreme view that language is just a behavior like any other human behavior nor on Chomsky's extreme position that our grammars are in our genes. There are other possible explanations, including logical requirements on communication, coupled with the nature of society and culture.

Michael Tomasello's psycholinguistics research group at the Max Planck Institute for Evolutionary Anthropology in Leipzig, Germany, is one of the leading research teams working on language and its emergence from membership in society. And this team's research is unburdened by either behavioristic or Chomskyan assumptions.

Another major reason for the fading influence of Chomsky's theory is the perception by many that the theory has become too vague and untestable to make much out of it these days. Many in the linguistics community at large find Chomsky's current research program of little use in their own efforts.

A third problem for Chomsky's theory of language—and the issue that I want to pursue here—is the simple fact that languages are less alike than Chomsky imagined, and their differences are profound.

If the Pirahãs were philosophers and linguists in the Western sense, they would be unlikely to develop a linguistics similar to Chomsky's. Contrary to the Cartesian concept of creativity, Pirahã cultural values limit the range of acceptable subjects and acceptable ways of talking to a narrow range within immediate experience.

At the same time, the Pirahãs love to talk. One of the most common comments I hear from visitors to the Pirahãs is that they seem to be talking and laughing together constantly. The Pirahãs are not reserved in their behavior, at least not in their own villages. As they lie around the ever-burning fires of their huts, they often bury potatoes or tubers in the coals to roast slowly. Talking about fishing, spirits, the last visit by a foreigner, why the Brazil nut trees yielded fewer nuts this year, and so on, Pirahãs pause to pull up a hot potato, open it, and ruminate almost literally as the conversation progresses.

They just don't talk about many things. But neither did my family in Southern California when I was growing up. We talked about cattle, field yields, boxing, barbeque, honky-tonks, movies, and politics, with a few other issues. No one in my family would be interested in "Cartesian creativity" either. Maybe linguists need it, though, because they talk about a much greater variety of topics? I don't think so. Most linguists I know, in fact most university professors I know, have if anything as narrow a range of conversational topics as the Pirahãs. Linguists talk about linguistics and other linguists much of the time. Philosophers talk about philosophy and philosophers and wine. These are pretty much the conversational parameters most of us operate within—our profession and our coprofessionals. Of course, to do all of this talking within the confines of a single language, our language has to be adequate for all the academic disciplines, professions, trades, and so on.

We often think that what we know is "portable"—as though what we learn about perceiving and knowing the world in San Diego will enable us to perceive and understand the world competently in Delhi. But so much of what we think we know is local information, based on local perspectives, that is no easier to use in a new environment than a 110-volt appliance in a 220-volt power source. A linguist, for example, who studies linguistic theory in a modern university and then travels to the field for research, if she is sensitive to her new environment, will soon learn that her theories are not a precise fit with the languages that she encounters. Theories can be useful if they are locally adjusted. If they're not, they can be like a Procrustean bed, in which facts are stretched and chopped to fit.

This is especially true for theories that language (or grammar, depending on the author's terminology) is innate. Although these theories can look very appealing in the classroom, they are difficult to reconcile with the facts in the field. Chomsky and Pinker suggest that nature (biology) is the principal explanatory tool for understanding the evolution and current form of human grammars. They propose a universal grammar (Chomsky) or a language instinct (Pinker), either of which would be part of our genome. These views have had a major impact on research in human psychology and language for decades. But there are other potential explanations of the psychology, evolution, and form of human grammars and languages. For example, we know that B. F. Skinner's view was that language is simply the product of environmental conditioning—all nurture, not nature. And we also know that Chomsky's devastating review of Skinner's theory in 1959 showed that Skinner's model was unequal to the task of accounting for the emergence of language either phylogenetically, in the species, or ontogenetically, in the individual. On the other hand, Chomsky's and Pinker's approaches to the problem, laying the core aspects of language exclusively at the feet of nature, are fraught with problems too. The Pirahã evidence of no recursion and cultural constraints on grammar are counterexamples to the idea of a universal grammar. The best account of the origin and nature of language is more complex than any simple dichotomy.

If this theory is inadequate, though, what are we left with?

We are left with a theory in which grammar—the mechanics of language—is much less important than the culture-based meanings and constraints on talking of each specific culture in the world.

And if this is correct, it has profound implications for the methodology of linguistics research. It means, again, that we cannot study languages effectively apart from their cultural context, especially languages whose cultures differ radically from the culture of the researcher.

This also means that linguistics is not so much a part of psychology, as most contemporary linguists believe, as part of anthropology, as Sapir believed (in fact, this could mean that psychology itself is part of anthropology, as Sapir also believed). Linguistics apart from anthropology and field research is like chemistry apart from chemicals and the laboratory.

Sometimes, though, as we study these cultures, the lessons we learn range far beyond our scientific objectives. I was learning something about my own spirituality from the Pirahãs that was to change my life forever.

Part Three CONCLUSION

17 Converting the Missionary

SIL missionaries do not preach or baptize. They avoid pastorlike roles. Rather, SIL believes that the most effective way to evangelize indigenous peoples is to translate the New Testament into their language. Since SIL also believes that the Bible is literally the word of God, then, it is reasoned, the Bible should be able to speak for itself. So my daily activities among the Pirahãs were mainly linguistic, trying to figure out the language well enough to do a good translation of the New Testament. As I progressed, I would work on translating sections and test my translations with different people in the village. In free times during the day, I would often talk to people about my faith and why it was important to me. There was no more to my missionary activity than this, typical for SIL members.

One morning in November 1983, after I had spent about fourteen months off and on living among the Pirahãs, I was sitting in the front room of our house in the village drinking coffee with several Pirahã men. It was about ten o'clock and the day was getting hot, a heat that would intensify until about 4 p.m., when it would gradually begin to relent. I was facing the river and enjoying a midmorning breeze on my face as I talked to the fellows about boats they had heard going down the Marmelos River, a mile or so from the village. Kóhoibiíihíai entered and I got up and poured him a cup of coffee—we had an assortment of nonmatching cheap plastic cups in our kitchen. The coffee was weak and very sweet.

As he took the cup from me, Kóhoi said, "*Ko Xoogiái, ti gi xahoaisoogabagai*" (Hey Dan, I want to talk to you). He continued, "The Pirahãs know that you left your family and your own land to come here and live with us. We know that you do this to tell us about

Jesus. You want us to live like Americans. But the Pirahãs do not want to live like Americans. We like to drink. We like more than one woman. We don't want Jesus. But we like you. You can stay with us. But we don't want to hear any more about Jesus. OK?"

Although SIL never allows its members to preach among indigenous peoples like the Pirahãs, Kóhoi had heard of my faith many times in conversations with me and in helping me translate small portions of the New Testament.

Then, referring to the previous American missionaries among them, he added, "Arlo told us about Jesus. Steve told us about Jesus. But we don't want Jesus."

The other men present seemed to agree with him.

I replied, "If you don't want Jesus, you don't want us. My family is only here to tell you about Jesus."

I said I had to study. The men rose and left to take their turns fishing as other men arrived back in the village, making canoes available.

This information shocked me. And it presented me with a clear moral choice. I had gone to the Pirahãs to tell them about Jesus and, in my opinion at that time, to give them an opportunity to choose purpose over pointlessness, to choose life over death, to choose joy and faith over despair and fear, to choose heaven over hell.

If the Pirahãs had understood the gospel and were nevertheless rejecting it, that was one thing. But perhaps they had not understood it. This was a strong possibility, since my speaking ability in the Pirahã language was still far from native.

On another occasion during that first period with the Pirahãs, I felt I understood their language well enough to give my own story about why I accepted Jesus as my savior. This is a common practice among evangelical Christians, called "giving your testimony." The idea is that the worse your life was before you accepted Jesus, the greater the miracle of your salvation and the greater the motive of unbelievers in the audience to accept Jesus too.

It was in the evening, just after my family had finished dinner, about seven o'clock. We were still cool from our baths in the Maici. This was when we made coffee for the people and they would come sit with us in the house and just visit. During these times I would talk about my faith in God and why I believed that the Pirahãs should want God too, as I did. Because the Pirahãs had no word for *God*, I used a term that Steve Sheldon had suggested to me, *Baíxi Hioóxio* (Up-high Father).

I said that our up-high father had made my life better. Once, I said, I used to drink like the Pirahãs. I had many women (exaggerating somewhat here), and I was unhappy. Then the up-high father came into my heart and made me happy and made my life better. I gave no thought to whether all these new concepts, metaphors, and names that I was inventing on the fly were actually intelligible to the Pirahãs. They made sense to me. This night, I decided to tell them something very personal about myself—something that I thought would make them understand how important God can be in our lives. So I told the Pirahãs how my stepmother committed suicide and how this led me to Jesus and how my life got better after I stopped drinking and doing drugs and accepted Jesus. I told this as a very serious story.

When I concluded, the Pirahãs burst into laughter. This was unexpected, to put it mildly. I was used to reactions like "Praise God!" with my audience genuinely impressed by the great hardships I had been through and how God had pulled me out of them.

"Why are you laughing?" I asked.

"She killed herself? Ha ha ha. How stupid. Pirahãs don't kill themselves," they answered.

They were utterly unimpressed. It was clear to them that the fact that someone I had loved had committed suicide was no reason at all for the Pirahãs to believe in my God. Indeed, it had the opposite effect, highlighting our differences. This was a setback for my missionary objectives. Days went by after this in which I thought long and hard about my purpose among the Pirahãs.

Part of the difficulty of my task began to become clear to me. I communicated more or less correctly to the Pirahãs about my Christian beliefs. The men listening to me understood that there was a man named Hisó, Jesus, and that he wanted others to do what he told them.

The Pirahã men then asked, "Hey Dan, what does Jesus look like? Is he dark like us or light like you?"

I said, "Well, I have never actually seen him. He lived a long time ago. But I do have his words."

"Well, Dan, how do you have his words if you have never heard him or seen him?"

They then made it clear that if I had not actually seen this guy (and not in any metaphorical sense, but literally), they weren't interested in any stories I had to tell about him. Period. This is because, as I now knew, the Pirahãs believe only what they see. Sometimes they also believe in things that someone else has told them, so long as that person has personally witnessed what he or she is reporting.

I decided that part of the difficulty for receptivity to the gospel was that the Pirahãs at the village of Posto Novo where we currently worked had too much contact with caboclo culture and had come to see that culture as more compatible with their way of life than American culture, which is how they perceived the source of the gospel. I reasoned that if I moved to another village beyond the reach of the river traders, the gospel would have more success. There were two such villages that I knew of, one next to the Transamazon Highway and another more isolated yet, perhaps a day's trip downriver from the Transamazon and three days upriver by motorboat from where we now lived.

I talked this over with Keren. We decided that before we made any decision we would take our first "furlough," our first trip back to the United States in over five years. This was a time to report to our financial supporters, to rest, and to assess our progress as missionaries.

On our furlough, I thought again of the challenge of the missionary: to convince a happy, satisfied people that they are lost and need Jesus as their personal savior. My evangelism professor at Biola University, Dr. Curtis Mitchell, used to say, "You've gotta get 'em lost before you can get 'em saved." If people don't perceive a serious lack of some sort in their lives, they are less likely to embrace new beliefs, especially about God and salvation. The linguistic and cultural challenges are enormous. I didn't even speak Pirahã well yet and was certainly unaware that it had characteristics that almost guaranteed that no message from the first century could be communicated.

We decided to move to another village, the more isolated one. We moved upriver about 150 miles to the village of Xagíopai, six hours downriver from the Transamazon Highway. The Pirahãs of this new village welcomed us warmly. For the first few years in this new location, we slept in tents and reached the village by taking the Transamazon, either by hitchhiking, renting a mission vehicle, or traveling on our own small off-road motorcycle, then taking our motorboat down the

Maici to the village. Our supplies were carried to the river by pickup truck from the SIL missionary compound.

We had something to offer this group of Pirahãs that was new: the just-translated Gospel of Mark in Pirahã. I had worked very hard on this; it was finished a few weeks before our definitive move to the upriver village.

Before releasing the translation for use among the Pirahãs, however, SIL required me to schedule what it calls a translation "checking session." I persuaded Xisaóoxoi (his Portuguese name is Doutor) to come to Pôrto Velho and spend a couple of weeks at the missionary compound to work on checking the quality of my translation. Wycliffe Bible Translators' director, John Taylor, who had studied classical languages at Oxford, agreed to check my efforts. In our first session, John held his Greek New Testament in front of him and asked me to ask Doutor, in Pirahã, how he understood particular sections of Mark's gospel. Doutor listened to my first question, but barely looked up at me, focusing instead on picking at a callus on his heel. The air conditioner was on. When he lost interest in his callus, Doutor pointed at the air conditioner with his lower lip and asked, "What's that?" Then he repeated the question for the doorknobs, the desk, and just about every other object in the room. John was at first worried that Doutor didn't understand my translation.

And I was nervous because I so wanted this translation checking to be a success. I pressed Doutor until he finally responded directly to a question. We quickly got into a routine of a couple of hours per day. By the end of two weeks, John was convinced that Doutor understood Mark's gospel. One of WBT's checking requirements is that the native-speaker helper must not have played any role in the actual translation, that is, that they come to the checking "cold," with no vested interest (as a helper might) in the outcome.

But Doutor's understanding bothered me more than it pleased me. If he understood as well as he seemed to, why did it have so little impact on him? Doutor could not have been less interested in or affected by the "message" of Mark's gospel. When we returned to the village, I recorded Mark's gospel in my own voice for the Pirahãs to listen to. I then brought in a wind-up tape recorder to play the recording, and I taught the Pirahãs how to use it, which, surprisingly enough, some of the children did. Keren and I left the village and returned a few weeks later. The people were still listening to the gospel, with children cranking the recorder. I was initially quite excited about this, until it became clear that the only part of the book that they paid attention to was the beheading of John the Baptist. "Wow, they cut off his head. Play that again!"

Perhaps they weren't listening to the whole gospel because of my accent, I thought. To solve this problem, we decided to have a Pirahã man record the translation on tape. I would say a line and then he would repeat after me, as naturally as possible. When it was all done we had a studio add music and sound effects, in addition to professionally editing the tape. We thought it sounded great.

We had multiple copies made and purchased more hand-cranked cassette players. Within a few days Pirahãs were playing the translation several hours a day. We were sure that with this new tool we would now be successful in converting the Pirahãs.

The recorders had hard green plastic cases with yellow handles. The first time I showed a Pirahã how to use one, I sat by Xaoóopisi, whom I was just getting to know, and showed him how to crank slowly to keep the electric power steady. We listened. He smiled and said that he liked it. I felt good and got up and left him to listen alone.

The next evening I saw a group of men sitting by a fire at a beach on the other side of the river from the main village, eating fish and laughing. I paddled my boat over to them, with a recorder. I asked them if they wanted to listen. "Sure," they all said enthusiastically in unison. I knew that they liked new things to break the monotony. And they did not disappoint me.

I cranked a bit and listened to the beginning of the Gospel of Mark. I asked them if they could understand it. They answered yes, they could understand it, and paraphrased it back to me so that I could see that they did understand it. Night had fallen and we were sitting on the sand by the light of their fire talking about the gospel. It was what I had always dreamed of.

But suddenly, Doutor, one of the four men, asked me a question.

"Hey Dan, who is that on the tape? It sounds like Piihoatai."

"It is Piihoatai," I answered.

"Well, he has never seen Jesus. He told us that he doesn't know Jesus and that he doesn't want Jesus."

And with this simple observation, the Pirahãs signaled that these tapes would have little or no spiritual influence. They had no epistemological grip on their minds.

But rather than give up, we supplemented audio recordings of Mark's gospel with a slide show of commercially produced pictures of New Testament scenes—Jesus, the apostles, and so on.

The morning after one evening's "show" an older Pirahã man, Kaaxaóoi, came to work with me on the language. As we were working, he startled me by suddenly saying, "The women are afraid of Jesus. We do not want him."

"Why not?" I asked, wondering what had triggered this declaration.

"Because last night he came to our village and tried to have sex with our women. He chased them around the village, trying to stick his large penis into them."

Kaaxaóoi proceeded to show me with his two hands held far apart how long Jesus's penis was—a good three feet.

I didn't know what to say to this. I had no idea whether a Pirahã male had pretended to be Jesus and pretended to have a long penis, faking it in some way, or what else could be behind this report. Clearly Kaaxaóoi wasn't making this up. He was reporting it as a fact that he was concerned about. Later, when I questioned two other men from his village, they confirmed his story.

The difficulty at the core of my reason for being among the Pirahãs was that the message that I had staked my life and career on did not fit the Pirahãs' culture. At the very least, one lesson to draw here was that my confidence in the universal appeal of the spiritual message I was bringing was ill-founded. The Pirahãs were not in the market for a new worldview. And they could defend their own just fine. Had I taken the time to read about the Pirahãs before visiting them the first time, I would have learned that missionaries had been trying to convert them for over two hundred years. From the first record of contact with the Pirahãs and the Muras, a closely related people, in the eighteenth century, they had developed a reputation for "recalcitrance"—no Pirahãs are known to have "converted" at any period of their history. Not that this knowledge would have dissuaded me. Like all new missionaries, I was prepared to sweep aside mere facts and believe that my faith would ultimately overcome any obstacles. But the Pirahãs did not feel lost, so they didn't feel a need to be "saved" either.

The immediacy of experience principle means that if you haven't experienced something directly, your stories about it are largely irrelevant. This renders them relatively impermeable to missionary efforts based on stories of the long-ago past that no one alive has witnessed. And this explains why they have resisted missionaries for so long. Creation myths are no match for this demand for evidence.

Surprisingly, this all resonated with me. The Pirahãs' refusal to believe something just because I said they should was not completely unexpected. I never believed that missionary work would be easy. But there was more to the reaction I was having than this. The Pirahãs' rejection of the gospel caused me to question my own faith. This surprised me. I was no novice, after all. I had graduated at the top of my class from Moody Bible Institute. I had preached on the streets of Chicago, spoken in rescue missions, gone door-to-door, and debated atheists and agnostics in my own culture. I was well trained in apologetics and personal evangelism.

But I had now also been trained as a scientist, where evidence was crucial, where I would demand for any claim evidence similar to what the Pirahãs were now requesting of me. I did not have the evidence that they wanted. I only had subjective support for what I was saying, my own feelings.

Another edge to the Pirahãs' challenge was my growing respect for them. There was so much about them that I admired. They were a sovereign people. And they were in effect telling me to peddle my goods elsewhere. They were telling me that my message had no purchase among them.

All the doctrines and faith I had held dear were a glaring irrelevancy in this culture. They were superstition to the Pirahãs. And they began to seem more and more like superstition to me.

I began to seriously question the nature of faith, the act of believing in something unseen. Religious books like the Bible and the Koran glorified this kind of faith in the nonobjective and counterintuitive—life after death, virgin birth, angels, miracles, and so on. The Pirahãs' values of immediacy of experience and demand for evidence made all of this seem deeply dubious. Their own beliefs were not in the fantastic and miraculous but in spirits that were in fact creatures of their environment, creatures that did normal kinds of things (whether or not I thought they were real). There was no sense of sin among the Pirahãs, no need to "fix" mankind or even themselves. There was acceptance for things the way they are, by and large. No fear of death. Their faith was in themselves. This was not the first time I had questioned my faith. Brazilian intellectuals, my own hippie background, and a lot of reading had already raised doubts. But the Pirahãs were the last straw.

So, sometime in the late 1980s, I came to admit to myself alone that I no longer believed in any article of faith or in anything supernatural. I was a closet atheist. And I was not proud of it. I was terrified that someone I loved might find out. I knew that eventually I must tell them. But in the meantime, I feared the consequences.

There is a sense among missionaries and their financial backers that missionary work is a noble challenge—a feeling that you are putting your money where your mouth is when you volunteer to go to dangerous and difficult parts of the world in order to serve Jesus. And when the missionary arrives, he or she usually is able to begin right away a life that at once combines adventure with altruism. Obviously, this is tempered by the missionary's desire to convert people to his or her own concept of truth, but worse things are known and the relative effect of proselytizing varies from people to people.

When I reached the place where I was finally prepared to take the consequences and let someone else know about my "deconversion," some two decades had elapsed since my initial doubts. And, as I expected, when I finally announced my change of belief, it had severe consequences for me personally. It's a difficult decision for anyone to tell his closest friends and family that he no longer shares their foundational beliefs—the beliefs that make them who they are. It must be something like coming out as gay to unsuspecting close friends and family.

In the end, my loss of religion and the epistemological crisis that accompanied it led to the breakup of my family—what I most wanted to avoid.

The missionary martyr to the Huaorani people, Jim Elliot, said once, in a line that affected me for many years after I read it, "He is no fool who gives what he cannot keep to gain what he cannot lose." He meant, of course, that giving up this world, which we cannot keep, is a small price to pay to know God and dwell in a heaven that we cannot lose.

I have given up what I could not keep, my faith, to gain what I cannot lose, freedom from what Thomas Jefferson called "tyranny of the mind"—following outside authorities rather than one's own reason.

The Pirahãs made me question concepts of truth that I had long adhered to and lived by. The questioning of my faith in God, coupled with life among the Pirahãs, led me to question what is perhaps an even more fundamental component of modern thought, the concept of truth itself. Indeed, I decided that I lived under a delusion—the delusion of truth. God and truth are two sides of the same coin. Life and mental well-being are hindered by both, at least if the Pirahãs are right. And their quality of inner life, their happiness and contentment, strongly supports their values.

From the time we are born we try to simplify the world around us. For it is too complicated for us to navigate; there are too many sounds, too many sights, too many stimuli for us to take even a single step unless we can decide what to pay attention to and what to ignore. In specific intellectual domains we call our attempts at simplification "hypotheses" and "theories." Scientists invest their careers and energies in certain attempts at simplification. They request money from funding organizations to travel to or to build some new environment in which to test their simplifying scheme.

But this type of "elegance theorizing" (getting results that are "pretty" rather than particularly useful) began to satisfy me less and less. People who contribute to such programs usually see themselves as working toward a closer relationship to truth. But as the American pragmatist philosopher and psychologist William James reminded us, we shouldn't take ourselves too seriously. We are no more nor less than evolved primates. It is rather ridiculous to think that the universe is a virgin saving herself for us. We are all too often the three blind men describing an elephant; or the man who looks on the wrong side of the road for his keys, simply because the light is better there.

The Pirahãs are firmly committed to the pragmatic concept of utility. They don't believe in a heaven above us, or a hell below us, or that any abstract cause is worth dying for. They give us an opportunity to consider what a life without absolutes, like righteousness or holiness and sin, could be like. And the vision is appealing.

Is it possible to live a life without the crutches of religion and truth? The Pirahãs do so live. They share some of our concerns, of course, since many of our concerns derive from our biology, independent of our culture (our cultures attribute meanings to otherwise ineffable, but no less real, concerns). But they live most of their lives outside these concerns because they have independently discovered the usefulness of living one day at a time. The Pirahãs simply make the immediate their focus of concentration, and thereby, at a single stroke, they eliminate huge sources of worry, fear, and despair that plague so many of us in Western societies.

They have no craving for truth as a transcendental reality. Indeed, the concept has no place in their values. Truth to the Pirahãs is catching a fish, rowing a canoe, laughing with your children, loving your brother, dying of malaria. Does this make them more primitive? Many anthropologists have suggested so, which is why they are so concerned about finding out the Pirahãs' notions about God, the world, and creation.

But there is an interesting alternative way to think about things. Perhaps it is the presence of these concerns that makes a culture more primitive, and their absence that renders a culture more sophisticated. If that is true, the Pirahãs are a very sophisticated people. Does this sound far-fetched? Let's ask ourselves if it is more sophisticated to look at the universe with worry, concern, and a belief that we can understand it all, or to enjoy life as it comes, recognizing the likely futility of looking for truth or God?

The Pirahãs have built their culture around what is useful to their survival. They don't worry about what they don't know, nor do they think they can or do know it all. Likewise, they do not crave the products of others' knowledge or solutions. Their views, not so much as I summarize them dryly here, but as they are lived out in the Pirahãs' daily lives, have been extremely helpful to me and persuasive as I have looked at my own life and the beliefs that I held, many of them without warrant. Much of what I am today, including my nontheistic view of the world, I owe at least in part to the Pirahãs.

Epilogue   Why Care about Other Cultures and Languages?

The Hans Rausing Endangered Languages Project is housed at the School of Oriental and African Studies (SOAS) of the University of London. The project is funded by a donation of £20 million from Lisbet Rausing, the daughter of Hans Rausing. The goal of the project is to document languages from around the world that are in danger of extinction.

Why would anyone give £20 million sterling to study languages spoken mainly by powerless tribal people in parts of the world that are, to put it lightly, off the beaten tourist trails? After all, one could easily make the case that languages come and go and that their disappearance, or their spread, or the emergence of new languages, is governed by the forces of natural selection. A dying tongue is an inconvenience for those who need to learn a new language because their own is no longer viable, but little more than that. In fact, if one believes that the Tower of Babel was either literally a curse or merely symbolic of some human problems, reducing the number of spoken languages and homogenizing or "globalizing" human languages could be viewed as a good thing.

On the Rausing Project's Web site, they put part of their rationale for the interest in endangered languages this way:

> Today, there are about 6,500 languages and half of those are under threat of extinction within 50 to 100 years. This is a social, cultural and scientific disaster because languages express the unique knowledge, history and worldview of their communities; and each language is a specially evolved variation of the human capacity for communication.

This sounds persuasive to me. Think of what the Pirahãs' combination of language and culture has taught us about human cognition. Now think of all the similar lessons that could be learned from other endangered languages.

Languages become endangered for at least two reasons. They are endangered when the people who speak them are in danger. The Pirahãs are down to less than four hundred speakers. They are a fragile people because they have little resistance to outside diseases and are being exposed more and more to the outside world, often with the government of Brazil exercising little effective control over who enters their reservation. So the Pirahã language is endangered because the Pirahã people are endangered—their survival as a people is threatened.

Another reason that languages become endangered is what we might call the effect of "market forces" or natural selection. The speakers of some minority languages, such as Irish, Diegueño, Banawá, and others, begin to switch to national languages (English, Portuguese, and so on) because it is economically advantageous to do so. Banawá speakers of Brazil move off their land to work for Brazilians because they have come to rely on industrialized goods. This in turn places them in environments where speaking their own language can make them the object of ridicule, and where, in any case, Portuguese is the only language that is useful for working with Brazilians. So Banawá has begun to disappear.

In this second sense, however, the Pirahã language is not endangered because the Pirahãs are not interested in using Portuguese, or any other language, at all. Certainly they feel no pressure to stop speaking Pirahã in favor of any other language.

A more general question worth asking in light of our discussion of the uniqueness of pairings of languages and culture is: What is the loss to those of us who don't speak the language that has disappeared? Is there really any loss to us? Clearly there is.

The number of languages actually spoken in the world at a given moment of human history is but a small fragment of the perhaps infinitely large total number of possible human languages. A language is a repository of specialized cultural experiences. When a language is lost, we lose the knowledge of that language's words and grammar. Such knowledge can never be recovered if the language has not been studied or recorded. Not all of this knowledge is of immediate practical benefit, of course, but all of it is vital in teaching us different ways of thinking about life, of approaching our day-to-day existence on planet Earth.

One of the groups I have studied in addition to the Pirahãs is the Banawás, one of the Amazonian Indian peoples that make curare, a fast-acting and deadly strychnine-based poison used on blowgun darts and arrows. The ability to make this poison is the result of centuries of lore and experimentation, encoded in the Banawás' language in the terms for plants and procedures. All this is in danger of being lost, as the last seventy remaining Banawá speakers gradually switch to Portuguese.

For many people, like the Banawás, the loss of their language brings loss of identity and sense of community, loss of traditional spirituality, and even loss of the will to live. To save languages like Banawá, Pirahã, and thousands of others around the world will require a massive effort by linguists, anthropologists, and other interested individuals. We need, at a minimum, to identify which languages are endangered around the world, to learn enough about each of them to produce a dictionary, a grammar, and a written form of the language, to train native speakers of these languages as teachers and linguists, and to secure government support for protecting and respecting these languages and their speakers. This is a daunting task, but a vital one.

The view of this book is that every language and culture pair shows us something unique about the way that one subset of our species has evolved to deal with the world around it. Each people solves linguistic, psychological, social, and cultural problems in different ways. When a language dies without documentation, we lose a piece of the puzzle of the origin of human language. But perhaps more important, humanity loses an example of how to live, of how to survive in the world around us. With terrorism and fundamentalism threatening to sever the ties of trust and common expectations that bind societies together, the examples of endangered languages become ever more precious and their loss ever more damaging to our hopes for survival as a species.

Groups like the Pirahãs offer novel, deeply useful, and alternative examples of how to deal with perennial and ubiquitous problems such as violence, rape, racism, the treatment of disabled members of society, child-parent relations, and so on. The fact, for example, that no Ama-

zonian group that I have worked with has "motherese," or baby talk—
that is, a special, watered-down way of talking to little children—is
interesting. The Pirahãs' lack of baby talk seems to be based on the
belief of Pirahã adults that all members of the society are equal and
thus that children should not be treated any differently from adults, by
and large. Everyone has responsibility for the community and everyone
is cared for by the community.

Looking more closely at Pirahã language and culture, there are
other, equally important lessons for us. The Pirahãs show no evidence
of depression, chronic fatigue, extreme anxiety, panic attacks, or other
psychological ailments common in many industrialized societies. But
this psychological well-being is not due, as some might think, to a lack
of pressure. It is ethnocentric to suppose that only industrialized societies can produce psychological pressure, or that psychological difficulties are found only in such societies.

True, the Pirahãs don't have to worry about paying their bills on
time or which college to select for their children. But they do have life-
threatening physical ailments (such as malaria, infection, viruses, leish-
maniasis, and so on). And they have love lives. And they need to
provide food every day for their families. They have high infant mortal-
ity. They regularly face dangerous reptiles, mammals, bugs, and other
creatures. They live with threats of violence from outsiders who frequently invade their land. When I am there, with a much easier life than
the Pirahãs themselves have, I still find that there is plenty for me to get
worked up about. The thing is, I do get worked up, but they do not.

I have never heard a Pirahã say that he or she is worried. In fact, so
far as I can tell, the Pirahãs have no word for *worry* in their language.
One group of visitors to the Pirahãs, psychologists from the Massachusetts Institute of Technology's Brain and Cognitive Science Department, commented that the Pirahãs appeared to be the happiest people
they had ever seen. I asked them how they could test such a statement.
They replied that one way might be to measure the time that the average Pirahã spends smiling and laughing and then to compare this with
the number of minutes members of other societies, such as Americans,
spend smiling and laughing. They suggested that the Pirahãs would
win hands down. In the more than twenty isolated Amazonian groups I
have studied over the past thirty years, only the Pirahãs manifest this

unusual happiness. Many others, if not all, that I have studied are often sullen and withdrawn, torn between the desire to maintain their cultural autonomy and to acquire the goods of the outside world. The Pirahãs have no such conflicts.

My own impression, built up over my entire experience with the Pirahãs, is that my colleague from MIT was correct. The Pirahãs are an unusually happy and contented people. I would go so far as to suggest that the Pirahãs are happier, fitter, and better adjusted to their environment than any Christian or other religious person I have ever known.

Acknowledgments

I would like to thank the people who have made the experiences recounted in this book and the writing of it possible. Foremost among all are the Pirahãs. They have taught me many things over the past decades of my life. Their brilliance, their beauty, their patience, their faithful friendship, and their love for me and my family have made my world a better place.

Next I would like to thank the employees of the Brazilian National Indian Foundation (FUNAI) in Pôrto Velho, especially Seu Osman and Seu Rómulo, for their support of my research for many years. Osman and I began working with Amazonian Indians at nearly the same time. I have always been impressed by his selfless dedication to the cause of Brazil's Indians.

My former wife, Keren, was with me through most of the experiences recounted here, and I thank her for many memories. Shannon, Kristene, and Caleb helped me come out alive and sane through every danger and trial. Without my family none of the experiences and lessons in this book would have happened. The changes documented in chapter 17 have strained our relationships, but as the apostle Paul rightly declared, love is greater than all other feelings.

Steve Sheldon, who preceded me as missionary to the Pirahãs, supported me as a friend and as a mission administrator for many years. From first introducing me to the Pirahãs all those years ago, to typing my Ph.D. dissertation, to corresponding with me about all sorts of issues and questions for over thirty years, Steve has helped me more than I can say. In particular, I want to thank him for the example that he and his predecessor, the first missionary to the Pirahãs, Arlo Heinrichs, set in their relations with the "straight ones." Many Pirahãs still recall how Arlo hunted for them and fed them during the measles epi-

demic of the early 1960s. Old men credit Arlo and Steve for the continued survival of the Pirahãs as a people. I hope that the medical help I
have provided to the Pirahãs for these past three decades has been some
small repayment for their inestimable contributions to my own life—
that the children who would have died but now are living because of
something as simple as an injection of chloroquine or penicillin will
remember Paóxaisi.

I could not have written this book without the generous support of
my colleagues at Illinois State University. I cannot imagine a warmer,
more helpful academic home. My colleagues in the Department of
Languages, Literatures, and Cultures have all tolerated my enthusiasm
for this project. ISU's president, Al Bowman, has been encouraging on
multiple occasions. Gary Olson has been the most helpful and encouraging dean I have ever had and it is a pleasure to acknowledge his support here.

I also want to thank people who have helped me by reading and
commenting on drafts of all or parts of this book. Some of them have
made so many detailed comments that the book would have been
greatly inferior without their generous help: Manfred Krifka, Shannon
Russell, Kristene Diggins, Linda Everett, Mitchell Mattox, Mike Frank,
Heidi Harley, Jeanette Sakel, Ted Gibson, Robert Van Valin, Geoffrey
Pullum, Cormac McCarthy, C. C. Wood, and John Searle. David Brum-
ble, my former dean at the University of Pittsburgh, made contributions far beyond the obligations of friendship. With humor and
directness, he made suggestions that helped me say some things more
clearly.

Over the past twenty-five years, my research on Amazonian languages has been supported by the National Science Foundation, the
National Endowment for the Humanities, the European Union (via a
grant for Characterizing Human Language by Structural Complexity),
the Arts and Humanities Research Council and the Economics and
Social Research Council of the United Kingdom, and the Fundação de
Amparo à Pesquisa do Estado de São Paulo. Thanks to all of these entities for allowing me to use the tax dollars of Brazilian, European,
British, and American citizens for the study of endangered languages of
the Amazon.

The New Yorker photographer Martin Schoeller was incredibly generous in making available his photos of the Pirahãs for this book. *The New Yorker* writer John Colapinto was helpful indirectly in setting a high standard for writing about my life among the Pirahãs. Many times while writing this book, I drew inspiration from John's "deathless prose."

My editor at Pantheon, Edward Kastenmeier, has given generously of his time to discuss this book with me on numerous occasions, always trying to help me describe the Pirahãs more effectively and to let them stand out as the rightful focus of these pages. John Davey, my editor with Profile Books, also offered many useful comments and words of encouragement throughout the writing.

Finally, but most important, I want to thank my agent, Max Brockman. It was Max's vision that made this book a reality. His confidence convinced me that perhaps I could do this.

Index